7 50

NC

MW00452003

The Far Side
of
My Dreams

Carole L. Mercer

Copyright © 2013 Carole L. Mercer
All rights reserved.
ISBN-10: 91484867165
ISBN-13: 978-1484-867167

DEDICATION

In loving memory of my darling daughter,
Sarah Ann Mercer

September 30, 1977 - May 24, 1997

CONTENTS

FULL CIRCLE

ACKNOWLEDGMENTS

*Thank you to
Carol Kirkham,
my good friend,
and to my friend and editor,
Lisa Peterson.*

*Without your help and support,
this book would
never have happened.*

Carole

PROLOGUE

In the beginning there is a mess.

We all experience some mess in our lives. My messy life is unique. Come share my mess, come be unique with me. I guarantee that you won't become dirty. Tired maybe, but dirty, never. You will laugh often as we step along the messy path that carries me beyond my dreams.

I think that we are all searching for who we are. Secretly, we hope to open a magic door, step through and there we will stand, "Found and finished." I believe we do not *find* ourselves, but we *create* ourselves.

I have learned that I already know right from wrong. I just sometimes like to believe that the "right-versus-wrong" rules don't apply to me. But the right rules apply to me as well as the wrong rules. I have made my share of mistakes with no one to blame but myself.

I also know that I am a kind person, but people perceive that kindness is a weakness. Kindness is not a weakness. Kindness is a right choice.

Terrible things can and do come along in your lifetime. You don't get much choice of what comes. But you do get a choice of how you handle it.

I have an interesting life. I like unusual, strong people. I am an unusual, strong woman. People can be and often are attracted to the strength in the beginning of a friendship, but later tire of being around a strong, independent and opinionated woman. I've created that woman from a child who was painfully shy.

Laughing often is one of my best ways of coping with and cleaning up the mess-ups in my life. Come walk with me, arm-in-arm, as we stroll through my story-telling. Let us laugh at the adversities, cry at the sorrows, and step out on the other side of my dreams a new and happier person.

Here is my story.

BEGINNINGS

CHAPTER 1
HORSE CRAZY

I should not start with "once upon a time."

So.... Once upon a time, I was born into a family of non-horse people. My parents were sure I was an alien born into their non-horsey family. Horse people like big, hairy animals that step on your toes, eat too much grass, and poop often. A perfect definition of a horse for the non-horse person is as follows: The front end of a horse bites, the back end of a horse kicks, and the middle of a horse is the most uncomfortable place in the world to sit. My parents didn't even really like horses.

I loved horses from the moment I first could see, smell, or touch a horse. I cannot recall that first moment. My childhood in the 1950s is spent living at a small veteran's hospital nestled in the foothills of Wyoming's Big Horn Mountains. My earliest childhood horse recollection fills my mind, with the sights and sounds of horses roaming in the vastness of 10,000 rolling BLM (Bureau of Land Management) acres behind my parent's home at Fort McKenzie, Wyoming.

The first horse I can actually recall is a big, brown gelding named "Fisher." Fisher lived behind the Fort McKenzie house somewhere on those 10,000 BLM acres. I must have been about four-years old. My mother used to tell me about one winter when she looked out the kitchen window and could barely see me wandering out into the blizzard to "check on Fisher" to make sure he was okay. I still can feel his warm, sweet, sage-and-grass breath on my shoulder as I reach out to touch his frozen, whisker-covered muzzle. I love this huge horse who towers over me. Fisher must be 18-years old. He lets me crawl under him, over him, and up his hind legs to sit on his back. Fisher remains my perfect first horse. Because he is so old, Fisher only walks or stands still. For a small child living in the beauty of Wyoming's wild, Big Horn Mountain foothills, Fisher becomes not only my first horse, but my first equine love and friend.

I don't know who owns Fisher. He lives out on the vast prairie and I climb all over him. He no longer lives on the 10,000 acres. I do not know what happened to him. One day he simply melts out of my memory.

My next memory is "Silver," a golden-palomino gelding of unsure ancestry. I never question why a golden horse is called "Silver." I just call him Silver. He too lives on those 10,000 acres. I own a wonderful picture of me sitting proudly in a huge, elegantly hand-carved western saddle on Silver's back. My dark brown hair is done up in pigtails and my left hand is jauntily perched on my hip. I dream of racing into a rodeo arena as the Sheridan, Wyoming rodeo queen on this old palomino gelding. The glitter is gone from his golden coat. The spark in his eyes glows dimly. But I love this tired old champion of imaginary arenas. Then he too fades out of my memory.

To this day I do not know what happened to those old horses. I was a small girl of four and five years and knew nothing of death, nor the disappearance of the life force that comes with death, and with old horses.

When I am 10-years old I finally own a mare named "Dhobi." Dhobi means "gold" in Arabic, or so I am told. Dhobi is a palomino, Morgan-Arab cross, known today as a Morab. I ride her all over those 10,000 acres; on the map that's more than 390-square miles of open land. I learn to saddle her and think I am riding her. Interestingly enough, I didn't know how to *really* ride. I think I mostly just sat on her as she wandered around those vast acres that nestle up to the Big Horn Mountains.

I have a unique and wonderful childhood. We find the cottonwood trees, secreted in the giant gullies of the prairies. You can only find the trees by seeing the tip-tops of the fluttering leaves. Deer and cattle shelter under the trees during the hot summers and the freezing winters.

A man built a dangerous earthen dam across one gully to hold back the spring melt of snow from the Big Horn Mountains. I am forbidden to go to those waters, but Dhobi and I spent many hours patrolling the edges of the deep and dark water.

I ride down to Soldiers Creek, named after Custer's 7th Cavalry that patrolled the area in the late 1800s "protecting" the settlers in and around the settlement of Sheridan. I ride across the smooth, shallow waters to places I could never walk by myself. I discover the companionship and freedom that riding a good horse brings to a small girl child. I go places with the horses that I cannot go by myself, and I am never alone when I am riding. I am one with my horse, wandering on those prairies.

Now I wonder what my parents thought of my long absences on

horseback. They must not have known where all I rode or how far I went. We lived in an age of innocent, confident security that has evaporated in today's world. I thrived in an era when we had no television. My parents simply trusted that I would not be hurt. And, I never fell off.

CHAPTER 2
GOING PLACES

My non-horsey parents were like living with grandparents. I was born very late in their lives. Dad retired when I turned 12. Retirement, for them, was to a large, one-acre lot south of San Francisco, California.

I experienced total culture shock as my horses were left behind and I experienced urban living. My Dhobi was given to some friends who owned a ranch in Montana. Alone for the first time, I wasted away until I discovered a horse community about five miles from my parent's home in Atherton. I had found Woodside.

I am 12-years old and miserable in town. I bike (uphill both ways of course) to Woodside every day to happily clean stalls in exchange for riding lessons, and I practically live at the Canada Stables barn. Owners Jack and Lois Melville make sure that I have horses to ride all though high school. I replace the wilderness of Wyoming with excursions in nearby Huddart Park, where I can wander 900-acres of old logging roads among California redwoods. I manage to live and survive suburban life because I have horses to ride and keep me content.

Horses came and went in my life as I married, went to college, moved to Los Angeles, and taught school. I had a daughter, divorced, moved to Palo Alto, remarried, and bought my little daughter, Sarah, her first pony.

Pepper is my first pony too. He is 11-hands high and a P.O.A. (Pony of the Americas). I ride him everywhere, Sarah perched in front of me. We just go. Sarah and I also hitch Pepper to a two-wheeled, pony-sized spring-wagon. I made a comfy bed in the back of the wagon and Sarah, aged 3, often took her afternoon nap in the wagon as I drove Pepper on the smooth back roads of Los Altos Hills, California. One of my most cherished photos is of Sarah and the neighbor's Jack Russell dog, Geraldine, sitting snugly-wrapped in a blanket on a very cold, winter's day whilst I drove them down a country road. I love this generous pony. I drove him everywhere.

Next I buy Chular's Valentine, my first Morgan, and I begin driving horses seriously. I buy carriages and carts and drive my horses and carriages all over town. I start a carriage club called "The Peninsula Carriage Driving Club." The club is social as well as competitive. I meet like-minded horse and carriage people at meetings, dinners and competitions. At one time I have six carriages stuffed in my garage.

This idyllic life makes another turn and I divorce again. Pepper and Valentine are sold for the money to help buy a ranch in Oregon where my daughter Sarah, now 10, and I start our next chapter.

CHAPTER 3
INDEPENDENCE

I started my first new life in 1986 by purchasing a 50-acre ranch, three miles outside of Eagle Point, Oregon. Eagle Point is a small town just outside of Medford, Oregon. Medford is just 20 miles from the northern border of California. Interstate 5 runs smack dab through Medford. And here is where my mess and my dreams are created together.

I flee the San Francisco Bay Area, leaving behind two bad marriages. Squished in the front and only seat of my old, blue and white, 1979 Ford pick-up is my hope of a new start in life on my new, private cattle ranch. I am now the owner of 50 broken-down acres of farm land.

Sharing that seat sits Sarah, bolt upright beside me, along with two boys, Trevor (9) and Steve (8), borrowed from wealthy parents who are eager for their sons to spend a couple of weeks on a cattle ranch away from the suburbs. On the floor of the cab, looking up with soulful eyes, scrunches my Lhasa Apso dog, Popsie, aged two. I captain the driver's seat, ready to start a new life on my ranch.

` The trip from Woodside, California to Eagle Point, Oregon is quick. The journey lasts six hours while I keep one eye on the road and one eye on the rear view mirror for the highway patrol's flashing red light. In those days I drive too fast. Not anymore. Life is better at 55-miles per hour.

We settle on our Rolling Wheel Ranch. The ranch is 50-acres of irrigated hayfields and pasture. There is an old, four-stall horse barn. The barn is complete with falling down fences and a rugged 50' x 60' tin-sided hay barn. The farmhouse is an A-frame built in the 1970s with a rickety deck that is rapidly collapsing. There is an above-ground swimming pool that desperately needs repair to hold water. There is also a dirty, filthy, three-car garage.

All of this mess is perfect for my new start, as I had been living in a beautiful, ranch-style house in a wealthy suburb of California. Waiting for me in Oregon is a perfect mess of a ranch house, barns and fields. I can hardly wait to release the independent cowgirl raging within my soul.

I find my true home on this ranch. Yesterday, I stepped out of my raw silk, San Francisco suit. Today I will climb into my fashionably tight Guess jeans and onto a big red tractor. I begin the greatest adventures of my new lifetime by bumping across my field pulling a hay rake, before I've even unpacked. I begin the creation of who I will become.

CHAPTER 4
HAY AS AN ART FORM

Personally, I am convinced that farmers and ranchers qualify as gamblers.

My vet, Jim Perry, once told me that, "Ranchers are the only people who can go broke six times in a row and can hardly wait to go back again next year."

I think he is right. He certainly is right about the state of my cattle when I desperately call in the middle of the night, due to a cow crisis of some sort.

When I lived in California, I had no idea what goes into making a bale of hay that winds up in my barn loft. All I know is if I call the hay guy and pay him enough money, then 30 hay bales appear in my loft.

I buy the ranch and learn to make that hay.

Picture me as I step out of my straw-colored, raw silk city suit and my three-inch, russet brown '80s high-heels and into my dark-brown Bass penny loafers and my snazzy, designer Guess jeans. The city girl loafers and jeans take me down to the hayfield and I find myself sitting on a big, red Allis Chambers tractor. The rear tractor tires are taller than me and I am 5'6" tall. This huge red tractor belongs to the man who I have hired to cut and bale my hayfield.

Haying is an art form. If you have a good hayfield, Mother Nature is willing to play along with you, and if you are lucky, very lucky, you will get a good crop of hay. Here is a weather report so you can understand hay weather. Haying usually begins as the weather turns sweltering hot. The very day after I arrive, haying starts. I know NOTHING about haying or tractors. Fortunately, I can drive a stick shift automobile. My dear Dad made sure I could drive a stick shift car, teaching me to drive in a black, 1958 MGA. I silently thank him for that piece of education now. In my far-away past, I also owned a 1960 VW stick-shift.

A clutch is a clutch. Put your foot on the tractor clutch. Depress the clutch and shift. Take your foot off the clutch as you press down on the gas and, if you are extremely fortunate, the behemoth under your body will magically rumble forward. If the clutch action is not perfect, you lurch forward with a giant, violent leap. I can drive a tractor well because I know how to release the clutch.

I contract a couple of local men with hay equipment to cut, rake, and bale the hay that flourishes in my field. The man I hired drafts me to power the huge tractor across the field. He drives another huge tractor in front of me and I follow him on the giant red tractor. I will be raking the hay that he cuts. The smell of a newly-cut hayfield is the amplified smell of a lush, fresh-cut city lawn. The smell multiplies in intensity because of the many acres in a hayfield. Your olfactory senses can be overwhelmed. You are awash in the dewy, green essence of life. Walt Whitman understood farming. In his **Leaves of Grass** he writes, "All flesh is grass." I am made of flesh, and I am now grass-baptized in my hayfield.

First the hay is cut, like a giant mower rolling across the lawn. Then the hay dries lying in the field. I have to wait a day and rake again. The hay must be dry enough to rake into windrows. I must make perfectly straight lines as I rake. Fortunately my past saves me again, for I have sailed and know how to pick a spot on the horizon and drive straight to that point. You then make a nice, curvy turn and pick a point on the opposite fence line.

The trick to raking is that you need to watch behind you to make sure that the rake picks up all the flat, cut grass and neatly piles it into well-defined rows. After the rows are raked and have properly dried, someone comes with yet another tractor pulling a machine called a baler. The baler scoops up the rows of dry, loose hay and pounds it into a solid bale of hay.

The baler's plunger compresses the hay in the baler. The

compressed bale is mechanically wrapped with wire or twine string and is popped out the back of the baler onto the ground. The new hay bale then lies on the field, ready to be picked up and stored in the barn.

This critical feed stuff that maintains all types of livestock through the starvation of winter has a careful science to it. Too wet, and it will decompose and possibly combust in flames. Too dry, and it loses the vital nutrition animals need to survive. To accomplish this ideal moisture-level, the raked hay is often baled at night so the correct amount of moisture is on the hay. I go to sleep at night with the sound of "bum, bum, bum, bum" pounding away in the hayfield.

The bum, bum, bum of the piston, plunging the hay into bales, will sound for the rest of my life on this ranch. I can hear my neighbors baling in the warm summer nights. I hear my tractor guys baling when my fields are ready. *Bum, bum, bum* is a reassuring lull-a-bye that all is well.

During the rigors of hay season, no extra pair of hands go un-blistered. My moving boxes from the elegant home in California lay untouched and unpacked. The borrowed boys and my daughter are quickly put to work.

The small, ten-year-old children are instantly drafted into ranch-ife labor. They struggle to help the local men load and unload the solid, 120-pound bales of rich alfalfa. They are quickly assigned more appropriate jobs.

The boys gleefully master the ability to drive a giant tractor they can barely see over the steering wheel of. My 10-year-old daughter retreats to her room and thrusts herself into her one salvation, her books. I give up the tractor-driving to the small boys and retreat to my kitchen. I begin one of the most traditional roles of a woman on a ranch. I cook for my first hay crew.

Sarah will retreat into reading for the majority of her life. She loves to read and completes **The Great Books** series by the time she is 13. Her mind is photographic. She also turns into a runner. And of course Sarah knows how to ride. But in this foreign environment of a small, broken-down ranch, Sarah finds her place and escapes the heat, dust and blistered hands. Sarah reads, for we have no television.

I can and do cook. I created gourmet dinners for my ex-husband and his business associates. Now I cook for real. I cook for truly hungry, hard-working, grateful men. This entire farming/ranching business is about food and what we eat. All flesh is grass and I am busy with a hay harvest. The two-boy, two-man hay crew can and do eat. A hay crew will devour an entire 15-pound turkey with all the trimmings. The potatoes, stuffing, cooked peas and carrots disappear from the table and then the men and boys look around politely and inquire about dessert. Two apple pies disappear. Just how hard and how willing a hay crew is to return to work at your farm next year often depends upon how good the food is this year.

Of course, I also need a tractor, and I buy an almost new Ford F-1510, four-wheel drive. The tractor comes accessorized with a loader, a scraper, an auger, and a bush hog. The cost of haying equipment is too much money for only three weeks of work a year. I am not a mechanic by nature, so it is better to pay for my hay work than fight the easily broken machinery myself and lose a crop in the process.

I foolishly bought a used baler for my first hay season.

I wisely sold the baler right after my first hay season.

Why did I sell the baler? A farmer needs to know what equipment she needs to bring in the hay. You need mechanical ability and hay equipment. Anyone who wishes to stay out of the destructive net of farm debt never buys any new equipment. In fact, I have never even known farm equipment that started out new. A farmer who needs equipment goes to farm auctions to acquire the used mowers, hay rakes, and balers necessary to cut, rake, and bale the life-sustaining grass or alfalfa that grows to feed your cattle, or to sell the grass crop to other ranchers and farmers for their livestock.

In all the years that I hay my fields, I only own one tractor (I still have the small, blue Ford F-1015 I bought *almost* new 27 years ago. I call it my "girl tractor." It is just the right size for me. It is big enough to get the job done, but not so big that I get myself into trouble. It comes with a front-end loader. That loader will often save my workload-life in the future. The tractor and I become a two-man team. I just need it to work all the time. Equipped with my newest farm tool, I am still so new at this game.

The back end of a real tractor comes with a PTO (Power Take Off). The PTO powers things that drill and cut. I have a post-hole digger (it drills holes) and a bush hog. That is a giant, four-foot wide lawn mower that runs off the back end of the tractor. The bush hog is attached to the PTO, and the diesel engine of the tractor powers the blades. I hate the bush hog because it is so darn hard to attach to the

PTO, but I need it, so I learn how to attach it to the tractor. This bush hog can cut small trees up to three inches in diameter, weeds, and brush, all of which live to invade hayfields, pastures, and other places you don't want to be a mess.

I teach myself how to attach the PTO implements. I cry and swear often during my early tractor education, but I teach myself and I learn. If I do not learn, I will lose the ranch, a mess I can't afford. Everything here depends upon my shoulders bearing the burdens I have picked for myself and my daughter. I cannot afford to fail.

I love the tractor's blade, I find it so easy to attach. I own a scraping blade to smooth the farm roads and knock down the ever-present ant hills that flourish in my upper pastures. I use the tractor often. I would not be able to run the ranch without my knowledge of the functions and the use of the little blue Ford tractor.

Once the hay is cut, raked, and baled, those beautiful bales must come out of the field. The real work of haying now starts. My hired-man hay crew leaves the "bringing in the bales" to me. The visiting city boys go home, leaving half the bales for me to pick up. After all, I didn't hire the crew to bring in the 60 tons of hay that is sitting out in my field. I only hired them to "cut and bale" the field.

So I do the job. Sarah is pulled from her books and learns to drive my tractor. I walk behind a tractor driven by my little 10-year old Sarah. The tractor pulls a flatbed trailer. I lug those huge 120-pound bales onto the flatbed trailer with every ounce of my 120-pound body. Never again do I allow anyone to make bales heavier than 60-65 pounds. I call this smaller size of bale "girl bales."

I find a neighbor kid to stack the bales on the flatbed as I struggle to toss them up on the trailer to him. Young kids aren't strong enough to pick-up or stack heavy bales. The young kids get to drive the tractor.

This team develops a rhythm. Once you fill the flatbed you drive up to the barn and unload the bales. You tightly stack the bales in the hay barn as you unload them. I pick up all the bales. I bring in that crop with the help of two, 15-year old neighbor boys and me. I am so tired that I cry and cry. The boys drive the tractor. Sarah gets off the tractor and puts together the meals that I cook the night before. I cry some more. Sarah doesn't cry. She is so tough. She gently tells me "you bought the farm, you have to make it go." I am so tired that even the muscles in my face sag. I am exhausted from lifting thousands of pounds of hay in the course of hours.

But I do it. I get the hay in the barn. And I discover that I cannot be around alfalfa. I am deathly allergic to alfalfa once it is cut. I must reseed my hayfield from alfalfa to grass hay.

The best part about hay season is you work in temperatures of above 100-degrees. Just as the sun is rising you get up to pick-up bales, and you quit when the sun shines too hot. Southern Oregon is really, really hot in the summer.

I always salt my hay as it is stacked in the hay barn. I buy 100-pound bags of rock salt from the Grange Co-op and sprinkle it over each layer of hay as we stack it in the barn. The salt draws out the moisture that might be left in the hay and thus prevents spontaneous combustion if the bales should begin to rot due to dampness. The other plus of salting hay is the cattle and horses will drink much needed water in the winter, as the salt makes them thirsty.

I continue to raise hay for the next 20 years. There are always more hay stories to follow. I no longer cry as much as I did with my first crop. Yet some years I still weep over the sheer exhaustion of this work.

Eventually I learn to haul hay with my team of Morgan mares. The horses are easier to use than a pick-up truck as they are both the truck and the driver. I hitch up the bay mares to an old wooden hay wagon. I drive them down the steep hill to the flat, bottom land of the hayfield. There I get off the wagon seat and drive them from the ground. I drive the mares up to a bale in the field, pick up the bale, and lug it onto the back of the wagon while they wait. I load the hay one-bale-at-a-time. I pick up bales, stack bales in the wagon; drive the full wagon up the steep hill to the barn; back the wagon into the barn; unload the hay; stack the hay and return to the field for another load. Together, the Morgan horses and I can load and stack a ton-an-hour in the barn with no costly diesel fuel burned.

While I am bringing in the hay with the horses, I learn to hire a crew of kids to haul hay as well. The kid crew is usually teenage boys who have an old, run-down, half-alive pick-up truck. I have a small, flatbed trailer to attach to their truck. One boy drives the truck while the other two load the trailer and bed of the truck. One boy stands on the back of the truck. One boy tosses the hay to him and it is stacked. The walking boy is the tosser. He tosses the hay to the stacker. The driver must be skilled as well, to keep a slow, even speed as he navigates the rows of hay bales to avoid jarring the vehicles and knocking the stacker off balance. The hay is carefully stacked on the truck and trailer to avoid the tragedy of having loosely-stacked bales tumble off as they head up the steep hill while leaving the field.

The high school boys carefully back the truck and trailer into the barn to unload and re-stack the fragrant bales there. As Sarah gets older, I often draft her to help drive and stack hay. I pay her the same rate as I pay the boys. Haying must be done and I need everyone who can walk to help me get the hay inside the barn before bad weather can ruin it. I cook all the necessary food at night so I can feed my hay crew during the day. Sarah is finally out of the kitchen and out of her books. She is being paid to bring in the hay.

With the high school boys, Sarah, me, and the Morgan mares, we get 40 to 60 tons of hay into the hay barn for winter feed for the cattle. There is no romance about haying. Hay is hard work in grueling, hot temperatures. The hay must be cut, raked and baled before any freak rainstorm pelts the hay with water and ruins the quality and dryness. Summer rains always come at the wrong time in the cloudless summer skies of southern Oregon. If rain comes, you can bet someone's hay is being ruined in the fields

CHAPTER 5
STRUGGLING WITH RANCH LIFE

I raise hay. I cut, rake, and bale the life force of the sun in my hayfield and pile the result into my hay barn. I have about 40-tons of hay stacked and packed into the barn. I now have too much hay. I need something to feed it to.

I own one Morgan horse that came with me to Eagle Point, Oregon from California. The mare is Suzi; an overly-fat Morgan. Suzi is not going to eat all that hay. She would like to try, she is a (voracious) Morgan after all. But this is not the hard-earned, sparse mountain hay that hard-working, early-day Morgans were celebrated for thriving on. It is protein-filled alfalfa, rich enough to cause harm if overeaten.

So I proceed with a brilliant plan that borders on stupidity. I purchase three Quarter horses. I think I need lots of equines to feed this winter-I have tons of hay in the barn. Never before in my life have I owned *tons* of hay. I feel very wealthy.

Totally embracing my cowgirl fantasy, I fancy that I will have the next cutting horse champion. The Quarter horse mare has a colt at her side and is in foal for the spring of next year. Talk about a ready-made trio of horses!

I am also "training" a big Quarter horse gelding named "Tony." He will make a great roping horse when I buy my herd of cattle. Suzi is my pleasure driving and true ranch-work horse.

I must think I have lots of time on my hands. I believe I am really thinking wisely. Unbeknownst to me, I am NOT thinking. I am dreaming, unreal dreams. As I progress in my ranch life, I learn to tell the difference between real and unreal dreams. I learn to concentrate on the *realistic* dreams and just to think, not act, on the unreal dreams.

Sarah steadfastly stays in her room reading. I make her help me with ranch chores. If she does not help, I will not take her to the small, town library in Eagle Point. Withholding books from Sarah motivates her, unwillingly, to help me with my dreams. Farming is not Sarah's dream.

My cinder-block horse stalls have four, inconceivable feet of old, smelly, foul sheep manure piled up in them. My tractor will not fit through the stall doors, so I proceed to dig out all four stalls by hand. To this day, I still see the stain marks from that manure on the stall walls. I fill wheel-barrow after wheel-barrow with the foul excrement and slowly wheel the manure into a small, garden field where I spread the smelly fertilizer by hand. As I dig into the stinking stalls, the manure has begun to compost and is hot and steamy. The wheel-barrow and my number two back hoe (a shovel) clean all the stalls. I become passionate about picking-up poop. Never does one find a pile of poop or a huge manure pile on my property today. I pick and spread horse poop every day on my farm. I religiously pasture-harrow the field every other day. I much appreciate a "poop-free" environment. The grass and fields on my ranch are mostly sparkling green and clean.

While southern Oregon is murderously hot in the summer, the nights are thankfully cool, down to 80 degrees. The west brings a cool breeze most summer evenings. You can smell the cool breeze that picks up each evening around 4 P.M. On the still, hot summer nights, I sit outside on my deck and enjoy the air.

I have the above-ground pool-lining fixed. Sarah and I climb into the pool regularly. The cool water is a life-saver. I skinny dip. There is no one other than Sarah here. She lives in the pool, but she insists upon wearing her swimsuit. Remember she is only ten years old. No skinny-dipping for this modest child.

The first-cut hay is stacked in the barn. The hayfield thirsts for water. Rain does not fall during the summer in southern Oregon. You must irrigate the fields in order to get a second crop of hay and keep your fields productive.

Now all I have to do is to figure out how to put together the wheel line and the 15-horsepower, electric water pump that goes into Antelope Creek so I can irrigate the hayfield.

A wheel line is a monster sprinkler system on huge wheels. I have 23 sprinklers that spray water out 24-hours a day during the irrigation season. Mostly I don't care about important details. If I did care I could tell you just exactly how many pounds-per-square-inch (P.S.I.) of water pressure comes from my huge water pump. The pump sucks water from the creek into the wheel line and onto the hayfield.

I find four neighbor men who know how to place the pump next to the creek. We attach a 15-foot siphon pipe to the intake nozzle on the pump. We then attach the rubber hose to the pump outlet and wire the electrical pump into the electrical box by the creek in the hayfield. We prime the pump by dumping 20-gallons of water into the siphon pipe. I then touch the start button on the electrical box and wait for the pump to fill all the underground pipes in the field with water. Filling the vast amount of underground pipes takes about five to seven anxious minutes. Then, slowly, the above ground wheel line pipes start to fill and the sprinklers slowly begin to spray water on the mowed hayfields. Suddenly the water pressure is correct in all the pipes and the 18 Rain Bird sprinklers begin to throw 40-foot circles of water across the field.

I am relieved that I can make the water come out of Antelope Creek into the underground pipes, into the wheel line and onto the field. The sprinklers make a "click, click, click" sound. The clicking of the Rain Bird permeates my mind for 20 years. If the sprinklers go off in the middle of the night, I wake and walk down into the hayfield to restart the electrical box. I have just 20 minutes to restart the pump before the pipes all drain back into the creek. I do not want to re-prime the pump in the middle of the night. A stop in the clicking is as stimulating as a crying baby is to an attentive, new mother.

I have hand lines as well. Hand lines are 20-foot long, three-inch aluminum pipes that fit into each other. They must be moved once a day and I have 20 hand lines to move.

I hate the hand lines, but move they must. I pick up the pipes one-by-one and move them 30 yards to the next riser and hook them up. If I do not mate the pipes exactly into the next pipe I get a blowout of water and must turn off the hand lines, empty them, and refit them. I learn to be very careful about putting the hand lines together. There is no hurry in this tedious, strenuous job. Here I learn to care about important details. I make the moving of those hand lines a chore that Sarah must help me with each day. At ten, she cannot resist, but she hates the job. I try every trick in a single parent's book.

Trying to make a hard, difficult job fun does not work.

After much nagging and many threats, Sarah gives in and helps me move lines. We slowly become a small, farm team.

I listen to the click, click, click of the sprinklers all day and all night long. Little do I know that for the next 27-some years, every summer, my life will revolve around the "bum" of the baler and the "click" of those sprinklers.

At sunrise I get up to move the lines. Mornings are full of smells. The wet, field grass smells alive and growing. The dry spot where I roll the wheel line to absorbs the water like a dry sponge. The odor coming from the ground is like a small rainstorm. A family of red tail hawks, that have for generations lived in the 70-foot tall cottonwood trees that line Antelope Creek, wait for me to move the line. As soon as the water hits the dry ground, the underground world of the hayfield moves to the surface. Moles and gophers become breakfast for the hawks. I provide the wildlife food that they catch and take to their stick nests deftly nestled high in the cottonwoods. I can hear the chirping cries of their fledglings. Late in the summer, I watch the hawks teach their babies to fly and hunt. I learn about my red tails hawks all summer long. I am not only self-educated about running wheel lines, but am educated by watching the hawks. I learn their calls and can chirp to the babies as well. I have in-depth conversations with the hawks. I have no idea what we are talking about, but I learn to imitate their sounds.

I also have a great horned owl family that lives in the cottonwood. I become fluent in "hoot owl" language. I can mimic their calls perfectly. The owls come down to hunt in the field in the late evening when I once again move the lines. They also hunt at dawn. The hayfield is alive with food for both carnivores and herbivores.

I am relieved that I figure out how to drain the wheel line, pull-start the Briggs and Stratton gasoline motor on the pump, move it with the forward/backward lever, reconnect the hoses to the wheel line, and get the water sprinkling. I then move the hand lines 30 yards to the connection at the water pump. In the beginning I fight for every drop of water that comes pumping out of the creek. I have no idea how to do anything with this irrigation system. Only by horrendous trial and many errors do I figure out this cumbersome watering method.

I still cannot pass a field that is being overhead-watered without feeling great compassion for the time, effort and expense that goes into making dry ground green. I develop a love-hate relationship with my lower 20-acre hayfield that exists to this day.

This water is not free. I pay the power company about $15 a day for the electricity to run my pump. Hay grown by electrical pumping is very expensive.

My upper fields are flood-irrigated. I believe that the ancient Aztecs and Romans first recognized the power of water as it flows downhill. Flood irrigation is simply flooding the ground. Flood waters turn brown-ground green too. Man-made ditches bring water to my upper fields every two weeks for 36-hours. It is my job to open the flood gates and make sure the water flows downhill. I carry a shovel at all times and move water by opening and closing gates and cleaning the ditches with my shovel.

If you walk the fields, you develop a "farmer's foot." I can feel the difference between irrigated ground, almost wet, and dry ground, simply by walking across the fields. Flood irrigation is simple, direct, and not a high energy-consumer. Water works by Mother Nature's gravity. I just have to keep the ditches clean and the water moving. I love flood irrigation. I do pay the Eagle Point Irrigation District for the ditch water. No irrigation water in the west comes free.

My summer revolves around water. I pay the Rogue Valley Irrigation District for my hayfield water. Unused water is wasted water and wasted money. The water in the creek is not free. I move the wheel line daily. Moving the line takes me a couple of hours each and every morning because I still have no system and do not understand all the mechanics. I gradually gather more knowledge of the system and if everything goes well, I can get it done in an hour-and a-half. I walk the entire time as I have no four-wheeled ATV to ride.

I learn to move irrigation lines off a horse with Sarah behind me on the saddle. I ride the horse down to the fields and tie it under a shady cottonwood tree. Now on foot, I open one sprinkler valve to release the water pressure so as to not turn off the pump. Then I drain the wheel line. While the wheel line drains, I turn off the hand lines and Sarah and I move them. The hand lines are turned back on and I move the wheel line. I then reattach the wheel line to the underground water system and turn the wheel line back on. The open valve is turned off so the under-ground system can build pressure to pump the sprinklers that are watering the hayfield.

We then go back to the horse and ride home to start my barn chores. I am always, always working. I fall asleep working at night, dream about working, and wake-up to working the next day. Never in all of my life have I worked as much as I am working physically and mentally on my first summer of ranching.

Somehow the first months of living on a ranch slip away from me. Suddenly September comes. Sarah starts school. She is in the sixth grade and doesn't know any children at her new school. Like me, Sarah creates herself. She decides to become a straight "A" student. The school bus picks her up at the end of our quarter-mile driveway and she rides to school with the not-always-so-nice neighborhood farm kids. Sarah likes the school and makes some good friends. She likes most of the classmates and they like her, so she is making the best start possible for a painfully shy child.

For her 11th birthday, Sarah has a party. I have seven sixth-grade girls here for hot dogs, cake and ice cream. And I have hay down in the field. Rain rolls in and threatens the cut hay. Sarah's birthday party turns into a hay-hauling ordeal. I quickly teach one 11-old girl to drive my old white Ford Bronco as it pulls one flatbed trailer across the field. I teach another little girl to drive the tractor as it pulls a small flatbed trailer.

The little girls start walking to pick up this second cutting of September hay. The bales are light but the girls are small. Slowly I realize that there are strange trucks appearing in the field. My new neighbors are arriving to help save my hay. With an unusual array of girl children and old neighbors, the hay is pulled from the field and stored in the barn before the rain can ruin my crop. I again feed a hay crew. Everything in the refrigerator is cooked and served. There is not a crumb of cake nor a drop of ice-cream left in the house. All the girls, except Sarah, think this is the coolest birthday party ever.

Even today when I run into a now 32-year old woman who was at that party, she'll say, "Sarah's hay party was the neatest party I ever went to. I got to drive the tractor."

I try to do some substitute teaching to supplement my non-existent income. Not much work comes my way. Real life is emerging on the ranch. I need money.

I need some type of cash flow here on the Rolling Wheel Ranch. Oh yes. The ranch now has a name. The name comes from the wheel line rolling across the lower fields, watering the growing hay, and because of my love of the rolling wheels on my carriages. I have a brand too, "RWR." My brand is registered with the state of Oregon for cattle and horses. I have the horses, but I need the cattle. No money is coming in, I might as well spend my savings on cattle. I can make money raising cattle. After all, I own a ranch that has *lots* of grass.

I know nothing about cattle.

I fabricate another idea that borders on the brilliance of stupidity. I decide I want all-black, registered Angus cattle. I still harbor city girl ideas of how a ranch should look. I want everything to be neat, clean, and all the livestock should be the same color.

Over a period of several months, I have learned to bale hay, move irrigation-lines, flood irrigate, feed a hay crew, keep an above-ground swimming pool algae free, collect firewood for winter, marginally fix fences, and to clean up a very dirty and unkempt ranch. I now think I can run a herd of cattle.

I think all my cows should match so they will look pretty in the fields. I think that mama cows simply go out into the meadows and baby calves magically appear at their sides. I see the mamas and babies everywhere in all the meadows and fields surrounding my farm. By the end of September, I find a herd of 20 registered black Angus mama cows and nine babies. Come January and February, I expect 20 newborn calves. I can just see the dollar signs being born in the fields.

Life goes on. I am busy rebuilding fences so *my* cows will stay home. I am building a pond to collect the winter runoff for use in the summer. I am building paddocks for the too many horses I have purchased. I am building gates so I can move the cows from one field to the next. My freshly-built, crooked gates actually open and close. The fences sag in places, but at least the wire is up off the ground. I begin a lifetime romance with what I call my "cobweb" fences. Mostly these fences work. I am the tiny spider who constantly spins a thread to keep the fences together. I am always spinning fence webs on my ranch. It seems to me that as fast as I build fences, another section of fences falls down. Repairing fences is a lifetime job on a ranch.

My dad flies up from Atherton, California for a visit. My mother died seven years ago, so she never knows I am destined for ranching.

My dad is proud of Sarah's achievements in school. He just looks at me, and says, "Whatever possessed you to buy a ranch?"

I smile and reply, "I have always wanted to be a cowgirl. Remember I grew up in Wyoming."

My dear old dad just shakes his head. He is in his late 70s. When he leaves, his words of wisdom are short and to-the-point, "Good luck. You are going to need it."

"Bye, Dad," I reply. I think I am filled with luck.

I am still learning to ranch every day. There is an enormous amount of pride taken in raising cattle and hay (remember, I haven't raised a calf yet, I just bought this herd). All my hay is in the barn and the cattle have been turned out to pasture. One of my favorite pastimes is to ride my Morgan mare across my 20-acre hayfield and watch the cows. The other day my dogs and I walked down to Antelope Creek and enjoyed the autumn leaves turning all shades of color. I feel like I am in an English watercolor landscape.

An epidemic of cow pink eye jolts me back to reality. This epidemic is not a school child's pink eye epidemic, but a cowherd pink eye epidemic. I had no idea that cows ever have any problems. Remember, I know nothing about cows.

I call the vet. Dr. Jim Perry arrives. Jim is still my vet today. The man never hurries. The man never moves quickly. The man never speaks loudly. The man never gets excited. He is one hell of a vet.

Jim says, "Looks like we have a problem with pink eye."

I say, "Oh, my God. What am I going to do?"

Jim says, "Looks like we will have to give those cows shots."

I look at him like *he* is the crazy person who bought a herd of cows and has to admit that he knows nothing about them.

"*Shots!*" I say, "I don't ever handle needles. Needles make me faint even if I am not going to get the shot. I never have given a shot to anything."

Jim says, "Looks like you are going to learn."

My eyes and mouth gape open in total surprise. I stare. I thought that the vet is the one who gives shots. The thought of *me* actually giving a shot to a cow or any animal never entered my mind.

I ask, "Just where do I give the shot?"

Jim continues with his easy drawl, "Looks like you have to give them the shot in the eye."

I think I am going to faint. "Can't you just give them the shot?" My tone of the voice is begging.

Jim continues, "Carole, if you are going to be in the cattle business, you have to learn how to take care of the cows. You can't be calling me to give these cows shots every couple of days. Why, you have 20 cows with pink eye and the nine calves are coming down with it too. You can just watch and I'll show you how, and then you will just do it."

I look at him aghast. He's the vet, not me. I didn't go to college to be a vet. Vets give the shots, not me. I faint when I get a shot. I know I'll faint when I give a cow a shot.

We begin to run the cows though the squeeze-chute. A squeeze-chute is a large, metal, mechanized device that clamps down on a standing cow from each side so you can safely hold the cow still when you need to doctor her. Jim shows me how to attach the nose clamp so I can snub down the head of the cow and then give her a shot in the eye.

I almost faint.

I cannot faint because I have all my savings tied-up in these cows. Fainting is the false way out. There is no easy way out of this mess. I open my eyes, pick up the needle, and begin to give the cows shots. I have to give shots every three days for nine days. I cannot faint.

I relearn one of the very first lessons in ranching. *I do most of the work.* My hands then were the hands of a boy. I had no fingernail polish, no long nails, and many calluses. My hands will grow to be the hands of a working man. At this writing, my fingernails have not seen nail polish in 27 years. In the winter, no matter how many gloves I wear and lose, my chapped thumbs and fingers split open and bleed. I slather on cream. Nothing helps my hands except "Bag Balm."

The cows recover and I survive. I am introduced to the real life of a cattle ranch. My cows have not even started calving. Oh boy, do I have a world of knowledge to learn about cows.

I need to wean the big calves off the pregnant cows. The only creature I have ever weaned is Sarah. She still loved her baby bottle as a two-year old toddler. Weaning her off her bottle was a series of losing the bottle and having her believe my motherly white lies about losing it. I weaned Sarah with deception.

I cannot very well "lose" the cows.

I decide I will separate the nine calves from their mothers. Somehow, I manage to perform the trick of separating possessive mothers from clingy calves. I move the mothers away from the babies by riding my Morgan mare between them. I think I am a real cowgirl now.

As time goes by, I will discover I am very good at handling cows and their calves. I am quiet and slow. My method works. In the beginning I just did not know I have a quiet, hidden way with cattle. My method of separating mother cows and their children is simple. I am slow and quiet.

I pen up the newly-weaned calves. Fortunately for me I have a nice, sturdy corral. I feed the babies hay. The sad babies call for their mamas and the sad mamas call for their babies. My ranch sounds like an out-of-tune symphony of tubas playing a very sorrowful song. The song goes on for three days and nights and then suddenly, mothers and babies accept the separation. The music stops. Slow and quiet is better than loud and fast. Slow and quiet gets the job done.

I learn that I cannot simply turn those big calves back in with the mothers. If I turn the babies back in with the mothers, the mothers and babies go back to nursing. I must keep the separation permanent and take them to the auction to find a buyer for the calves. I will keep all the cows to produce future calves I can sell for a profit. Or so I think.

I cannot keep up with all the ranch work and the new Quarter horses. So I sell the Quarter horses and barely break even. The only horse that I have now is my big bay Morgan, Suzi.

I need to brand and vaccinate all the cows. I climb on Suzi to gather them. I sift and sort the cattle from her back. I am in my English saddle, which is not a traditional saddle for working cattle. I don't have a traditional western saddle, just the English one. Suzi does an admirable job. I never get off her to open or close a gate. At one point I think I am actually aboard a REAL cutting horse. No cows get away from Suzi. I never get my feet muddy.

The far neighbors come over and help organize my cattle drive to another neighbor's squeeze chute and sorting pens. I do not own any necessary cattle equipment. I rented a chute from the Grange during the pink eye epidemic. This cattle drive is the first of many drives to come into my life in southern Oregon. Many of the cattle drives that I take part in will be with other people's cattle.

Driving cattle down public roads takes a certain amount of organization. You need people on horses and people in trucks and people on mechanical four-wheelers. Some people race ahead of the cattle and block driveways, so the cows don't gallop through flower or vegetable gardens or raid hay barns. The entire drive needs good people. The far neighbors know enough people and we make the two-mile drive smoothly. We manage the entire cattle drive with two men, two woman, and two little kids on horseback. Then you add a pick-up load of little kids. The pick-up races in front of the herd to drop a little kid in each driveway to block the cows. The pick-up truck is usually driven by a wise and experienced grandmother. Remember that this drive takes place 22-years ago. Kids could still legally ride in the back of pick-up trucks.

My heifers need their "bangs" shots. Only a certified vet can give that shot. This shot prevents brucellosis in cattle. As we run the cattle through the shoot, I am so nervous that I am shaking. I cannot even brand my own cattle. My greatest achievement is that I give an old, limping cow a shot of penicillin. Wow. Big deal. Then I learn that I must give her another shot in three days. Gulp. Giving shots to cattle gives a whole new meaning to "cowpoke." I'm the one who faints at the sight of needles. I have managed to give shots in the eyes, and shots in the neck. I guess I will learn to brand too.

I later help to pull a calf belonging to another neighbor. The calf is born backwards and is miraculously alive. I used to think that cows magically have their babies in the meadows and eat grass. Little do I know how much work, effort and risk goes into raising cattle.

Winter settles in on my first year in southern Oregon. I now must feed my mama cows daily. I have a feedlot by my barn. The cows come into the lot through the terribly sticky mud to be fed. The feedlot is a muddy, sticky mess mixed with cow manure I can't possibly clean promptly in the mass of moving bodies. I am weight-lifting now, but my barbells are haybales. I toss down lots of bales of hay every day. In the beginning of winter, I think I have too much hay. Now I worry about not having enough. I hope it lasts. I hope I last. The rain keeps coming. The feed lot mud and mire deepen. I must do something.

I contract for delivery of rock for the feed lot. The rock man says that I must hire a bulldozer to move the mud. The dozer price is $45 per hour plus travel time. I have no spare change. I climb on my little Ford tractor and move the mud and barnyard goo myself. The rock man shale rock and deposits it in a large pile. I *slowly* spread the rock around. I use the front-end loader to pick-up the tractor equivalent of teaspoons of shale rock and spread it down the path to the field to make a solid, rock road for the cows to walk on to reach their food by the barn. I order more rock. This time the rock man brings "three-quarter-minus gravel," a mix of stone 3/4" big or less, to put on top of the shale rock. I move that rock teaspoon-by-teaspoon and level the feedlot and the path to the field. I am totally amazed at what I can do with my girl tractor. When pressed for money, I function. I build my first road on a budget.

Substitute teaching dries up for me. I teach only two days in December. My barn full of hay looks more and more empty. Hopefully things will get better in January.

What fun. On December 24 we wake up to SNOW. The snow continues to fall gently for the rest of the afternoon. My dear old Dad is visiting Sarah and me this Christmas season. We are so excited about the snow that we jump out of bed, toss on our winter boots, mittens, scarves and coats, and outside we go. Sarah and I make a couple of good snowballs and hold a great snowball fight. Splat! Her aim is perfect. I get the snowball on the back of my head.

Three neighbor girls come over to play. The four girls run and play in the snowy hayfield for a couple of hours. Snow angels and snow sculptures abound. They troop into the house, warm-up, dry their wet clothes in the drier and then out they go again.

I cannot stand to miss all the fun. I grab my lariat and a Flexible Flyer sled that hangs on the shop wall, just in case snow ever falls. I saddle Suzi and we all head out to the field. I now have a proper western saddle as well. It is a cheap saddle, but a saddle with a horn none-the-less. I wrap a lariat around the horn and the other end of the rope is on the sled. We have a glorious time on a sled ride around the 20-acre hayfield. The kids sit on the sled and Suzi and I pull them around at every speed with snow flying in their faces. What a wonderful day. When we are all wet and cold, we go up to the house and I put Suzi away. The kids peel out of wet clothes and we gobble down hot soup. Next year I will have a real sleigh.

December 25 comes softly with the quiet of falling snow flakes.

Our first Christmas in Oregon is white. We awake at 5 A.M. and check for presents from Santa. Sarah and I find none. I build up the fire so the house will be warmer when we try again later. By 8 o'clock, the house is warmer and Santa has arrived. Grandpa (my dad), Sarah and I, plus the dogs, Popsie and Dolly, open the presents and chow down breakfast. I feed the hungry livestock and we jump into the pick-up and hustle off to the little country church held in the tiny, one-room school house located just a quarter-of-a-mile from our ranch.

Grandpa wants to know what to wear to church. I assure him that it is very casual. It is a simple little church and the minister has his Levis on. He is also wearing a patch of cow manure from his barn. He too feeds his stock before he comes to give his sermon. I find something very humbling about attending a small church where everyone knows everyone else and we all visit the stable on Christmas morn to feed our hungry stock.

After church, we are invited to our neighbor's house for dinner. Dinner is late because another neighbor's bull has escaped and is busy feasting on the hay in our near neighbor's barn. One more act of Christmas spirit consists of herding the one-ton bull into a trailer and sending him back home.

Grandpa and I take the Christmas tree down on December 26. Sarah leaves for a visit to friends in San Francisco. Grandpa leaves on the plane for his home on Tuesday. I find myself gloriously alone for the week after Christmas. The quiet time alone moves in slow motion.

The calving of my cows is yet to come.

CHAPTER 6
FIRST CALVES OF THE FIRST YEAR

My first calf is born in January on Friday the 13th.

We have six inches of snow, so all the schools in Eagle Point are cancelled. Sarah and I do a mama cow walk. We put on layers and layers of clothes and meander around the snow-covered fields searching for any newborn calves. I find our first calf, freezing cold and on the wrong side of the fence from his mama. Running on the adrenaline of finding my first calf, I shove the baby back under the fence for his mother to bond with. The mama cow had decided she will not accept this cold creature and does not allow the calf to nurse. She kicks him hard every time he tries to suck. Oh great. Here is my very first calf that I have ever produced, and I have problems already.

The baby needs warm milk, and he needs the antibody-rich colostrum in that first milk. I put my arms under his belly and manage to hoist him up as I stagger under his healthy, 80-pound weight. He only weighs 40 pounds less than I do, and my carrying him is hampered by my many layers of heavy clothing. Sarah went back to the house long ago, being smart enough to see that looking for calves in the snow is not an Easter egg hunt.

The mama cow is hot on my tracks. What am I doing with the baby, her baby, that she does not want? Cows, even when they do not want their babies, are very protective of their newborn. Fortunately she does not stomp me down but follows right into the empty horse barn. I know nothing about orphaned calves, but I am totally determined that this cow and her baby are going to mother-up. This mama cow needs to let her baby nurse out her swollen and painful udder.

I manage to rope the mama cow and tie her up in the horse barn. I have no idea how I achieve this rodeo act, but I do. I then get a halter on her head while she is trying her best to kill me. I manage to blindfold her and tie up a back leg, preventing her from kicking. I get a bucket and I, who have never milked anything, milk her out by hand. She wants to kick the heck out of me, but I am so quick. I am quick and I milk like I am in a contest. I milk. She kicks. She misses. I milk.

Using a glove for a nipple, I feed the baby the vital colostrum milk. Now that her tight udder has been relieved of pressure and the calf has gotten enough warm milk to manage on his own for a bit, I introduce the calf to the milked-out mama cow. After I have risked my life to milk the mama cow, her bag is not so tight and doesn't hurt. The calf nurses slowly, but it nurses. I still have her securely tied-up and blindfolded.

The mama cow had been feeling a little excited from the confinement, so lots of manure has exploded from her hindend during this project. Now she can't see me, and she can't smell me, because I am covered with that manure from head-to-toe and I smell like her surroundings. Risking my life, and Sarah's future, to raising cattle and ranching is powerful dangerous stuff. And I will not trade my ranch for a warm, safe, inside job for anything. This living, breathing calf and the life we are creating for ourselves is reward enough. I leave the cow tied-up for now and feed and water her daily. After a week of nursing her calf with the halter restraint, the two have bonded and my first calf lives.

At 11-years old, Sarah has a job too. She feeds 16 head of cows every night. She gets paid a dollar-a-day and relishes her own spending money. I am glad to have her help. I am feeding a total of 30 head of stock a day. My excess of hay is getting low and I am selling off six cows to avoid running out of hay. But I am getting a good price for these animals. I can always build my herd back up next fall.

Christmas came with snowflakes and January comes with baby calves. I also buy a new Morgan horse. The New Year also brings monsoon rains. My most important criteria for becoming a rancher is to absolutely love the outdoors. I must love being outdoors unconditionally and without any reservations. While I ranch, I live with Mother Nature and her whims and whiles, her mercy and mirth. While an office worker will shudder at having to walk from their car to their building, I will be surrounded by freezing rain, icy winds, smouldering heat, picturesque sunny days, and every mix in between from the moment I leave my house until all chores and problems have been finished, every day. Currently I am living with winter monsoons.

Today a new baby bull arrives around 2 P.M. I manage to give the bull calf his "welcome to the world" vaccination without a problem soon after he is born. Best I get him vaccinated and ear-tagged before he grows beyond the weak strength of a newborn.

I then feed all the cattle, horses, dogs, child and myself, and retire to the warmth and comfort of my hearth and home. About 8 P.M., the cattle are conversing in a most discomforting manner. The mama cows are not contentedly lowing, but bellowing in alarm.

I climb into my wet-weather gear and out into the deluge I go. I find the first problem. Another brand new baby is on the other side of the fence from the mother cow. It must be a ritual for these babies to get pushed under the fence. I crawl over the fence and push the baby back underneath. I have not a dry spot on my body in the cold, wet rain. I fix a gap in the fence as I want no more babies on the wrong side.

Then I notice that the other mama cow is still calling her baby. She brought him up to the feed lot through the MUD.

Mud! Oregon mud is known as *black sticky*. Black sticky is black, gooey, terrible clay. In the summer the clay is cement-hard and seems to crack open into a foot-wide crevice that drops down at least ten feet. We claim you could hide a body in the cracks during the summer. In winter, the rains transform the brick-hard clay to sticky mud and the cracks collapse shut. The top of the mud is slick as snot and as deep or deeper than the tops of whatever boots you wear. When you walk in this goo, you become taller by several inches with each step you take. Either you cannot get the mud off your boots or you cannot get the boots out of the mud.

My road that I built into the feedlot does not hold up to the cows tromping on the rock. The cows wade in the black sticky up to their bellies to get to the feeders. I think that next spring I will build another road to solve the messy problem (ha ha on me).

Here I am, dressed in my yellow slicker, my slicker coveralls, my fisherman's hat and my cold, rubber boots. Dark is everywhere and Mother Nature is busy pouring rain on everything. Dark and Mother Nature are a defiant team tonight. I must rescue the calf because the calf is stuck in the MUD. At this point I have no wish to become stuck in the mud too, but the calf must be rescued. I arm myself with a shovel and adrenalin. I dig the calf out. The calf reunites with its mother. My boots stay united with my feet. (Always leave your rubber slicker pants on the outside of your boots. This technique prevents the mud from overflowing into your boot tops and the boots are less likely to fill with liquid mud and cold, wet manure.)

I slog through the black sticky back to the barn. I must return the shovel to its spot in the barn or lose track of it for future rescues. If I let go of the shovel, I am lost in the sea of mud and the shovel will disappear to parts unknown. On my way I discover that my Morgan mare Suzi has broken out of the barn. I catch her and return her to her stall. The new Morgan gelding "Woody" takes all this rainy-night activity in with wide eyes. I pause to explain to him, as simply as possible, that I do NOT usually cavort at night in my bright yellow Big Bird outfit in the pouring rain.

I carry my trusted shovel in-hand and am not overjoyed to see a flood in the horse barn. I now dig trenches at 9:45 P.M. so the barn will not flood due to the monsoon weather Mother Nature is providing. All I can think about is the 110-degree weather I enjoyed last summer; as hot and dry then as it is wet and cold now. When I awake in the morning, the monsoon changes into six-inches of snow and ice. Such is the mind and personality of Mother Nature in southern Oregon. The climate changes here are so incredibly different from the eternal spring of California. At least the monsoon-to-snow does not encourage the magnitude of population and traffic as the eternal spring in California.

I think about my vanishing, romantic life as a rancher. The next time I sink my teeth into a MacDonald's burger, I think about the freezing rainy nights, the sunny days for growing hay, and the alley rider who pushes the cattle into the packer's pen at the auction. I see the endless, eternal work it takes to get the beef from birth to market. I am barely learning about the path from start-to-finish in the livestock industry.

But I now have a paying job. My good neighbor lady, Miki Perry, related to the good Dr. Perry by being married to his son, Mike, finds me a job. I am now "riding the alley" at the livestock yard every Thursday. Miki finds me the job because she can ride very well and she already works at the auction yard, every Thursday. She knows I am desperate here in my first year, and she chooses to help me out.

"I think you can ride the alley," says she.

I say, "OK." I again have no idea what I am getting into.

So I show up at the Rogue Valley Livestock Yard to ride the alley. I push the cows off the scale while I am riding my Morgan, Suzi. Then I follow the cattle down the narrow, dark, freezing alleys to the waiting rider who opens the proper pen gate. I carry a numbered paper and hand it to the gate person. I trot back to the scale and Suzi and I repeat this process for the next four to eight hours, depending on the number of cattle being sold.

Riding alley is the best education I get in the cattle world. I see thousands of cattle of every breed, variety, age, wellness, lameness and temperament. I ride this alley off and on for almost 17 years. My last alley ride is for the Jackson County Cattlemen's Sale. I am the only woman in the group working the scales. I no longer have cattle and I now ride the alley on my dressage saddle and my old Morgan mare Birdie. I have come full circle. The sale yard is torn down soon after this sale to make way for a Dutch Brothers coffee café.

I continue to be startled by my passion of ranching, cows, weather and the outdoors. Ranching is hard work. I love what I am doing. The work is not just work. I find an enjoyment and a fulfillment from what I do. A calf is alive because I heard the mama cow bawling. I push the calf back to the cow on a dark and stormy night. The horse is safe in the stall because I put her there. The barn is dry because I dig a trench late at night to keep the water out. The sun will rise tomorrow on a new and different day that may even include another calf on the Rolling Wheel Ranch.

No new calves this morning. I still own just three calves. Two bulls and a heifer. Mama cows are not so different from people mothers. Two cows form a babysitting co-op. The other cow develops a "latch key" program. She hides her baby and tells the calf, "Stay put. Don't let anyone in. I have to go to work." A cow sees her primary job as filling her stomach and gossiping with other cows.

Some days Sarah and I manage to go skiing. Sarah and I go to Mount Ashland. I only drive one hour before we put on our skis and skim downhill. We have a wonderful time. The snow is good. Sarah is a good little skier. The next couple of runs we go down she skis right past me. We leave the ski hill at 4:40 P.M. and sit down to a quick dinner. All the ranch chores are done by 6:30 that night. I am getting better at driving on snow. The ol' Bronco that I bought is wonderful with its four-wheel drive.

January trudges on with poor weather. We experience relentlessly cold, wet, damp weather. This is depressing weather. I walk out into the far pasture to check on the heifer calf born last week. Her mama is the latch key cow. I find the baby dead. I think she died of neglect. My small bull calf is not looking good. So I give him a shot of antibiotics. I keep giving shots for three days. The death of these babies is like the weather: cold, damp, depressing.

My neighbors' calves die too. The neighbors are sympathetic and understanding but not mushy. A reality of life is that you have death. Death is so removed from the Saran-Wrapped meat counters of everyday city and urban living.

Death is new to me. In the years to come I learn much more about death.

I meet the neighbors. Over the years, some neighbors become good friends. Other neighbors become good enemies. I wave at some neighbors and with others I have a delicate truce. Farm people's report cards often state, "Does not play well with others." We may not play well with each other, but in a pinch, we help one another out.

One night I have nine people over for dinner. While we sit at the table I receive a call from a person looking for a horse to buy. I pass the phone from person-to-person until someone has just the right horse to sell. I am certain that the person who called thinks they dialed a crazy person's house. We all laugh about passing the phone until we achieve the right person/horse combination. I am just beginning to feel like I might belong here. I am just beginning, but the feeling of belonging is starting to take hold. I do have a ranch, and I am making friends.

Now I want to plant my flower garden. I do not feel so badly when flowers die. I do feel badly about the baby calves dying. The babies are so full of life one minute and so stiff, cold and dead the next minute. I must have courage to be a rancher. The emotional highs and lows are so pronounced. A dead calf represents a torn up $100 bill plus the all the work and nine months of time and feed it takes to make that calf.

By the end of January of my first year, I move into "graft and corruption." At the stockyards there is a shipment of three-day old Jersey/Angus calves coming across the scales. Sooo...I take the chance and buy one. She is a heifer and with the help of Mother Nature, Father Time, and the knowledge of the neighbors who know so much more than I, Sarah and I "graft" this calf onto the childless mama cow. Lo and behold, the mama cow lets this orphan calf nurse. I hope the calf lives through the night and grows up. Now I have $120 tied up in this non-registered Angus/Jersey cross. But better I take a gamble than I take a total loss. I go up to the barn twice tonight to see if she is still alive. I hope that the morning will shine brightly on me and the baby will still be alive.

Tonight I also must give the bull calf his shot of antibiotics. My newly developed technique is simple. As I grab the calf by the tail with my left hand, jab, and inject the shot with the right hand. This baby is feeling stronger. I grab and shoot, the calf jerks. My feet crash out from under me and down I go in the muddy, grassy, wet field. I am cold, wet, and yucky but realize how funny I must look at this moment.

I do not sit on the cold, clammy ground very long. I must develop a better technique. I may just rope him the next time. One more day of shots and he should be better. I hope the weather holds for my babies. Cold nights and mornings, 20 degrees until about noon, and then up to 40 degrees. On the north side of the house, the ice is an inch thick and never melts.

Bingo! The next morning I own another bull calf. This little guy is born today, the last day of January. I weigh him in at 90 pounds. I don't want to leave him in the field where the other calf died, so I ask a neighbor and his son to help me move the calf. I drive my truck into the wet field and pick up the calf with the help of Larry. I cannot bench press a 90-pound, wiggling calf into the back of the pick-up. Mama cow runs behind the pick-up truck while I hold her calf and Larry drives. I hope that the upset mama cow does not jump into the back of the pick-up with me. At the barn I slip the calf into a small stall and mama cow follows right behind me.

I've learned from previous experience and the good advice of neighbors: "Always keep the calf that you are handling between the mama cow and you. A mama cow rarely hurts her calf to get to the person handling the calf. Never take your eyes off the mama cow."

I practice this advice when I give the calf his "welcome to the world" shots.

The new calf is strong and good-looking. So far I own three live bull calves and one grafted heifer. The mother cow with the grafted baby is a wild woman. She protects her new grafted baby with deadly force.

I feed 34 head of animals every day. I toss 12 bales of hay into the back of the pick-up every night and "push feed" out of the pick-up. The water main broke up at the barn when a cow stepped through the mud and broke the water line. I haul water to the cows in the barn. I fill a trash container from the house, and then siphon the water into the cow's water tank.

Today I clean the cow stalls and have nice bedding down for the babies. I have learned to keep one clean stall ready all the time. I never know when I will need a clean stall for my mama cows and a new baby.

The mud deepens here every day. The grafted pair must stay in the stall for a long time. Mama cow does not have much milk. I hope to NOT bottle feed this grafted baby.

February comes with more rain. More rain means more mud. I face the fact that I am not experienced enough to handle the cows, the mud, and my dwindling hay supply. I need to fix things up before I can raise cows. I know that the registered herd of cows must be sold. I *must* sell these cows.

With more rain and mud comes the prospect that the cows will begin to calve again. These cows will not have their babies when Mother Nature mixes sun and warmth into the beginning of February.

I do not look forward to dark, cold, wet, rainy nights full of baby calves. I learn what I do not want to learn. Ranching is hard work. Raising cattle is not all fun and games. I put the word out at the sale yard that I am selling my cows.

Three buyers call to visit on one day. The first buyer flies in on the wings of a vulture. He jumps out of his truck and makes a mean and unkind offer on the cattle.

"Those cows are ready to calve. Look at all this mud you have. Those calves aren't going to live." (Like I am not already aware of this problem with dead calves and too much mud.)

He makes a ridiculously low offer. "I'll just take them cows off your hands, Little Missy. I'll give you $100 for each cow."

I look at him and laugh, "You have got to be kidding!" I *intensely* dislike being called "Little Missy."

"You had better take my offer because there won't be any more offers besides mine."

I smile and hold back the tears. "No, I'll make it work before I will give this herd away."

I learn something about this man that holds true today, 27 years later. He is a cheat and will take advantage of a person when that person is in trouble. I am glad I learn what holds true to today. I use my knowledge of this cattle buyer carefully in my future experiences with him.

The second buyer never shows up.

The third scheduled buyer comes. He is only interested in buying 10 head for his boss, but Chet Wolf decides to buy the entire herd for the White Oak Ranch. I am saved from ruin and disaster. Chet returns on Valentine's Day to pay for and pick-up the herd, and a new calf is born. Chet is delighted. He came for 30 cattle and takes home 31.

Through this sale of my first herd of cattle, I meet the head of my future adopted family. The Wolf clan will play a very import part in my life in southern Oregon.

Relief floods my soul as the last trailer load of my cows leaves the ranch. My wallet is full and my hay is almost gone. I had less than ten days of hay left to feed cattle, and two months of feeding to go. The cost to keep the cattle quickly outpaces the money I might make raising them. I do not miss the mama cows or the responsibility of their calves.

Next time, and there *is* a next time, I will do my cattle differently. I need to learn more and own fewer cows. I think I will buy feeder steers and turn them out to eat the grass in my pastures. When the grass goes I will sell the steers. I think I have some people who will put my hayfield up on shares. I *think* I have the future whipped.

I am only knocked down briefly. And I have managed to find solid footing waiting for me in the deep mud of my first, terrible winter in southern Oregon.

CHAPTER 7
HORSES IN THE FIRST YEAR

I arrive from California with my Morgan mare, Suzi. I think I need more horses so I can ride them and sell them.

I buy buckskin Quarter horses because I believe I will make a try at being a "master cutting horse trainer." Then I discover that the entry fee for a cutting horse competition can be as much as $500 for just a few minutes in the arena. And I have not a clue on how to cut cows or train that type of horse.

So I buy another Quarter horse gelding that I think will be my roping horse. I have one western saddle and no idea how to rope.

I own lots of pasture and I keep horses cheaply until winter, when I find out that the horses eat more hay than my cows. I keep the Morgan because she is an easy-keeper. Suzi can eat sticks and still gain weight. The Quarter horses need quality hay and grain to stay in good condition.

I sell all of my nice Quarter Horse dreams. They all go to good homes. I am down to one horse again. I must learn to think better this first year of owning my ranch.

This first November I also limp around with my foot in a cast. While riding a horse, I kicked the horse's side to move it over to open a gate. I broke my leg in the process. I have a perfect spiral fracture. Just dumb luck. I didn't even know that it was broken at the time. The leg swelled up in my boot, so I am in a temporary cast without knowing it. The leg hurts like the dickens when I try to pull the boot off later that day. But I take the agony of pulling off my boot rather than resort to the standard practice of cutting the boot off to avoid damaging the leg more.

While I cook dinner I cannot figure out why I hurt so much. By 3 A.M., I know something is really, really wrong. After I put Sarah on the school bus at the end of the driveway, I drive to the doctor's office.

Not easy to do because I am in pain and can hardly put pressure on my left leg. My truck at this point is fortunately an automatic and can be driven with only my right foot on the pedal.

The doctor says, "What did you do to cause this spiral fracture?" The doctor, of course, is looking at the x-ray of my left leg.

Says I, "I think I did something to my leg when I kicked a horse, but I am not sure what."

The doctor places a plaster cast on my leg. The rain pours down outside the doctor's office. The good doctor says, "Keep off the leg for a couple of days and then come back and I will put a walking-cast on your leg."

He then says, "I'll tell whoever drove you to the office to come and pick you up now."

I smile and say, "I drove myself. There is no one else."

Those words will haunt me for the rest of my life.

I drive myself home. Driving home alone may not be very smart, but I am alone and I have livestock to feed.

"Sure," I think as I hear the doctor's words in my mind, "Keep off the leg for a couple of days."

"Sure," I think. "Just *who* will do the chores and feed the cattle?"

Remember that Sarah is only 11-years old. I have cattle to feed and a ranch to run. I have no extra money to hire help. I stop and find crutches at the thrift store. I buy the crutches and I drive home. I limp out of the truck. I place the crutches under my armpits and swing my body with the help of the thrift store crutches to get in the house. I have cattle to feed. I place a plastic bag over my cast as rain gear. The bag lasts five steps. I know that I cannot afford to get the cast wet. I hobble up to the barn, find an old inner tube, cut the inner tube in half and slip it up, over my cast. I fold back the extra inner tube and secure it with a bungee cord.

I now have what I call my "Gucci" galoshes. I function on the wet ground with the inner-tube galoshes and crutches. I go to work at the sale yard, broken leg and all.

I *can* ride the alley with the broken, casted leg. I *can* feed the cattle. I ride Suzi without a stirrup for my left foot. I can step on her from the off side. I must function. My child is only 11 and she helps all she can. I have no medical insurance and no spare money to pay the doctor for another visit. In eight weeks I doctor myself by sitting on the back porch of the house and using a hacksaw to cut my cast off.

I must be crazy. I am in debt so deeply to this ranch that I have only one choice. I must function at all times and in all situations. I do not have the luxury of being lost in depression or crying. I must function or lose everything. I function. The leg heals perfectly.

Then I find a fellow in Grant's Pass who will insure me. I pay my first, private medical insurance premium. I never regret getting this costly private medical insurance. The medical insurance proves to be one of my wiser choices in this first year of ranching.

I decide to drive a pair of horses. I have always wanted to hook two horses to a wagon and drive them off into the sunset. The old man, Gerry Black, who lives next door to me on a hardscrabble ranch, drives horses. He is a master horseman. Gerry is in his 70s. Gerry agrees to help me put together a pair of light horses. My *dream* of a Morgan pair might just happen with the expert help of Gerry Black.

I buy a nice little Morgan gelding. This Morgan is named "Woody." Woody is a dandy little guy, only he and Suzi do not move alike and are not the same size. I sell Woody for a nice profit.

Soon I hook myself on horse trading. I use horse trading over and over to get myself out of tight financial spots that I put myself into when I buy my ranch. I usually can make a profit with the horses. *Usually* is the key word here. Sometimes I do not make money trading horses. However, most of the time, I make some money and can pay my ranch expenses by buying, training, and selling the horses.

Suzi stays on the ranch and earns her shoes at the sale yard. I drive her to a nice little single cart. I think I am on the top of the world.

In the winter Suzi pulls the flexi flyer sled in the hayfield for the kids. She truly is an all-around, versatile Morgan horse. But horses are social animals and Suzi needs a friend. I go looking for another Morgan mare.

This new mare must be the same size, color, and have the same way of moving as Suzi to create my dream team for the wagon. I think I am an expert on what to buy for a matched pair. I am not, however, an expert in what I buy. I prove to be as inept a buyer when I see the horses in person as when I buy them sight unseen. When I find a good horse, I recognize a good horse, but I also buy lots of not-so-good horses. Many times I sucker myself into buying the wrong horses. The "poor choice" horses always leave here better than when they came. I find a horse that I call Sally. Sally becomes Suzy's partner as a pair. I learn so much from Sally. Much of the learning is not what I want to know, but I certainly use the knowledge with other horses in the future. Sally is a great riding horse but not a good driving mare. I eventually sell Sally to a wonderful home and she is always well-loved and well-taken care of.

One Sunday I am invited to a neighbor's house to watch a new method of breaking colts. There are four unbroken two-year olds and three riders. One guy is a pro bronc-rider, another a young cowboy, and the third and last is another cowboy. They all look at me, and the bronc-rider asks, "Want to try?"

"Sure," says I, while inside my stomach a flicker of fear glows. Why do I not find the word "No" in my vocabulary very often?

So I climb off my English saddle, off my well-broke Morgan, and I try this "new" method of breaking horses. It turns out that a gentleman named Tom Dorrance is leading the group. I am so ignorant that I don't know who this old man is, but I do sense that I must listen to his every word of wisdom.

"Don't grab hold of these colts. Just go with them. If you grab hold of them they will BUCK," says Tom.

I force myself to be totally relaxed. The ride is *wonderful*. None of the colts buck. After a couple of hours, they are turning and moving well. We *never* move out of a simple walk. I have chanced to have been exposed to one of the greatest horsemen in history. I discover this concept that you must always be relaxed and go with the horse in the beginning.

I am invited back for the next session. The men are planning to work with ten young horses and they want me there. This training method is very passive. The key is no resistance and lots of forward impulsion. I must admit I am exhausted from "forced relaxation." My mouth is dry and my legs are shaking when I get off my colt. I *learn* a lot. The pro bronc-rider had busted up his knee and he needs a new method of training colts. He wants to try this different method, so his ranch has supplied the colts.

I am delighted to find pieces of the old West are still alive here. I love to sit with the old and young cowboys who make their living at this work, and listen to them talk. These men are always surprised to see me climb off my English-style saddle and sit up there with them. But riding English is no mystery. Riding is riding no matter what your style may be.

My best compliment comes when one of the old cowboys looks at me and says, "You are a pretty good hand with a colt. Will you come back to the next breaking party? We can use you."

I understand perfectly that they just need a warm body that listens to the instructor and follows directions exactly. My motive, of course, is to stay alive; I also come to the conclusion that while I used to claim that I am not a "brinksmanship person," that claim is NOT true. I *love* the brink. I actively seek out adventures. Sometimes my judgement is great. Other times I must crawl away from my mistakes. Like a gambler loves the risk of his game, I love brinksmanship, and I love life. And I am learning not to step over the brink. In brinksmanship, the fall can be very harmful when you step over the edge.

So far on my ranch adventures I have always managed to step back from the brink.

CHAPTER 8
OTHER PEOPLES' CATTLE

I lease out my fields to another man's cattle. I have fields and he needs grass. The time is the end of March, March 24 to be exact. The man turns his cattle onto my upper pasture. March this year arrives like a lion and creeps out on little lamb's hooves.

Calves are again being born on the ranch. The mud tries to dry up, and then Mother Nature laughs as she gleefully dumps buckets of water on the ground. The sticky mud turns to the consistency of wet cement. This black gumbo will grow anything but is treacherous soil. This soil can kill livestock as well as grow life-sustaining grass. The soil kills by bogging down the babies or causing infections in open sores of the older animals.

I spend one day and most of the night nursing a sick calf that "bogged" down in the feeding pen mud. Usually the mother cows are smart enough not to bring their babies up to the feed lot. This baby didn't listen very well to its mama cow. The past few days had been warm and wonderful so, "Why listen to my mama?" thinks the baby.

I had to get my Morgan to help pull the baby out of the mud. I drop a loop on the baby by climbing off the horse and slipping the rope around the back legs of the calf, then attach the other end to my saddle horn. The Morgan does the work and pulls the calf out of the mud with a steady, careful pull.

Naturally, that night Mother Nature throws a monsoon of water down from the skies. The baby gets pneumonia. I bring the calf down to the house, warm him up, and watch him die. Death is so difficult to cheat once Death makes his mark on a living being. The next day Death repeats himself. Another calf is lost.

I am very tired of the cattle business, mine or anyone else's. Needless to say, we move the cattle to another field. The grass isn't really up yet, but the man leasing the fields cannot stand to lose another calf. I cannot stand to watch the babies die in my kitchen. In the ranching business, livestock dies. I have never been exposed to so much death anywhere before. We are not neglectful with these cattle. The deep mud is the killer. Mud remains a problem over the years. I eventually haul in so much rock and humus that the problems with the mud diminish, but sticky mud problems never totally disappear.

I find new calves at the auction yard to graft onto the motherless cows. I move the mothers into a close, small pasture with no mud. One cow takes her new calf, but the other mother is not interested in raising a child that is not her own. I personally thank God that I am not learning all this information about death and grafting calves with my own cattle now. I find learning so much easier with someone else's. And I am being paid to learn with another man's cattle.

Never again do I drive by fields of cattle and envy the "rich" rancher. Every cow, bull, calf and steer represents hours of hard labor and some deaths of calves or cows. There is a high, hidden mortality rate in the domestic animal world. No wonder ranchers and farmers all jump to the sales pitch of the wonder drug salesmen. No one likes to lose an animal. Yet at the same time, I ponder the futility of it all. I struggle to keep these cattle alive, only to sell them to be killed and eaten in their future.

I meet a most remarkable woman. I meet her because her daughter, Jenny, and my daughter, Sarah, become friends in school. She is about 32-years old. Her name is Donna and she moved from Belmont, California 17 years ago. She and her husband own a small dairy farm. Donna and her daughters run the farm. They own 55 head of cattle. These cows *must* be milked twice a day, every day of the year. Donna milks five cows at a time with an automatic milking machine. She milks at eight in the morning and then again at 8 P.M. It takes her five hours, from start-to-finish, doing the entire herd. She puts in ten hours of work a day, every day. I must add that Donna is also raising three daughters. I stand in front of her and I am so impressed.

The dairy herd must be fed. All the dairy calves must be bottle-fed by hand. I think about Donna every time I drink a glass of milk. I think I am busy with 30 cows out in the fields that are raising (or trying to rise) their own children. I am not even milking the cows.

Donna tells me, "Ron and I milked all the cows by hand the first five years of the dairy farm. We could not afford the milking machines." Ron is Donna's husband.

I learn that in the mid-1980s, not all farms and ranches are high-tech.

Donna and I visit while she works. I help her as best that I can. I learn that I love to pressure wash the holding pen after the cattle move into the milking parlor. The milking parlor contains ten stalls on two levels. Five cows walk to their stanchions to be milked. Feed waits for them on their own plates. Each cow knows the order of its place and almost always goes to her own pen. The headgate is closed to keep her from leaving too soon, and the cow's udder is washed carefully. The suction tubes of the milking machine are applied to each of the four teats of the cows. While the cow munches on her grain, she is milked with the steady, rhythmic pressure of the machine. When the five cows are finished, their headgate releases, they walk out the door and then the next five cows are ready. There is a steady rhythm of gates closing, cows munching, and milking machine throbbing.

The holding pen is made of roughed-up concrete flooring, to prevent slipping, and tile walls. While the cows are waiting here, the holding pen is liberally "painted" with liquid, mud, and soft, splashy cow manure. My job is to pressure wash the walls of the holding pen when the last cow goes into the milking parlor.

I have no idea why I like this job and I don't care why. I suit-up in yellow construction rain gear, turn on the large pressure washer, and go at the job. I start with the 15-foot high ceiling. Yes, there is cow manure on the ceiling too. That bit of artistic work is done with a deft flick of the cow's tail as the wonderful manure is still plopping out of the cow.

I then hit the sides of the walls. Top down, then bottom up. The floor is next. I can wash the holding pen in about an hour. Washing the pen occurs twice a day. The slurry of nutrient-rich water and manure goes to a septic system and is later pumped into a truck and then onto the pastures and hayfields that will convert this messy black gold into rich grass for the cattle.

As I watch all this and occasionally visit with Donna as she milks, I know that I am very fortunate because I am convinced I am partaking in the very last glimmer of yesterday. The life of the little farmer may be gone forever in 20 years. Small farmers just cannot make a living in this high-tech industry. What the high tech world loses are people like Donna who know how to make an honest and decent living for herself and her young family as they care for their cattle and fields with sustainable methods. Their home is not fancy. Their wood stove warms their family like my wood stove warms Sarah and me.

While feeding hay out of the barn on a winter afternoon, Donna and I compare calf deaths. We are both saddened by that terrible, powerful moment when the light in their eyes goes out, never to return.

The light is the same with people too, we both agree,

"And none of us ever knows what the terrible future holds for us," says Donna. "When you watch a person die or see a person in death, their light is gone forever."

"Yes," says I. "That light is never to be called back by anyone or anything," I continue, with a new wisdom from fresh experiences.

One of my very best experiences at the dairy farm is when Ron holds his birthday party in the milking barn. I am sitting on the milking parlor steps in a blue-denim cotton dress, eating birthday cake. As one of the cows walks out of the barn past the steps, she deftly lifts her tail and ejects hot, wet cow manure down my back. We all laugh hysterically.

Fortunately for me there is a shower in the milking parlor restroom. I stay in the dress and take a very long, hot shower. Also fortunately for me, Ron's birthday is in July and it is a hot summer night. I go back to the party clean and wet, and I will *never* sit on the milking parlor steps again.

When you sit in a hay barn on a cold, wet, spring night and talk about death juxtaposed to life, the hard work it takes to raise a family, plus care for all the domestic animals and crops too, I become aware that food does not come easily to grocery counters. Food comes from the great sweat and toil and losses of people we seldom know.

People with cattle start to call me to help them out. I meet many small farmers and ranchers because of my work at the Rogue Valley sale yard.

A neighboring rancher calls on Saturday for help to push cattle up into the back hills. The grass in the foothills is starting to grow in this cold, wet spring time. I am late in joining the cattle drive. Of course they have already left when I pull-in with Morgan horse, truck and trailer.

Rule one: never be late to work.

I follow their trail of hoof prints through the muddy hillsides. I trail them for about an hour and cannot find them. I see the cattle, but no cowboys. I cut down the hillside to see if I can ride back with them on the return to the trailers. No luck. The cowboys are waiting for me back at the trailers. I am ten minutes late all day long. I enjoyed trailing them, but I am fussed at for riding alone. The cowboys make a good point. I am riding in new country. They invite me to go help at the ranch, so I take a muddy horse and watch them rope a couple of cows out of the pasture. I am no help here. I don't know how to rope and I ride in an English saddle.

Sometimes it feels very strange for me to be living alone so much without another adult to have as a sounding board. I sometimes wonder if my life will always be filled with others, but still alone. I am surprised that I don't feel lonelier, but in actuality I am rather content with my life.

Spring comes. Before living in the country, I thought of spring as a time of rebirth, with calves, lambs and colts out in the fields and the fruit trees blooming. I now know better. Spring is also a time of death. Spring is the time of the dying of the weak and the weak newborn animals. Spring is the time when I see one small branch on the peach tree struggle to bloom and then wither and fade into the grayness of the dead trunk of the tree.

Winter is the time of sleeping. Spring awakens those that will be strong enough to face life and the bounty of summer. Fall is the time of abundance, of harvest, and reaping the toil of spring and summer.

I am tired of trying to save animals. I bring yet another weak calf into the kitchen. The calf is born on a cold night in the murderous mud. I warm it up using the hair drier and rub it until it is warm. The calf's internal temperature stays very cold. Gradually I warm it up. I use a large soda bottle for a baby bottle. I cut a finger off a leather glove for the nipple. I tape the nipple onto the bottle with duct tape (no ranch can run without duct tape). I now have a bottle baby. I do such a good job of warming up the inside of the calf that he now has a fever. His temperature just keeps going up and up. This calf in the kitchen dies too. No miracles. I learn this fact over and over. I cannot save everything. Death is stronger than life in some cases. I, as a calf paramedic, cannot save this calf.

I talk to other ranchers and they too experience failures. They too nurse calves in the kitchen that die. One neighbor finds a foal in her field. The foal is a newborn. No mother. No nothing. None of us know how it got there. The foal dies too.

But most calves and foals live. Some of the babies born out in the cold, wet nights live and thrive and frolic through the warm spring fields. The living babies are the ones that we celebrate, and understand with the pride and joy of living, and that we will contribute to the abundance of food that ranchers and farmers raise for the unknowing urban population to set upon their bountiful tables.

CHAPTER 9
MY DAD

My first spring on the ranch is a time of struggle. My father comes to live with Sarah and me. My father is dying this spring. I receive a call on Thursday, March 31, 1990, that my father is hospitalized. I quickly run out of the house after the phone call from the doctor at Stanford hospital, and rearrange livestock to fend for themselves for several days. I think that I will be gone just a couple of days.

I grab Sarah and I climb into the Ford pick-up truck. I drive like a crazy woman. I have one eye in front of me and one on the rearview mirror. I am speeding all the way to San Francisco, California from Eagle Point. Usually the trip takes a good seven hours. Sarah and I arrive in San Francisco in five hours. My sister comes from Boston. My truck blows up on the Bay Shore Freeway on my way to the San Francisco Airport to pick her up. I sit on the freeway for two hours in broad daylight before anyone stops to help me. All the "yuppies" driving with their cell phones won't even call in for help. My truck blew a rod though the engine. I have it towed to a garage. I don't remember how I get back to the hospital. My sister finally reaches the hospital by taking a bus. Our dad is dying of congestive heart failure.

I bring Dad home with me to die. He is flown up in an air ambulance. I drive his old Mercedes back to Medford. Sarah is such a good traveler. The instant she gets in a car, she goes to sleep. Dad stays overnight in the ranch house with us and takes another turn for the worse. He goes by ambulance to the Rogue Valley Hospital. I will chase the ambulance several more times before Dad dies at my home, in his sleep.

I need round-the-clock care for Dad. I have been away from the ranch for 12 days. The ranch stays together, but I have a huge backload of work. I have also a huge front load of work ahead of me. I really know very few people here. I have no friends to call upon for help. I am on my own with a small, 11-year old child and a dying, 80-year old father.

I do not find this experience with my dad to be a burden. I am just 40 and I have the energy of youth still in my body and my mind. I see myself as a captain of a ship, and I put together my crew carefully.

My crew is an excellent group of professional caregivers. They consist of six women and one not-so-excellent teenage boy. The boy does not last.

My job is to NOT do the crews' jobs, but to let them do their own job with their own skills. Each woman comes with her own skills and her own way of caring for Dad. These women also wind up taking care of Sarah and me. I step out of my kitchen. The kitchen is in excellent hands. The care they give to my dad is beautiful and kind. These are special women. I am proud to be the captain of this ship. The journey is a cumbersome one in many ways, but the voyage is as important as it is difficult. You learn the most about life by facing death.

I give up the few substitute teaching jobs and the one long-term teaching job that I had gained since Christmas. I need the money, but I cannot be everywhere at once and I need to be at home. I learn to tear down my 400-foot wheel line and put it back together. I thread pipes. I read, read, read, read the tractor manuals and ask everyone at the Grange and tractor shops how to best do farm and ranch work. I think I will even tear apart the electric motor for the small pump, to see if I can get it to run better. I never do tear it down. I know that it is too much for me at this moment in time. I fill the potholes in the driveway. Dad complained that the holes made a bumpy ride in the ambulance coming and going to the hospital. Now the traffic that rolls into Rolling Wheel Ranch rolls in quickly. Such are the results of a smooth driveway. Pot holes, as with most messes, slow everyone down.

I fix the water pressure gauge on the swimming pool and clean out the green algae that lurked in the pool all winter long. Sarah and her school friends are swimming and having a wonderful time. I find someone to rebuild the deck around the pool, so we are turning into a real house and ranch as well. My dad loves being wheeled out on the deck for a few minutes to watch all the noise and activity going on here. We are glad to have him with us. I love having all the nurses' aides, my dad, and Sarah's friends all running in and out of the house. The house feels so alive, even as my dad is slowly dying.

One day I wheel Dad to his Mercedes and help him into the car. More than anything, he wants to go fishing. I drive him, complete with his portable oxygen tank, to Little Butte Creek. Right under the aqueduct is a place where I can drive the car into the water. Dad sits, with his window down and his fishing pole sticking out the window. We don't talk. We just enjoy.

He fishes while I sit and remember all the times he took me fishing as a child in Wyoming. He often tired of untangling my line, so he taught me to fish with kitchen twine and a float. He calls that "indian fishing." I am quite good at fishing with the white kitchen twine and float.

Finally he says, "I am tired and I need to go home."

I know that he doesn't mean my home. He means his home in Atherton, California. So right there, he and I make a pact that I will not ever sell his home in California. He gives me power of attorney. He keeps the power of a father. I respect his wishes. I will not sell the home while he is alive. I will wait until he dies. He is a good father and I am a good daughter.

Business done, I start to back the Mercedes out of the creek.

We are stuck.

Not a problem. The main road is only about 15 feet from the creek. I wade into the creek and flag down a man with a truck and a winch mounted on the front bumper, who I wish had been handy when I broke down in San Francisco.

The man laughingly pulls us out. My dad and I are quite a sight. An old man on oxygen wearing a black overcoat and a black fedora hat, fishing out of the window of an old Mercedes parked in the middle of the creek. Somehow the man who pulls us out of the creek knows that fishing is important, even when the fish are not biting. He acts like he pulls old men, daughters, and Mercedes out of Little Butte Creek all the time.

Dad now has a *new* adventure to talk about. He spends so much time talking about his past. He tells me about the time that he and Roy Hunnel went Jeep camping in Wyoming. They forgot to set the brake on the Jeep in camp and the jeep rolled into the lake. The Jeep is only about two-feet deep in the water, but it will not start. They cannot push it out and all their cans of food get wet. The labels float off and they never know if they are going to open a can of peaches or beans. After a couple of days, a guy comes by and pulls the Jeep out of the shallows of the lake. My dad has been stuck before.

He is drifting toward death. I am the captain of his ship and I want to make this journey from life as smooth as possible. I have a huge responsibility.

Some days I cannot take the pressure of a houseful of wonderful nurses and my dying father. The chugging motor of his respirator clunks all night and day. The endless "chug-chug" of the machine is the sound of my dad breathing. His lungs work less and less.

I escape with a blanket and a book and drive the tractor down to the creek. I pretend to be working on the far side of the fields. I quietly rest my inner soul under the trees and tightly wrap myself in the blanket to hold myself together. I have my daughter projecting life and my dad losing it, both under my roof. I gather inner and outer strength from these quiet outdoor moments. I need the strength to guide my ship across these rough, emotional waters.

Occasionally a captain must take a lonely watch. I journey to the funeral home to make the necessary arrangements for Dad's eventual death. I go alone because essentially, I am alone in some parts of this journey. Life is always interesting and filled with difficult, hard, and cruel moments. I also make the decision to register my own funeral arrangements right then, so that Sarah will never be faced with the weighty decisions that I am making for Dad.

My dad celebrates his 80th birthday. He grows more and more disoriented. I find him a small little dog that is content to lay by his side day-after-day. I keep Dad's wallet tied to his wrist. I have $1,000 in the wallet. Then I go in his room and ask, "Dad, can I have money for the groceries?"

He carefully peels off $200. He knows to the very penny how much money is in the wallet.

"Here," he says, "get ice cream too."

When he goes back to sleep, I carefully replace the money. I know that it is very important that Dad thinks he provides our food. He is always the provider for the household, and I want him to believe that he still is providing.

Sarah and I talk about what we will have tied to our wrists when we are dying.

Sarah says. "I want my Guess jeans." (remember, she is only 11)

I say, "I want my horses tied to my wrist."

Sarah says, "I guess you will be dying in the barn then."

We both laugh.

My dad's brain gets less and less oxygen. His heart is beginning to fail more and more. His mind becomes clouded. He thinks I am stealing his money. I tell him that I invested his money for him. He wants his check, so I write him a check for two-million dollars on my bank account. He endorses it in a quavering hand. Dad is thrilled. He is at last a multi-millionaire.

"Deposit this check!" he commands.

"Certainly," says I.

I walk out of his room with the largest check I have ever held and carefully rip it into tiny pieces. I deposit it into my trash can. I think it is the best money I have ever "spent."

Dad is so thrilled. He brags to everyone how rich he is. Best to die still owning your own house and rich. This no-good, torn-up check is the best, last gift I give my dad before he dies.

Dad is a good man. He lived through the Great Depression. He can out "cheap" anyone. For your Christmas gift, he would open a savings account and receive a "free" gift. I would receive the free gift for Christmas and he would keep the savings account. He made me work for everything as a child.

He also made sure that he takes me fishing and comforts me when I am unhappy.

My dad is a good dad with his own particular set of incongruities. He is never late for anything. When you invite him to dinner, he is an hour early. He *never* misses a plane or train in his life.

But his breathing is becoming much labored. He dies in his sleep on July 15, 1990. I arrange for him to be cremated and sent to South Dakota to rest beside my mother, who was buried there seven years hence. I get a call from an antique aunt-by-marriage who lives in South Dakota

"Carole," she says. "Where is Gerald?" (my dad)

I think that she is not thinking well. "Auntie, I sent him to you several weeks ago to be buried."

"Well, Carole," she states, matter-of-factly. I can tell by the tone of her voice, nothing is wrong with *her* thinking at all. "Gerald is NOT here."

I call the funeral home. I discover, much to my amusement, that the funeral home has forgotten to send off my dad. They are so embarrassed that they will not charge me to ship him to South Dakota.

I possess a very strange sense of humor and have to enjoy it at this moment.

I carefully explain my dad to the funeral home.

"You could not have given him a better send off. My dad was a doctor. He did not think he was going to die. He was a wonderful cheapskate and was never late for *anything*. He did die. Now he gets to travel to his own funeral for *free* and he is *late* for his own funeral. *Perfect!*"

I call my Aunt and explain that Dad is on his way. Her bridge club holds a small ceremony for him.

I miss my dad and I am in huge debt from his illness. Eventually I get it all straightened out and most of the medical debt is paid from his estate. I captained his ship and I fulfilled my filial duty.

His oxygen pump no longer chugs in the house. The house is strangely quiet.

I go down to Antelope Creek and weep under the cottonwood trees.

CHAPTER 10
SARAH

This chapter is my most difficult story to tell. I love my daughter very much. I am a good mother, and Sarah is a wonderful daughter. We have our regular "mother-daughter" squabbles, like all mothers and daughters. This chapter on Sarah's life is about our early days at the ranch in Eagle Point, Oregon.

I buy the ranch for me, and for her. The day when she goes to a Laker's basketball game back in California changes my life. Sarah is picked up by the nanny and driver of very wealthy friends. The two girls, aged 9 and 10, sit in the press box to watch the game. I decide, at that moment, Sarah needs to meet the real world of real and average people. Not just people of privilege. I am recently divorced and decide she needs a childhood on a ranch. Besides, I want to be a cowboy.

Now is the time to move. I move her to Oregon just as she is about to start the sixth grade.

I show her the ranch for the first time in April 1989. The ranch house is small and cramped. The horse barns are filled with sheep manure. The hay barn is full of stagnant, moldy hay and Mother Nature tosses buckets of water all over the ground. The ground is wet with mud. The front yard of the horse stalls is filled with metal junk, twisted wire, and waste wood.

I start to cry. "Buyer's remorse" is what the old realtor calls my panic.

Sarah gently puts her hand in mine. "You bought it. Make it work, Mom."

I cry harder, unaware just how hard I will have to toil to make my dreams come true. I can only hope that the dream is not a nightmare. I want more than anything to prove to myself and to Sarah that I can succeed after two terrible divorces.

I bribe Sarah with the promise of a pool and a puppy. I make good with both bribes. She gets a Red Heeler pup named "Dolly" from the pound. I later name a black Morgan mare "Dolly" after this wonderful dog. Sarah and the dog love each other. The outdoor pup steadfastly refuses to come in the house. Dolly buddies up well with the other dog, Popsie. Popsie comes inside the house and sleeps by Sarah regularly.

I have the pool fixed. Two men come out and replace the liner. One of the men later becomes the producer for my horse videos, but here I digress and get ahead of myself. The cool water of the pool saves us this first summer. Southern Oregon is *hot* in the summer. We swim every day. I skinny dip and then climb back into my sweaty clothes that in a matter of a few minutes have dried stiff in the hot sun. I go back to my farm work somewhat refreshed after my dunk in the pool.

Sarah began swimming when she was only four months old. I took her to the YMCA program called tadpoles. Sarah loves the water.

I make good on my bribes and these bribes make good for me.

I proactively call the local school and ask for a list of kids who will be in Sarah's new sixth grade class. I then invite the kids and their mothers over to meet us. The kids swim. Sarah makes friends and I get to talk to adult women who know something about farming.

September rolls around and Sarah catches the school bus at the end of our quarter-mile driveway. I walk her up to the bus for the first time. I cry after she gets on the bus. I am now alone on the ranch.

Sarah is awarded the "Student of the Month" at her elementary school. This award is the beginning of the many, many academic awards and honors she achieves while attending the Eagle Point School District. Moving to Southern Oregon is good for Sarah. She blossoms, but remains a shy and private child.

For Halloween, we carve our RWR brand into the smile of the pumpkin and Sarah goes off to school dressed as a Gibson girl. Sarah can almost wear my clothes. I laugh about the time, when it comes. She is almost as tall as I am, and I am five-foot six-inches tall.

This first November, Sarah makes the honor roll. She is a much better student than I ever was. Her love of reading focuses on everything and all of her subjects. I tell her that never in my school days did I do as well as she is doing in school. Sarah has made a huge effort to excel in her new environment, and excel she does. I am very proud of my amazing daughter.

Sarah is working at her job feeding 16 head of cows every night. I pay her a $1-a-day and she relishes having her own spending money. I cannot force or trick her into working for no pay. I am glad to have the help as I am feeding a total of 30 cows every night.

Some days I can talk Sarah into going for a ride with me on the Morgans. She rides beautifully, but does not have my love for horses. Her love is books and reading.

I feel so proud of Sarah. Tuesday is a substitute teaching day for me and is also the awards assembly at Little Butte Elementary School. Sarah is on the "A" honor roll, is a National Geographic Contest finalist, and has perfect attendance added to her list of honors. It is extra nice for me to be sitting in the gym and seeing her stand up for all of her well-deserved honors.

Occasionally I try to get Sarah and myself off the ranch. We discover that we can go skiing on Mt. Ashland. It is so nice to just jump into the old Bronco and drive off to the mountains and be there in an hour. Sarah is getting quite good at skiing. She zips down the mountains. She even zips down the pretty difficult ones. I turn around to see if she is behind me and I cannot find her on the hillside. I feel panic rise in my heart.

Sarah calls to me from below, "Hey Mom! Here I am!"

Sarah passes me on the slopes. She will continue to pass me on her many achievements. Thank goodness, I now know to look ahead for her, not just behind me. Sarah continues to grow up.

Easter comes. We weave Easter baskets out of the willow tree branches that crookedly grow by our crooked front gate. Sarah and two of her friends dye eggs from a neighbor's hen house. Some eggs come already the color of the summer sky. The other eggs are speckled brown. The girls use natural dyes to color the eggs and they line their homemade baskets with hay from the barn. They then fill the baskets with the "natural" eggs. We have a grand day by making beautiful stuff.

Sarah and I buy a teacup poodle and we name her "Tricksie." Sarah and Tricksie go to dog school. Neither one likes it very much, but both learn dog manners: come when called, sit when told, stay when you must stay put. Popsie knows all the dog rules already. Only Dolly decides that she doesn't need to go to school, but prefers to learn the dog rules at home. Dolly is home-schooled before home-schooling is popular.

Even while her grandfather is living with us, Sarah continues her good work in school. She has some fears about "Grandpa scaring her friends because he is so sick."

Those fears pass. Her friends come and play and swim and hold wheelchair races on the deck. The nurses all befriend the children and life goes on aboard this strange ship that I am captaining.

A couple of weeks after Dad dies, Sarah and a friend are playing outside by the pool. They are playing "high jump in the pool" with a pole. I tell them several times not to play with the pole. They do not listen and manage to poke a hole in the bottom of the pool. All the water goes rushing out of the plastic liner. Needless to say, I am now facing a major repair on the pool liner. Sarah gets to make a healthy contribution to the cost. She is busy finding as many baby-sitting jobs as she can. She is also cleaning lots of stalls, washing dishes, and working on any odd-job that an 11-year old country girl can find to make some money. She wants to swim again. The beginning of our second summer in southern Oregon is hot.

I will continue to intersperse Sarah stories throughout my book. She is a complete part of me, and I yearn for her every day.

CHAPTER 11
LESSON OF THE COPPER POT PONY

After buying the ranch, as you will recall, I dabble in Quarter horses, but my heart is with Morgans. So I follow my heart and I begin to dabble in buying and selling Morgan horses. I discover that I can buy, train and sell Morgans easily as long as the horse is a "classic Morgan," with an upright, arched-neck, compact body, and kind disposition. I buy and sell two-to-four horses a year. I am not a big-time operation. I just get the horses going really well and then I sell them for a profit. I have a talent for making very nice, safe, trail horses.

This sideline brings me to a couple of horses that I will call "Chuck" and "Samson." These two horses have lots of old time Brunk and University of Vermont breeding in their background, which are breeding lines that a good majority of Morgans today come from. Samson is black and Chuck is the color of a shiny, copper pot.

A friend of mine who lives in La Pine, Oregon calls me one morning and says, "Carole, there are two Morgan horses over here that this guy wants to sell."

"Are they broke?" I ask.

"Nope! But they do lead, so you might be able to get them into a trailer."

Buying horses is easy. Getting the 800-plus pound horse into a small, fairly dark trailer that makes scary, metal noises when they step inside is very difficult if the horses are not used it.

"OK," says I. "How much?"

"Not much. You might even be able to trade something," says my friend.

Please remember that this conversation takes place almost 25 years ago. Oregon and especially La Pine was still very rural and fairly western-oriented. A person could trade a material object and lead a new horse home.

I call the number that my friend gives me.

"Hello," I say. "I understand you have two Morgan geldings for sale. Are these horses registered, and do you have the signed registration papers?" This is a very important question to ask in the horse-trading business, just as important as it is with cars.

"Yes to both questions," comes the answer.

I now commence horse-trading. "How much do you want for both horses?" The geldings are not babies. I will have my work cut out for me.

"I want $100 for both horses and papers."

My heart breaks. I don't have $100. Plus I have to pay for the fuel to drive three hours from Eagle Point to La Pine and back with a heavy, loaded trailer.

"Would you be willing to trade something for the horses?"

"Sure. What do you got?"

My eyes sweep around the house. I had just picked up a huge, 20-gallon copper pot at a yard sale for $10. The pot is an antique and worth a considerable amount of money, maybe even $200 or $300.

"I have my *mother's* antique copper pot." At this exact moment in time, the copper pot becomes a family heirloom.

The guy on the other end of the phone says, "Bring the pot and if I like it you can have the horses."

I drive the three-hour trip in my old pick-up, hauling my old stock trailer. I follow the directions to the guy's house in La Pine. I see the horses. He sees the copper pot. I soon head home with my new horses. I don't know what happens to my old copper pot in La Pine, but I do know what happens to the two horses.

I sell Samson the black horse to a neighbor who eventually sells him to someone else. At that point Samson disappears into the mists of ownerships.

Chuck, on the other hand, continues to resurface in my life for the next 25 years.

First I sell him to a trainer in California. That trainer sells him to another trainer, who sells him to a lady named Nancy Summers.

She and Chuck fall in love with each other. Nancy Summers boards the horse at another lady's barn, in Sacramento, California. I don't know either of these women at this time.

Then, seven years ago I meet both women. Nancy Summers tells me how much she loves Chuck and thanks me for him. Chuck and Nancy win lots and lots of ribbons together.

I tell Nancy the trainer the copper pot story, but we never tell Nancy Summers, because she paid thousands of dollars for the horse. Nancy Summers died this past summer. Chuck is still living and is used by a little girl who rides him and shows him. The little girl and the geriatric but very healthy Chuck are still winning lots and lots of ribbons.

I bought, from the Nancy Summers estate, the western show saddle that she won so many ribbons on with Chuck. The instant I swing up into that saddle (that would have cost thousands of dollars new, and just about as much used) and sit in the seat, it fits me perfectly. I make no adjustments.

The copper pot horse has come full circle as I ride in the saddle that Nancy Summers used on Chuck. When I ride my "Western Ride and Drive" performances in Nancy and Chuck's beautiful saddle, I think that these performances all started thanks to the help of a $10 copper pot.

Chapter 12
More Morgans

I meet the man who lives next door. He comes driving up to our shared, falling-down fence. Gerry Black is his name. Gerry seems to be an old man to me. When I first met him he was ten years older than I am today. I am currently 65 years old. Gerry drives up to the old fence in his old Ford flatbed truck. The truck is highway department yellow. It bounces across the non-road of Gerry's rolling oak savanna. How all the "stuff" on the flatbed stays put as the truck bounces along is beyond the scope of any one's understanding. The flatbed is loaded with rusty old horse shoes, piles and piles of sun-faded orange bailing twine, and moldy remnants of unused hay.

At 75, Gerry is still shoeing horses and does a fine job. He eventually becomes my farrier. I learn very quickly to take away his truck keys so that he does not leave a horse unfinished. Often he will get three shoes on a horse and decide he has to leave. Then you are left with a three-legged horse for a week or two until Gerry remembers to come back and complete the job. Gerry definitely lives in his own time warp.

I bring him gallons of coffee and Costco muffins while he trims and nails on the shoes. Sometimes horseshoeing with Gerry takes all day to get three to four horses done. He is an excellent shoer and a fabulous storyteller. I love the stories. I don't mind the time it takes to finish shoeing as I gather years of stories from him and learn much about horses at the same time. I just keep bringing him coffee and sweet muffins. I have never seen a man who can drink as much black coffee as Gerry Black.

Gerry is a huge man. Much of his largeness is simply fat. He can consume food and then more food. He says he "hobo-ed" to the west in the '30s with only eight, hard bread rolls in his shirt pockets. He makes up for that hungry period of time for the rest of his life. His hands are the size and color of small hams. He is still furiously strong at his age. While he is strong, he's not quick. When we start working his or my horses, his brain runs the show while my legs provide the quickness needed to hook and unhook wild horses in harness. We often meet over the cobweb fences that keep his herd of 12 to 20 massive, crossbred Belgian work horses off my irrigated lands.

Gerry knows how to drive horses. As I get to know him better, he tells me stories of digging irrigation canals with a slip (ditch digger), logging in the woods of the Cascades, and gathering wild horses from Pilot Rock to Mt. Shasta with his dear friend Buck. I meet Buck, who becomes a friend of mine as well.

These old men hang out on cold, winter days at the local (no longer standing) café called the "Milky Way." They sit there for hours drinking stale coffee and telling vibrant stories. While Sarah is in school, I often find my way to the café just to sit and listen to men who are vanishing into the mists of time and to learn their stories. I am so aware that I am living on the cusp of a time that will fade before my eyes. I must hear these adventures in my own life, or I will never have the vanishing opportunity again.

One morning Gerry says, "'Bout time we put together that pair of Morgan horses you have always dreamed of having."

"Sure," I reply. "OK, when do we start?"

Currently I have two Morgan horses on the place. My mare Suzie and Woody, my gelding. I use them for everything necessary on the ranch and often for the unnecessary things as well. I often just ride for the love and fun of riding.

I am so excited about driving my pair of horses. Gerry uses one of his very broke (i.e. well-trained) Belgian crosses, Jug, as a breaking horse with my smaller mare, Suzie. He hitches Suzie on the right side of the pair and puts the horses through their paces.

"Always break horses in the winter. They don't get overheated and mad," says Gerry. "You don't get mad either, too cold and wet to get mad."

He then drops another pearl of wisdom. "Never use a hammer on your wife or husband, your truck, or your horse. Use the tool as it is intended and learn how to use the tool."

Soon comes an additional pearl on this necklace-of-knowledge that I continue to collect from Gerry. "There are no shortcuts. Don't hide behind the problems. Drive the horse beyond the problem. If they won't stand, teach them to stand. You got to teach them to stand with only a silk string holding them and to pull the weight of the world behind them. A horse is very smart. Do the job right the first time."

I sit here with a master horseman upon an old, wooden farm wagon that has seen better days. The tongue of the wagon that goes between the horses is no polished ash or oak pole, but a tree with the bark still on it. Gerry drives the horses as a perfect pair. What I would give, if I had the funds, to send him to the elegant East Coast driving competitions. What an art this man holds in his hands. He can effortlessly drive a pair even with the crudest equipment.

Gerry begins to talk about putting together a four-in-hand of Morgans. A four-in-hand is the horseman's term for driving four horses harnessed in two pairs. One pair are the "leaders" and the second pair are called "wheelers." The wheelers are the bigger horses and are the closest to the heavy carriage and the front wheels. The wheelers help slow the carriage when stopping and do most of the work while pulling the carriage forward. He wants to drive four finely-bred Morgan horses hitched to his old, pieced-together wagon.

I start looking for the perfect four Morgans, and continue to look for the next 20 years, until I figure out that driving in pairs is good enough for me. At one time I own and drive three pairs of Morgans and can put together a four-in-hand from that group. I can drive the four horses by myself, but realize just how dangerous and fool-hardy that really is. I step back from that treacherous brink, and keep to my pairs.

Now let us return to Gerry.

One of the best parts of learning to drive a pair is the experience of gathering up Gerry's horse that we will use as a partner to each one of my horses.

"You cannot train a horse by the clock," says Gerry.

Gerry lives by his own time and sees the world only through his eyes. He NEVER has his horses ready for our lesson when I show up with my Morgan. I ride my mare over to his old wooden pole barn. Since he doesn't have his horse ready, I ride out on his 250-acres in search of the big horse herd and run them into the barn. I have a surreal experience on these crisp, fall mornings, searching out the horses that are the color of fall leaves, and watching them gallop to the barn with their hooves thundering and their manes flowing behind them as their breath steams the air.

Yes, we could lock-up old Jug in a stall so we wouldn't have to re-catch him each morning, but then I would miss my golden leaves, the running, bucking freedom of draft horses, and my gallop. For the first time in many years, I have the most precious commodity of all things. I have *time*. I enjoy my ride rather than worry about saving time by having Jug locked-up

I am forever grateful for my formal-driving lessons from some of the best drivers in the world while I lived in California where I drove Pepper the P.O.A. pony and my first Morgan, Chular's Valentine, with the carriage club.

All those hours of driving amidst polished leather, gleaming brass hardware, and perfectly shaped carriages in California carries me to a height of appreciation of formal driving that I would never have obtained if I did not have the detailed art of "perfection" behind me. Now, I am content to sit beside a master driver disguised as Cinderella, covered in farm dirt, wood smoke, and dirty clothes while driving a scrap-heap across bumpy fields; knowing fully well, in my heart-of-hearts, that Gerry Black is incredibly able to drive any golden coach to the ball. Such is the silken fabric of my dreams that are slowly weaving into the rough cloth of my reality.

From those rough yet sensitive ham-hands, I learn to drive pairs very well and with great joy and purpose.

Gerry and I went thru a bunch of Morgans before we finally had a really nice pair of matched bay Morgan mares. I called them Birdie and Tessa. I learned so much sitting next to him on the hard, wooden seat as we thumped and bumped over his non-existent ranch roads. We fed hay in the winter to his horses. I have never forgotten his words while we were feeding his loose horses one winter morning.

"Mercer," says Gerry, "never let loose stock get between your wagon tongue and the seat. You will loose all control of the situation."

Someplace along the driving fun in his rough fields, either he or I decided that we needed to put together that four-in-hand of Morgan mares. I started hunting for two more matched bay mares. I found two smaller mares, Star and Flashlite. They were to be the leaders. I found more harness and we got all four going. Driving the four was tricky. Just getting them all harnessed up took an hour. Gerry watched from the old auto-tired wagon and gave me quiet instructions on how to hitch the mares up as four.

We had a problem. The leaders were bigger than the wheelers. It looked like the little wheelers, Star and Flashlite, were being pulled along by the bigger leaders, Bird and Tessa. I would have to start all over.

This putting together of a four-up happened over a period of about four or five winters. Gerry had gotten too old to help much and sold his ranch. I drove the four mares for one winter by myself, but finally realized that harnessing and driving them by myself was pretty dangerous and that the four mares were really two pairs. They drove ok, but not well as four.

I would ride one horse, pony one horse, and drive the two big mares in front of me. That method of exercise was easier than hitching them all up to the wagon. If I got in trouble I could let go of everyone and just ride the horse I was on. I never got in trouble, and I took those mares all over the farm.

I started riding and driving the four from horseback at local dressage shows for a fun exhibition. I used dressage shows because the people in the stands are so QUIET. To increase my ranch income, I did carriage driving for weddings at the ranch and away from the ranch. I taught carriage driving, mostly singles, and some pairs.

Once again, my horse trading and training was helping keep the ranch cash flowing, and achieving Sarah's directive to "Make it work."

CHAPTER 13
FIRST YEAR CLOSES

My first year of running the ranch draws to a close. While I am the captain of this magnificent ship, the ranch is commanding me.

I have lived in Eagle Point for 12 months. I am ready to cut hay once again. I arrived last June and the next day was cutting hay. June arrives again and I am ready to cut hay. I will continue to cut hay for the next 25 years.

I have bought and sold my first herd of cattle. I have bought and sold Quarter horses and Morgans to mend the fraying ends of my farming budget. Twenty-five years later, I am still farming and I am still working on those frayed ends.

Sarah blossoms under the rural school environment. She reaches for high standards of excellence and sets the standards that she will continue to meet throughout her educational experiences. She excels in the five years of public schooling she receives here in Eagle Point,

Oregon. Sarah graduates from Eagle Point High School as the valedictorian of her class. She is a National Honor Society student and is in the top 10% of students in the national SAT test. She receives a scholarship to her college of choice, U.C. Santa Cruz.

Sarah and I make new friends. Children come to the ranch and work and play together. I make lifelong and temporary friends in this ranching community.

Sarah's life and my life change radically because of the gamble I took when I began to live my dream. My life is going beyond my dreams.

CHAPTER 14
CATTLE, COWBOYS & COWGIRLS

I survived my first year on my ranch. I bought my first herd of cattle. I sold my first herd of cattle. I am way over my head with cattle.

Now, I know that I know nothing.

Fortunately for me I sold my first herd of cattle to a local ranch whose best manager handled the sale. By selling my first herd of cattle to Chet Wolf for the White Oak Ranch, I meet the head of a model cowboy and cowgirl family. This family helps define my life for the next 25 years.

Sarah and I are invited into the family's life. I learn how to gather, work, vaccinate, castrate, and brand cattle. I am very careful NEVER to learn how to rope. I don't want to rope, as I fear losing a finger should I not dally the rope correctly on the saddle horn. I solve the roping problem by ALWAYS riding my English saddle. No saddle horn, no requests to rope. Works great.

Chet Wolf arrives to take my black Angus herd on a cold, snowy Valentine's morning with his 15-year old son, Brian. This man and his son brought a large stock trailer. A stock trailer differs from a horse trailer. Instead of windows, long horizontal-slots act as ventilation on the sides of the trailer. Most stock trailers are goosenecks rather than bumper-pull trailers. These connect to the bed of the truck rather than the back bumper, allowing tighter turns while backing up and a less bumpy ride for the animals. In the 16-to-20 foot bed of the stock trailer, there is a center gate that can separate the front and back halves when livestock is in the trailer. That center gate is a "slam" type of gate. You *slam* the gate quickly whenever you get the first bunch of critters into the front of the trailer. This prevents them from changing their mind and stampeding back out. The back half of the trailer can hold a couple of horses or whatever livestock you might have sorted by size, sex, or dumb luck.

Chet and Brian quickly and expertly begin to load the mama cows into the trailer. The small calves are gently tossed into the compartment space above the gooseneck. This little space is safe for the calves. If the little calves ride with the big cows, they can be accidentally knocked down and fatally stepped on.

Sometimes the western saddles also ride up in the gooseneck compartment. The calves leave some poop behind during their visit. You learn to watch out for the "cow-ka-poopie" on your saddle seat when you pull the saddle out to ride. Sitting in calf poop is no fun.

Cattle dogs are also known to ride in the gooseneck section when they cannot ride in the bed or the cab of the pick-up truck. Very occasionally, I have seen a cowboy, or two or three, in the gooseneck when the truck is overflowing with men, dogs, and there is simply no other space anywhere to ride.

Only very young cowboys who are low on the cowboy hierarchy have to ride in the gooseneck compartment. Riding in the gooseneck is similar to being in a jail cell cubical. You cannot get out once the door of the gooseneck is slammed. The door only opens from an outer latch and you cannot open the gate to freedom from inside. Getting out of the gooseneck is often a hilarious joke for the "higher-up" cowboys. Much teasing occurs before the hatch is opened for the guys in the gooseneck. Everyone *knows* that the hatch will be opened, because all hands are necessary when it comes to working the cattle. But the young guys are often teased for a minute or two before they are put to work.

In October of the same year, Chet and his family invited me to gather cattle in the Cascade Mountains. Chet works for the Mill Mar Ranch every year gathering their cattle out of the mountains. I am asked to gather on the 1st of October.

"Gathering" cattle is a misnomer. You *hunt* mountain cattle. Not with guns, but with dogs, men and horses. Chet has incredible knowledge of the landscape and the cattle, the dogs, the riding and the roping.

"Wear your chaps, Mercer. And be prepared to ride," says Chet.

I find myself running my Morgan horse through the forests, over downed trees, crossing flooded creeks, and driving trucks and trailers on rough forest service roads that are narrow and hacked out of the hillsides.

"You even ride in the rain, Mercer," says Chet Wolf.

I innately understand that I am again living on a cusp of time that will never again exist. For the next ten years, I become one of the crew under the expert tutelage of Chet and his wife Terry, "the family of cowboys and cowgirls." I learn an incredible amount about cows, horses, and people. And myself.

So begin the chapters of my life called the "Gatherings."

GATHERINGS

CHAPTER 15
BOYFRIENDS, HUSBANDS & OTHER PROBLEMS

People always want to know, "Why are you single?"

I was not always a single woman. I have been married and divorced three times now and have two broken engagements under my belt. Finally, after years of trying to be in various committed relationships of one kind or another, I finally figured it out. I like being single.

I also figured out that I am married to my ranch. I love this ground and self-imposed lifestyle that is occasionally a life-sentence. All the glory of my farming and ranching success rests on my shoulders, as do all the disappointment of my defeats.

I used to think that my problems, that seem to just skip up the driveway, are caused by my being a woman. Then I listen to my men friends (and truly these men are only my friends, nothing else) and quietly I discover that their truck transmissions are not installed properly either, and they too have to return to the shop to get the truck fixed.

I am *not* alone in my world. And I now understand why jobs do not always get done immediately. A *fixed* problem has an obvious solution. A new problem doesn't always. I will often ponder about a particular problem for three weeks. Finally I figure out a solution in my head and am able fix the problem in 20 minutes. Easy!

I can hear my former self saying to the men in my past life, "What took you so long to get to that job? It only took you 20 minutes to fix it."

Now I understand that fixing the job in only 20 minutes takes hours of planning and pondering beforehand.

Much of the repair work on a ranch is simply trial and error, as each job is totally different from the one that came before. The jobs on a ranch are endless. There is always more to be done or something to be fixed. The job list can be as follows:

fix fence,
fix irrigation pipes,
replace hot wire in horse pastures,
fix more fence,
move irrigation pipes,
clean ditches for flood irrigation,
clean horse stalls,

pasture harrow fields,
clean horse stalls,
mow the lawns,
water the lawns,
clean the gutters,
repair the gutters,
change the oil in the tractor,
change the oil in the four wheeler,
change the oil in the lawn mower,
fuel-up the trucks,
change the oil in the trucks,
move the cattle from one field to the other,
fix the leak in the barn roof,
fill the pot holes in the driveway...

I think you can see that the chore list can go on and on.

Once you fix a problem, that chore will only need repeated maintenance.

Living on a ranch is like being the monarch of a small world. You run the village. A ranch has its own sewer system (septic tank), a water system that is usually a well, and there is usually a small village of people who live on the ranch. There is not always a place for the hired help to live, but often one finds a small village of help on a ranch when lodging is available.

I hire certain jobs to be done. I don't want to learn to fix electrical circuits. The electrician comes and does the job and then goes away. I don't cook, so I serve no cookies and pay only with a check. My checks are always good, my checkbook always balances. I never write a bad check.

I also hire a plumber to come and do the job. I can fix some outdoor plumbing problems, but leaks in the house still scare me. I can and have fixed the buried, five-inch irrigation pipe (that's a really big pipe) in my hayfield. I dig four-feet down to the buried pipe, repair it with a coupling joint at the break, and rebury it. I am a muddy mess during this project that takes place on a blistering, hot summer day. I can fix BIG pipes, but am afraid of little water pipes in the house.

Again, I almost never cook, so I serve no cookies to the plumber either. I pay him with the check that NEVER bounces and send him away.

I make an active choice. I love men. They are good brothers and friends. I do not make good choices about husbands or lovers. I am shocked when one man meets me and says, "You could have any man you want. You are bright, beautiful and intelligent. Why aren't you married?"

I think about his statement for several weeks. I come to my conclusion.

"I do not wish to be married, dating, or seeing someone. I am simply happy again with my single life. I almost destroyed myself once. I have come to grips with myself. I am finally very happy again."

I read a bibliography on Albert Einstein. He was a very interesting fellow who had an unusual lifestyle. I quote him about his life in his later years. I keep a copy of his quote on my kitchen counter. I understand what he is saying.

"I live in that solitude which is painful in youth but delicious in the years of maturity." –A. Einstein

My friends stop by frequently to visit. I have friends of all ages. My friends are people from young to old. I am now qualified as an old person. I adore my friends. I have men friends who are indeed just friends. I have woman friends who are indeed just friends.

I have many fine friends, many great acquaintances and a few good enemies.

I have no crystal ball. I have no idea if I will ever fall in love again at my new old age. I don't care anymore. I am happy within my own skin and person. I seem to be happiest when single. I think I will remain single. At this point, who knows and who cares? My life is working well.

CHAPTER 16
CATTLE GATHERING

Mill Mar Ranch sits high in the Cascade Mountains. The ranch nestles in an open meadow of about 100-acres. This meadow was cleared of timber by logging the giant evergreens. The tree stumps left behind were cleared by dynamiting the stumps out of the ground. In past days, beyond 40 years ago, a man could buy sticks of dynamite in the hardware stores. Many man-made mountain meadows were created from logging and dynamite.

The Mill Mar ranch started in the 1920s or 1930s as a dude ranch and was eventually purchased by the Pingle family. Chet Wolf and his wife Terry works periodically for the Pingles. Terry eventually takes a town job, but Chet usually heads the fall gathering operation at the Mill Mar. Chet has an extraordinary ability to be in the middle of the Cascade forest, totally surrounded by thick evergreen trees, mounds of downed sticks of trees, high thick brush, and know exactly where he is. He will know where the ranch is and where he saw you last. He not only knows where he is, but he knows how to get to any forest service road and how to return to the Mill Mar ranch. I and many others depend upon Chet's incredible sense of direction.

Western Cascade Mountain gatherings are pretty simple. Everyone drives their own truck and trailer up the forest service roads in a convoy. This expedition occurs during hunting season, so the deer and the elk hunters become unwitting cattle spies. The leader of the convoy, usually Chet, will spy a hunter's camp. Chet stops his truck and asks the hunters, "Have you seen cows?"

The hunters reply, "We saw just about three pair (a mama cow and her calf is one pair) just about a mile-up on the road."

All the cowboy convoy trucks shift into high gear and race to the spot where the cowboys spy the cows grazing along the roadside. A Chinese fire drill follows. Trucks slide to a stop by the side of the road. Cowboys and dogs fly out of the trucks and fling open the trailer doors. The cowboys then leap onto fully-saddled and bridled horses as the horses pile out of the trailer, and race off into the woods in pursuit of the cattle. Sometimes I am fast enough to head out of the trailer and into the woods. I learn to move quickly and not to be left behind by the crew of cowboys, cow horses and cow dogs.

If possible, the cattle are roped and tied to a tree. The trucks then drive as close to the tied cattle as possible and the cattle are winched from tree-to-tree to the stock trailer. If enough cattle are found at once, they are driven to a known holding corral. This small herd of five to ten head of cattle are driven through miles of dense forests and brush, or magically turned and chased into the open-door trailers parked by the side of the road.

If a large bunch of cattle are gathered, then the herd is taught to come to my cattle call. I ride in front of the herd calling the cattle,

"Come cows, come cows." Sometimes we can trail the cattle down the twisting mountain forest service roads. I often get to ride point (out in front of the cattle).

"Come cows. Come cows," I call for hours. The cattle learn to follow my voice and to follow my pace. I must set the perfect pace. Not so fast that the calves get tired, but fast enough to keep the cattle from disappearing into the brush and forest beside the roads.

The talented cowboys, dogs, and a few good women keep cattle from breaking from the bunch and racing off through the woods. I learn to call cows by "mooing" like a lost calf so the mama cows come to me. Mooing is a neat trick to know when the cows want to turn back into the forest. Being excellent mamas, they will come to a bawling calf every time. I cannot quit when the roads get rough. I have no sense of direction so I must listen above the bawling of cattle for Chet's voice, filled with the directions to the ranch or the corrals.

I love this gathering of cattle. I love the mountains and the forest and the excitement of racing through the brush after the men, dogs and cattle. I love the cusp of time that I experience during my cattle-gathering years. I love that I know that I am experiencing a time period that will only come once in my lifetime. I may spend ten years gathering cattle with the Wolf family, but I know that I am riding on a time warp that is fading into oblivion.

I never learn my way around the mountains. I learn instead to follow the "hurried" directions of Chet or to stay put when left behind. I was only lost once and gave directions in Spanish to three Spanish men in a pick-up to let the "Chief " (Chet) know where I am.

Chet got the message in pantomime and he arrived driving my truck and trailer, using my fuel, to retrieve the other cowboy and me who were very lost. We were sitting about three miles from the trailers. Luckily I had followed directions and stayed put.

Sometimes staying with Chet was more terrifying than getting separated. He convinced me that I was more afraid of the bears and "o'dark thirty" than I was of riding my horse down the "shortcut" back to the Mill Mar Ranch. The short cut was a five-million foot, straight-down drop to hell... but back to the ranch. Everyone went down the drop and I was at the top trying to find my courage.

"Do I get lost going home in the dark, or do I ride the horse over the cliff?" I said to myself.

I heard Chet's voice of encouragement. "Mercer! Come on. We are *going*."

I shut my eyes and opened my voice. Over the cliff I went, screaming all the way down. I only knew I was alive went Chet said, "Mercer! Open your eyes."

One time, when we were all road-hunting cattle and we could not turn the trucks around and we could not go further, since one side of the road went to up heaven and the other side went down to hell, Chet shouted more encouragement to me. "Mercer! Use your mirrors!"

Yeah, like right I was going to *back* a truck and trailer down a narrow mountain road. Yeah! Yeah! Yeah! So I carefully followed his directions. I turned off my engine and got my lipstick out. I opened the driver's-side door, adjusted the outside mirror, and put my lipstick on.

"Mercer! *What* are you doing?"

I replied, "I'm a girl. I'm using my mirror."

Chet offered to back the truck and trailer down the mountain. I said "Sure" and I unloaded my horse and rode down the mountain. I figured if the trailer and truck went off the road, he could jump and my horse would be just fine with me riding her.

Gathering cattle is a misnomer. "Gathering" sounds like putting Easter eggs in a pretty basket. Gathering cattle in the Cascade Mountains of Oregon means racing at breakneck speed though Douglas fir forests. Downed trees lie like giant, broken tiddly-winks on the forest floor. You cannot see the forests for the wall of short trees, medium trees and the tall trees. I ride on my Morgan horse and on my English saddle. I gallop though dangling willows, thick but flexible evergreens, and walls of thickets at full speed, in hot pursuit of the men on horseback. The horseback men are in full pursuit of the Catahoula dogs, that are in full pursuit of cattle that are running away as fast as cattle can run. Let me tell you, cattle can run in low brush. So can the dogs. I often come home covered with whip marks from the tree branches and many bruises from the larger tree limbs. And I love every exhilarating step.

The only reason I am racing after these cowboys is that they can and do disappear in a blink of a bush. I do not know where I am most of the time, and I have no idea how to return to my horse trailer or Mill Mar Ranch. I have a huge incentive not to become lost in the brush or echoing forest wilderness.

I start before dawn and come home in the dark. I spend long days riding in the mountains. We ride up, up, up to heaven and then down, down, down to hell. The Cascades are young mountains and have yet to be worn smooth by the elements. The Mill Mar cattle are scattered over 12,000 leased acres of rugged, craggy rock, dense forest, and surprise drop-offs.

Six of us ride the first day. I follow every rule laid out to me by Chet, "Stay where you were last seen! Don't move from that spot. I *will* come back and get you. Stay put or stay up."

I learn to keep up with Chet. I am one of the few people who can keep up with him and I am highly-motivated. When directional sense was doled out in heaven, I was in line for chocolate. I have absolutely no sense of direction. I have the up-and-down concept of directions, but nothing more. I keep up with Chet because I have no idea where I am.

The joke over the next 10 years becomes Chet asking me, "Where is the trailer, Mercer?"

I have come to believe that I was born into the wrong era. One morning I am driving my horses down my bumpy ranch roads. The next day I happily ride like a crazy person through the brush-filled mountains, chasing cattle.

"Gathering cattle" makes the experience sound like a stroll though the meadows. The movie *The Man from Snowy River* is easy compared to riding in the Cascades of southern Oregon. And like an addiction, I go back for more cattle gathering every chance I get.

We figure that we ride between 15 to 20 miles some days. Most of that riding is either straight up or straight down. We ride hard. The horses are tired. The dogs are tired, and the men are tired. I am tired too. Yet, I go back again and again for more rides and gatherings. There are huge pine tree shadows filled with "morning" frost at 3 o'clock in the afternoon. The aspen leaves are gold dollars still hanging on the branches. The huge maple leaves dump cups of delightfully dewey water down our backs as we ride under them on cold, foggy mornings. Once in a great while we surprise a bunch of elk. I catch a fleeting glimpse of their rumps as they bolt silently through the forest.

Six of us gather cattle today; six riders, six horses and four dogs. Bill rides a black gelding named Burn. Bill is a young man, about 20-years old. He is blond with a mustache and a great sense of humor. He jumps off his horse and pulls my young mare's leg out of wire when she gets tangled-up. The best line of the day comes from Bill, "I learned a lot of new words in the brush. Only when I used them in school, I got detention."

The next rider is Cory. Cory is young too. He is in his 20s. Cory is a big man. He easily stands over six-feet tall in his stocking feet. Cory is riding a 16-year old palomino Quarter horse gelding. Cory is re-training the horse to stand still after doing too much running in the arena as a younger horse. By the end of the day, the palomino is only too happy to stand.

Another rider is a part-owner of the Mill Mar Ranch. Over the years, I watch as the tragic story of the Mill Mar pits father against son and son against father and ultimately destroys the family relationship. Today is the present and none of us know the future. Allen is an ageless man with the deep tan of an outdoorsman. Turns out that he too used to teach school.

He and I chat as we ride down a cliff. We both decide that working cattle is not too much different than working with kids. Not that we think that kids are cattle, but the responsibility of moving living creatures safely from place-to-place can be similar.

Allen says,"Intelligent city people would not have ridden down that cliff following the cattle. The city folk are afraid of falling down the cliff."

I didn't tell Allen that *I* am terrified of going down this cliff after the cattle. I am even more terrified of being found out that I am terrified. Fear sometimes works wonders to make bravery blossom.

Allen turns to me at the bottom of the cliff and says, "I guess you aren't city folk."

I just smile and keep my mouth shut. I am sure that if I say anything I will cry. Best I just keep smiling in the face of my fears.

I pat my Morgan horse and whisper, "Thank you, mare, for carrying us both down that cliff."

The other two riders are father and son. Father is Chet Wolf and son is Randy Wolf. Randy is tired because his eight-month old daughter cried all night and kept him awake. Tired or not, these two men are the quickest and the best riders of the group. They race after a cow, rope her in the brush, and tie her to a tree before you can turn around and see where they go. They both are riding big, strong Appaloosas.

Then there is me. I ride my young, little bay Morgan mare. I ride in my English saddle and am greatly teased about not having a horn. I don't want to rope. I NEVER ride on a western saddle in all my years of gathering with these men. They always continue to tease me. I don't care. I will never rope a cow.

The cattle dogs are a motley crew of the descendents of Georgia bear dogs. The dogs respect their owners and are taught to work cattle by their owners. The dogs are great at the lunch breaks. They receive tidbits of sandwiches from their cowboys. Each dog has its own personality. One of the dogs you never hit to punish or she will bite you badly. You just holler at her. These dogs can hold a cow. They will grab hold of a tail, ear or nose, depending upon the bloodlines of the dog. The cow goes nowhere. These dogs hang onto the cow, no matter what the cow does. Dogs, like Ginger and Snowball, are part of the important working crew of men, horses and cattle. Without the dogs, we would have missed some of the cattle in the brush. I love these bear dogs as they bay when they are on the scent of the cows. I have one Morgan mare that learns to follow the scent and sound of the dogs. I never get lost when the cowboys use the Catahoula dogs. Eventually, when these dogs are replaced due to their old age with the popular border collies, I find gathering more difficult. The border collies hold the cattle with their hypnotic wolf-stare. They never bark.

The next day after my first cattle gathering, I wake up feeling like I have been beaten by sticks. When I look at my naked body in the hot morning shower, I see bruises on my arms, legs and torso. I acknowledge that I have been beaten by branches and sticks as I galloped though the forest. I now know why cowboys drink beer. The beer deadens the pains and aches of gathering. I can barely move. I never drink. Well I hardly ever drink. No beer for me with the men today.

Chet calls me tonight to tell me that they are tired too and won't ride tomorrow. I am relieved and disappointed at the same time.

Then Chet says, "Mercer, do you want to come on Friday? We still need riders."

"Of course!" I tell him. "I'll be there. What time?"

Says Chet, "Same time, before first light. O'dark thirty to be exact."

"OK. I'll be there," I reply.

I mean it, and I am there at the Mill Mar Ranch, high in the Cascade Mountains, before first light at o' dark thirty for the next 10 years of my life, whenever I get the "Cattle Call" from Chet.

Chet's cattle call is simple, "We will be gathering tomorrow morning before first light. Will you be there, Mercer?"

So is my reply. I rarely decline this September through October and occasionally into November phone call.

"Yes, I'll be there," I say, and I am there at the Mill Mar Ranch to have another wonderful adventure gathering cattle high in the Southern Oregon Cascade Mountains.

CHAPTER 17
I CANNOT STAY OUT OF THE CATTLE BUSINESS

I sell my first herd of mama cows. Then I turn around in six weeks and buy more cattle. I cannot stay out of the cattle business. I buy my ranch so I can be in the cattle business. I love cattle. Cattle fascinate me. I love how they smell. They have a sticky-sweet smell about them. I love how they move around in the pastures. I find I love learning about livestock. And I have so much to learn.

My neighbor Mikki Perry helped me get the job "riding alley" at the Rogue Valley Auction Yard. Mikki is one of the first people I meet in my new life. She lives about two miles from me and takes me under her stern wing.

I have no idea that being an alley rider is a plum job at the auction yard. Usually a person working at the livestock yard works their way up to riding alley.

The alley job is dangerous. If there is danger, then I stand in that line. I love cattle and the brinksmanship of flirting with danger. The cattle are in pens on one side of the auction stage and scale. The auction yard is a small pen surrounded by an antique room, filled with dilapidated theater seats. The white paint on the sides of the room is long faded into grey. In fact the entire room is grey. The auctioneer sits opposite of the curved 10-to-12 rows of theater seats. His job is to spy a small flicker of movement from the livestock buyers. The small movement is a signal that the person wants to make a bid. The men in the pen with the cattle watch the buyers for more movement and relay that bid to the auctioneer. Bidding is subtle and moves like wild fire. A person bidding has only seconds to make the bid.

The cattle are in the auction pen for only a couple of minutes. They are sold by the pound. After they are sold, the cattle are herded over a floating scale near the auction stage. The bidder visually estimates the weight of the cattle that he or she is buying. The cattle are pushed from the auction stage to the scale and the gate slams behind the cattle as they mill around on the scale. The weight of the cattle is then flashed on a screen to the bidders sitting in the theater seats.

A person can learn many things sitting in those seats. You develop an eye for the weight of the cattle. You develop an eye for conformation. You develop an eye for good cattle.

The cattle are driven up to the auction stage by a man on foot on the other side of the stage. The cattle go onto the stage where they are sold by the auctioneer. The cattle are then pushed out to the scale, weighed, and a paper sale tag is issued for the bunch or single cow in that consignment. The scale gate is then opened and the cattle are pushed by the gate opener to the alley rider. During this very brief time (several seconds), a pen lot-number is assigned to the cattle. The alley rider takes the number from the gate opener and pushes the cattle to a pen lot and the gate person, who is also on horseback.

This movement of cattle is like a huge ballet. If everyone does the job smoothly and in-sync, then the sweet dance of the alleyway works. One mess-up results in a traffic jam of huge and dangerous proportions. The alleys are very narrow and dangerous. The floors of the alleyway are slick with wet cow manure in summer. The cement floors of the alleyways are frozen with uneven lumps and slick manure in winter. You work at a brisk trot on risky footing because time is money. You don't dawdle. The cattle bawl and you can barely hear the pen lot number over the antiquated speaker-system in the maze of the backyards. This sale yard is right under the airport's runway approach. Mix in the occasional jet taking off one hundred feet overhead, and the discord of sounds is deafening.

The smell in winter is of heavy, sticky cattle-sweat hanging in the thick, freezing Rogue Valley fog. Summer brings the opposite conditions. The heat is trapped in the alley. The dust made of manure and sweat cakes every part of your body, your saddle, and your horse. Breathing is difficult. The sound dissipates more in the heavy summer air. In winter the fog muffles the sounds, but holds them at the same time.

I love the job. Mikki Perry teaches me well. I am always grateful for her stern and protective wing.

I learn about cattle in the sale yard. I learn how to estimate their weight. I learn how to move cattle in small, tight, dangerous places. I see every breed of cattle that anyone thought imaginable. I begin to recognize fellow rancher's cattle just by the way the cow looks. I learn about every disease known to cattle.

There are also horses that are run through the sale yard. In this time period there are no slaughter bans. I learn about the buyers, the traders, the horses. I see every problem and lameness and disease ever invented with a horse. Working at the sale yard gives me the best, hands-on experience I have had in my lifetime. I see everything.

The training that my Morgans acquire at the sale yard proves to be invaluable to me. Every Morgan horse I own works at the sale yard. They become brave, learn to do a job, and to take pressure at the yard. I get paid for working at the yard. I can hardly believe my luck. I ride for six-to-eight hours for the pay. No breaks, no stopping, just trotting up and down the alley ways. The horse learns the job. I am poorly paid but am richly educated. The pay is just minimum wage. The day's wages barely pay for the cost of hauling my horse there and back, but the education I receive working in the Rogue Valley Auction Yard is a priceless gift for the rest of my life.

I meet another woman at the sale yard. Her name is Karen Dollarhide. She comes from old pioneer stock. I continue to see, and cherish my friendship with, Karen Dollarhide. She is possibly the toughest woman that I have ever met. I have seen her take on a wreck in the alleyway when all the tough cowboys are jumping over the walls to get out of the way of a raging bull. There stands Karen, either on foot or horseback, and she turns the bull. I ALWAYS defer to either Mikki Perry or Karen Dollarhide when they bark an order to me in the alleyways. I grow to respect the bravery and knowledge that these women impart to me as we work.

Every Thursday for almost ten years I am at the auction yard riding my Morgan mares up and down the alleys. One mare, Birdie, so loves the job, I know I could step off her and she would know where to pen the cattle. Birdie learns the pen numbers as she listens to them being called over the loud speaker.

The cowboys at the yard give me a very bad time about my English saddle that I use in the sale yard. Freddy challenges me by saying, "Bring a saddle with a horn on it. We'll show you how to really ride those Morgans."

I show up the next week with my sidesaddle and wearing my sidesaddle skirt. I turn back cattle for five hours in the sidesaddle.

When I finally dismount, I show them the horn my top leg rests over, ask them to get on the saddle, and say, "Now show me how to ride a horse with a horn like this."

The cowboys never again tease me about any kind of saddle that I ride in the alley. I never do use a western saddle. I never want to use a rope.

Flashlight is a small Morgan mare that I use when I drive a pair. She gets her rotation in the sale yard along with all six of the mares that I own. Flashlight is a funny little horse. She is either really with you or she is off, thus her name. One time she and I were chasing a cow that leaped out of the alley onto Table Rock Road. Of course, Mother Nature is raining and its o'dark thirty at night. Flashlight is not bothered by the trucks blowing their horns nor the car lights flashing through the rain drops. She just chases the cow along the side of the road until we turn it into somebody's front yard. A cowboy with a rope jumps from his pick-up truck and tries to hand me his rope.

"I don't rope. No horn," says I.

The cowboy is incredulous in the dark pouring rain. "You don't rope?"

"Nope! I ride English."

His mouth drops open. "How the hell do you think you are going to catch the cow?" he says.

"I'll just hold her in this yard until the owner shows up." I reply.

That answer is more than the poor cowboy can handle. He moves the cow into a corner of the fence, tosses a perfect loop, catches the cow and has a momentary loss of memory. He tries to hand me the rope. "Quick dally it on your horn," he commands.

"No horn. English saddle," I repeat.

Just then the owner shows up with a broken-down trailer from which the wily cow has escaped. The two men manage to winch the cow into the trailer and tie the back door shut with the cowboy's rope.

"Damnedest thing I ever saw!" says the cowboy. "You can gallop a horse down Table Rock Road in the dark and in the rain. You can hold the cow. But by God, you don't rope. Never saw a cowgirl like that before."

I just smile, knowing that I have a good little Morgan horse under me who isn't bothered one bit by the cow, cowboy, rain, dark or traffic. And I still have all my fingers.

CHAPTER 18
MY "BROTHER" JEFF

I am no longer sure how Randy Wolf organized this local cattle gather on a Saturday afternoon, but he did. Randy organized Jeff and me into helping move a herd of about 50 cows from one field to the next field. Randy also needs to pull three bulls off the pasture.

These fields run right next to the Rogue River in Southern Oregon. These fields are also located next to the sewage treatment plant. The fields are liberally laced with downed wire fences placed to interfere with any easy movement of cows from one pasture to the next. You have to watch for wire with every step. The wire tangles the gather sometimes. Also sprinkled across the fields are grapefruit-sized rocks. The rocks are from a volcanic eruption which occurred millions of years ago. The rock helps in hindering the movement of cattle from one field to the other. The footing for the horses is terrible and you must move the cattle slowly.

Anyway, on with the story. Jeff and I arrive to help Randy in my, new to me, shiny, red, very clean, four-wheel drive, 1985 Ford F-250 pick-up truck. I am overly proud of my truck. We pull in with my old bumper-pull stock trailer and two of my Morgan horses loaded up and ready to go. I don't even remember which horses we brought. I'll have to ask Jeff to jog my memory about the horses. Jeff is 20 years younger than me so he can still remember everything.

I do remember that we start this gather about 2 P.M. and the sun is out. I must be home by 6 P.M. so I can go to a Shakespeare play in Ashland by 8 P.M.. By 4:30 the sky is tossing down water in buckets and has been throwing water at us for the last 45 minutes.

I have no idea what I am thinking. Never make any plans when you are going to do a simple job of moving cattle from one field to the other. If you have plans and a time when you have to be somewhere, something will go wrong.

We start to gather. Jeff is up on a great Morgan horse. I'm pretty sure he is riding my really good cow horse, the Morgan mare Birdie. I have no memory who I am riding, but you can be darn sure it is a Morgan mare. Randy rides some kinda young, half-broke Quarter horse colt. The horse is a big chestnut colt. Randy's red hair matches the color of the horse he is riding. Randy's temperament also matches the redheaded colt and the color of Randy's hair.

Somehow after lots of false starts we manage to get the herd of mama cows bunched up on the hill above the sewage plant. I keep reminding the men that I have to go to the "theater" and be cultural. My swan song of "going to the theater" becomes a joke. We have yet a bull to gather.

Randy and I leave Jeff in charge of the 50 cows and calves on the hill. Two of the three bulls are with the herd. Randy and I ride off to pick up the one bull that just doesn't want to go along with the cow party. Holding a herd of mama cows and two bulls is NOT easy. Jeff just keeps them contained. To this day the silhouette of Jeff sitting quietly on the hill holding that herd is imprinted on my mind's eye. He is doing a perfect job. He's quiet. The horse remains quiet, and the cows are happy to just be still. Jeff has it all under control.

Randy is a cracker jack of a cowman. He can ride anything and he can and will rope anything. Randy ropes the one bull off the green, red-headed colt. I am not sure of what all happens next because a lot is happening. At one point, Randy, the colt, and the bull are all in a race of some sort. The colt is bucking, and the bull is charging the bucking colt and Randy. Now Randy has dallied on pretty good, so where the colt goes so does the bull....

I am the cheerleader to this sporting event. I yell at the top of my lungs. "Let go! Get off! Let go!"

Randy is a true Wolf. "Get off" and "let go" are not in his vocabulary, yet somehow Randy is off the bucking horse, on his feet, and holding onto the end of the rope. Imagine a small boy running in huge leaps behind a Great Dane dog, and you get the mental picture of Randy holding a rope leash with a bull on the other end. In comic-book fashion they run over the grapefruit rocks and through and over the downed wire. I don't know how they all stay up in this race, but no one goes down.

Back to Jeff on the hill. Jeff is watching all of this activity from the top of the hill where he has managed to hold and settle 50 head of mama cows and their calves for a good 45-minutes of our bull hunting-and-finding. Jeff stares in total disbelief. The bull, Randy, and the bucking colt decide that the finish line to this pasture race is the peaceful herd of cows and calves.

In the last two minutes, all of Jeff's quiet work comes undone. Randy, with the bull on the leash, races towards the herd on the hill. The loose colt races behind Randy and is still bucking.

I race behind Randy, the bull, and the bucking colt and shout to

Jeff, *"Hold the herd!"*

The bull arrives at the "finish line" just a nose ahead of Randy. Randy runs really fast holding onto the bull leash. The colt comes in next and I am dead last. But the bull, Randy, the colt and I all blast into the rapidly evaporating herd of mama cows and calves.

Poof!

The herd disperses. Jeff's holding pattern disappears. What happens next is pretty unbelievable. Randy sling shots around and around the bull, trips the bull down, and sits on the tangled bull's head. I have no idea how he got the bull snugged up that fast, but like I said, Randy is a Wolf.

I have no idea how Randy has enough air to bark orders, but bark he does. Randy barks at Jeff, "Come sit on this bull! I'll go get the trailers."

Jeff just smiles and shrugs. Jeff has been on lots of gathers before. Jeff says, *"I'll* go get Carole's truck and trailer. *You* sit on the bull, Randy."

Jeff thrusts Birdie's reins into my hands. I am left holding the horses while Randy's colt races around me while bucking. The colt is having a ball. He's not mad. He is just having a good time.

Jeff catapults into my *new* truck, guns the engine, and goes leaping and bounding across the rocks and wire with my truck and trailer to where Randy and the bull are playing a game of bull fight. Jeff pulls my truck up right next to Randy's trailer. The men have now made a bull pen with the trucks and trailers, and my *new* truck and my trailer are part of the pen. It is still raining and everything, including my *new* truck is muddy and wet.

"Keep that colt out of here!" barks Randy.

"Like sure!" I think. I have my hands full. I'm on a horse, I'm holding horses with a loose young horse wanting to play. I cowgirl-up and catch hold of the colt's bridle. He stops. I smile. I have been on lots of gathers before too.

Again I am the cheerleader. "Don't hurt my truck. Keep that bull away from my truck!"

The two men have managed to get the bull into Randy's trailer and slam the trailer door shut. "Bang!" The bull is not happy in the trailer. We are happy that the bull is in the trailer. It took two men to wrench the bull in with the rope. I am so glad I am tending to the horses and not the bull. Finally all three bulls are secure in Randy's trailer.

"Let's go get those cows," says Randy as he gets up on the playful colt.

"OK," says Jeff. Jeff is always ready to ride.

I look at them both and say, "I have to go to the *theater*. I have to be home by six."

It is now 5:00 P.M. Mother Nature continues to throw water at us. We are soaking wet and covered with mud.

"We'll get it done," consoles Jeff.

And we do. Cows and calves are moved. Bulls are captured. I get home by six. My truck is filthy. I love gathering cattle with these young men. They are good men. I am an old gal.

I fall asleep watching Shakespeare.

CHAPTER 19
JULIA PINGLE

I meet Julia Pingle through Terri and Chet Wolf almost 18-years ago.

I gather for the Pingles' Mill Mar Ranch, and really just ride with the cowboys, mainly Chet and his family. I have a grand time, as do countless others who are drafted to help gather cattle.

Gradually I become friends with Julia. She is easily 50-years older than me. Eventually I am asked to stay with Julia at the ranch one January while the men all go to the Red Bluff Bull Sale. What a grand lady Julia is. We laugh and really get to know each other that weekend. I feed the cattle as she watches me out the window to make sure I don't fall off the hay wagon or get run over by the tractor pulling the hay wagon. A bald eagle sitting on a tree stump in the "stump field" just watches the entire feeding operation.

Of course a first-calf heifer decides to give birth early, so I have to tend to the cow-calf deal. The heifer doesn't want to take her baby. Julia solves the problem by lending her lovely bath powder to me. I powder the baby calf and powder the mama's nose. Everyone smells the same now, so the heifer decides that the calf must belong to her.

Julia also shares a wonderful scrapbook with me. She takes me back to her vaudeville days and her movies past. What a remarkable woman.

Another time both Sarah and I are up helping at a branding. Sarah is running the needles and accidentally vaccinates the darling, good-looking son of a local farrier. Sarah is so embarrassed that she flees to the kitchen and spends a delightful afternoon learning how to cook for a crew of hungry cowmen and women. From that afternoon on, Sarah says, "A woman's place at a branding is in the kitchen with Julia, learning to cook."

I think highly of Julia.

CHAPTER 20
MORE GATHERING

October 14, 1990. I am living in the magic cusp of time that will never come again in my lifetime. I am riding with the cowboys and I am gathering wild cattle high in the Cascade Mountains.

Some men dream of owning a sailboat and sailing the world to test their perception of reality. Me, I just want to sail through the woods of Southern Oregon at a fast gallop on my sure-footed, strong Morgan horses.

We are still gathering cattle. We have gathered daily for a week. We started on Saturday. By Friday, the rest of the days blur into one extended adventure. We all move slowly; the men, the horses, the dogs, and I. The cattle move like hot fire in the dry woods. We are tired, but the cattle are not. Some cattle runs come easily. The cow is captured and runs into the trailer or corral. The next bunch of cattle we find is really wild.

We add and subtract riders. Today we have Cowboy Bob. He has ridden with Chet before. Bob's horse is a pretty brown and white paint. The horse is easy to follow in the woods. I can see the white flashes of the horse as Bob races through the Cascade forest filled with the towering Douglass fir trees and the thick, short, replanted pines.

Suddenly we are on a run. The cows are wild. The cattle separate and pop out thru the woods like the sparks blown by the wind from a campfire.

Bill yells at me, "Stay on the cow!"

So I stay on the cow. This cow give Sally (my horse) and me a long, fast run. Finally the cow stops in a thicket and I commence to call in the cowboys.

The call is a "yodel," so you can be found in the woods.

I yodel, "Yoohoo!"

I yodel my call again, "Yoohoooo."

I am not the best yodeler. I manage to be loud enough to be heard.

Shortly Chet arrives with Bill, and Chet's 12-year old daughter, Melissa. "Where is the cow? And where is everyone else?" demands Chet.

"The cow is in the thicket, but I am not sure where everyone else is," I reply.

We all begin to make "cowboy noises" to drive the cow out of the thicket.

"Hup! Hup! Hup! Get out you ol' cow" says Chet.

No cow. She silently slipped out of the thicket, unnoticed by me. I am teased all the way back to the horse trailer about my horse race with the missing cow. The teasing is done in a good-natured ribbing. I easily laugh back.

Meanwhile, back in the woods, one calf has been roped and pushed into the stock trailer. Cowboy Bob meets us walking and leading his horse up the logging road. He has quite a limp as he held a lonely adventure with a cow. The cow he ran is roped. She turned on him and charged his horse. The paint horse bucked and Cowboy Bob fell off and hurt his leg. Bob is lucky as neither the cow nor the paint horse stepped on him. Bob's injury bleeds through his long johns and his jeans. The leg is not broken. Bob just sustains a nasty cut.

The roped cow is left tied to a tree so we can come back and get her. Even after Bob fell off, he managed to tie the wild cow to the tree.

This particular cow is wild, big, and angry. The men decide they will winch her from tree-to-tree. Just as they make their first move towards the tree where she is tied, the cow charges Chet. Bob's horse gets tangled in the rope and bucks again. Chet just scrambles out of the cow's charge.

We are now in an incredibly dangerous situation. The woods are soon filled with "blue smoke words" which I cannot write on this page. However, much to my surprise, I learn all the words and the sequence and am often startled to find myself occasionally swearing not like a sailor, but like a cowboy. This cowboy vocabulary is a very handy vocabulary to know when working cattle.

The escaped, angry dangerous cow is roped again. She is again tied to a tree.

Rancher Allen decides to back the stock trailer into the woods to the cow. Allen needs to winch a fallen pine tree out of the way. He has an electric winch mounted on the front of his pick-up. Allen moves the downed tree out of the way. He can now get the stock trailer to the cow.

At this point in the cow drama, Chet hollers at Melissa and me to, "Hold all the horses and *stay the hell out of the way!*"

Melissa and I are no dummies. We know to stay the hell out of the way. We move way back from the action. Twelve-year old Melisa and I even plan an escape path thru the trees. The thick parts of the woods are where we would go if we have to run from the escaped, dangerous, mad cow.

Melissa holds her dad's horse while sitting on her horse. I forget whose horses I am holding, but I have two horses to hold plus the mare I am riding.

Melissa and I know, no matter what happens, DO NOT LET GO OF THE HORSES. No matter where we run, HOLD ONTO THE MEN'S HORSES. Our job is not the job for the faint-of-heart. My heart may feel faint, but I must function and so must Melissa. Melissa is a 12-year old doing a man's job. I am just old and am also doing a man's job. We are part of this cowboy crew. We have no room for mistakes.

Picture the following scene:

Melissa and I cannot see what is happening behind the trailer. All we see is the tip of a fir tree twitching its top like the end-tip of an angry cat's tail. The dogs are screaming terrible dog words at the cow encouraging her to climb into the stock trailer. The cow is bawling terrible cow words back to the dogs and men. The men are sending select cowboy words into the pure, virginal mountain air. Finally the trailer door slams shut. Instant stillness fills the virgin mountain air. The men filter out from behind the stock trailer and mount the waiting horses that Melissa and I have been very quietly holding. We ride off quietly in search of more cattle.

This day, the cattle win. We find very few.

CHAPTER 21
MOUNTAIN GATHERING

I am busy gathering cattle again. I find myself in the Cascades on another day with another crew. I step into some very interesting family dynamics.

Chet Wolf has his entire family with him at this particular gathering. His wife Terry, both sons, Randy (21) and Brian (18), and daughter Melissa (12) make up one of the finest working crews on the

Mill Mar Ranch. This is a hard-working family who respects the orders Chet barks out. Chet in return respects and relies on his sons' abilities and knows that these young men will hang in and dally the rope any time he needs them. Terry and Melissa are always right where he wants them in order to stop or turn the cattle.

Allen, the ranch owner, and Allen's son Mark, are world's apart. Allen is the rancher, Mark is an economics professor. Today, on this gather, Mark invites a professor-friend to ride along. The undercurrent of family dynamics crackles. This is now, "The ride of Cowboys versus the Professors." I can feel the tension in the air. I place my bet with the Cowboys. We are, after all, riding in Cowboy Country. I am not sitting at a desk in a college professor's economics classroom.

I am driving my own rig as we have a total of ten riders. Randy Wolf and Bill ride with me and tease me about how slowly I drive my rig and that I drive a Chevy truck. All good cowboys in the Pacific Northwest drive a Ford. Allen and Chet sandwich me in between their rigs. The men can talk on their C.B.'s. I don't have a C.B. so I can only talk to Randy and Bill.

Randy has more than plenty of time to tease me. Randy is a mechanic. He lets me know about every strange sound my truck makes. I begin to feel like the truck is going to fall apart at any moment. I begin to panic.

Randy laughs. "Mercer, do you think I would ride in this rig if it was going to fall apart?"

I relax. We are at least 15 miles from the ranch and we have our horses.

Chet stops and asks some elk hunters if they have seen any cattle.

As I am next in line, I stop and make a joke, "I would like an order of two ham sandwiches and a couple of Cokes to go."

One hunter hands me an un-opened 7-Up and an untouched beef sandwich. Delighted with my luck and the fellow's winning sense-of-humor, I drive off with 7-Up in hand and eating the beef sandwich. Randy and Bill stare at me with wide-open eyes and mouths. We all laugh.

The young men want me to drive faster on the twisting dirt roads. I won't. Finally they understand they are stuck with a little ol' grey-haired lady in cowboy boots who is NOT going to drive 60 miles-an-hour on dirt roads. I keep track of Chet's truck by the dust cloud billowing ahead of us. Allen's rig is stuck behind me.

Cows are spotted and we are on a run. The cattle are captured and jammed into trailers. One cow escapes this hard-riding crew of cowboys. Chet's son Brian is after the cow. I am assigned the job of watching and help hold a new cluster of cattle. I have dirt in my eyes. I rub it and out pops my contact lenses, onto the forest floor duff. I crawl around for 45-minutes looking for the contact and by some mountain miracle, I find the lens just as we begin to move cattle down to the trailer to load them. As this group of cattle is loaded onto the trailer (often referred to as "the bus"), we hear from another hunter that there are more cattle just down the road.

We are on another run. I hear Melissa call to me, "Carole! You are losing candy bars!"

Sure enough, I am acting like Hansel and Gretel as my horse Suzi gallops down the road. My bite-size candy bars fly out of a hole in my jacket pocket.

"Oh well!" I holler to Melissa, "Maybe I can find my way back to the trailer this time."

I actually do find my way back by following the candy bars. The candy bar trail is the one-and-only time I ever can find my way back the trailer without Chet's help.

Chet says, "Following candy bars doesn't count."

We pull up from this maddening horse race down the mountain road just in time to watch Brian perform a new sport known as "gravel-skiing." Brian roped a cow. As he ties her to the tree, or maybe unties her to load her, the cow gets away. Brian is a Wolf. Wolf men do not *ever* let go of any rope they have ahold of. Brian holds onto that rope as the cow races though the woods, across the road, and down the road bank. Brian digs in his heels and leans back, much like a water-skier does behind the boat. The cow is not content to just run down the road. She jumps down the 20-foot bank. There goes Brian over the bank, grinning the entire time.

I hear Terry yell to Chet, "Don't kill him."

It takes us less than two seconds to look over the 20-foot drop. Father Chet and his horse dropped right over the "jump" in hot pursuit of son and cow. Father and horse are racing after son and cow, who are rocketing through the woods. Brian is still upright and still hanging on to the cow.

There is only one thing for the rest of us to do. Off the edge of the road we all jump after Brian, the cow, Chet and his horse.

Brian somehow manages to tie the cow to a tree. Then the team maneuvers her from tree-to-tree, up the 20-foot drop, and into the waiting trailer. She gets on the cow-bus for the ride down to the loading corrals.

I ride down the road gathering my candy bars. I joke with Chet and Allen about leaving a trail so I can lead them back to the trailer.

Good times. Busy times. They ask me back for the branding. Brian says he is going to teach me how to rope a cow. I tell him that I am not ready for "gravel skiing."

"Yes, you are, Carole, yes, you are," says Brian.

I try to remind them that I am a little ol' lady in cowboy boots. It takes my body a week to recover from this week of riding.

Yes, I go again and again, over a period of ten years. There are cattle and adventures waiting for us. We all recover. For a week we all walk slower: the men, the dogs, the horses, and me.

My body is slowly recovering from hunting cattle. I bowed out of going today because I am still catching up on my work left from being out gathering. I mow the lawns, clean the stalls and paddocks, feed all the inside stalled creatures, feed the dogs, turn out the horses, go food shopping, go to work at the auction yard. I am looking for some cheap cow/calf pairs for next spring. I do not purchase anything as cattle prices are too high and I need to sell some of my calves so I can buy more young ones and raise them up. So goes the cycle.

CHAPTER 22
STILL GATHERING

During the following years, three generations of ranchers fall out with each other. Great beauty often comes with a very high price-tag. Mill Mar Ranch owners pay the price of beauty within a ranching family. Grandfather and grandson take a stand against the man in the middle, the son of one and the father of the other. Allen does not ride at the Mill Mar Ranch this year. The family trio has split. I miss riding with Allen as does Chet. Chet and Allen have ridden many years together.

We are a new bunch of riders this fall day. The Cascade forest is dry and the floor is littered with the musty smell of fall. Old, dead evergreens that fell 50 years ago criss-cross each other. Their grey, bare bones look like a forest of skeletons collapsed across the forest floor. The smell is of autumn. Autumn mornings in the high Cascades are covered with sparkling, white frost and by noon the hot, indian summer sun beats down on the horses and riders. The cowboys and cowgirls shed layers of clothes as the day progresses. We push the few cattle we find down to the ranch. We move the cattle from the ranch pastures into the holding pens and sort them. A nice, easy day. We are ready to go back again and again. We ride four more days. The past and the present and the future blur into one adventure.

One day Chet arranges a miracle as Allen quietly meets us at a holding pen. The men ride together quietly and the beauty and strength transcends the harsh reality of a family division. We find only two head of cattle all day.

Allen leaves, and as we drive the trucks and trailers off the mountain and are careening down the narrow forest service roads, we see *cattle*. First we see only two, then three, then eight head. We unload tired men, horses, and dogs and are on a run after the cattle. We drive eight more head back to the ranch. By now it is DARK, but we return to the ranch with at least some pride under our tired skins. As the cattle are loading, one cow blasts through the holding-pen fence, making a hole the size of a Howitzer shell. We let her go. That cow has won her freedom for this day.

We ride another day with Allen. He recalls the surrounding land of his youth.

We have a grand time with cattle at Medco Ponds. We make a trap with the trailers and some loose hay. Chet is over-eager. He moves in too fast and close to the cattle. The cattle split out into the woods. We lose them.

Some days the cows win.

I ride back to the ranch along the highway. I am alone, but can follow the highway to the ranch. If I am on the road, I know where I am. I find three head of cattle and try to push them along the fence line. There are picnickers at the ranch gate. No way will those cattle turn by the picnickers onto the ranch road. The cattle scatter. I was so hoping to be a hero and bring in three wild cows by myself. So much for that scattered dream, as I watch the cows leap up the side of the roadway and disappear into the thick woods. Some hero.

The following weekends and some weekdays are spent gathering. After the gather is done, we move to the task of sorting and branding all the gathered cattle. This sorting and branding is a huge job.

The men and women who rope are on their horses. One person

ropes the head and one person ropes the heels of the calves. There are four people roping. This group of ropers is very good at their job. The calves are quickly brought to the branding fire.

Those of us on the ground crew start by "mugging" the roped calves. Mugging is done by a ground crew of young men. The calf is roped and hauled to the fire. The ground crew grabs the calf and puts it on the ground where it is given shots, doctored, and castrated if it is bull calf. The calf is then branded.

Only someone who has been to a branding understands the delicate dance of roping, mugging, branding, vaccinating, and the timing required. The sounds are deafening. The mother cows call for their babies, the calves cry for their mothers. The dust, burned hair, and the sounds all melt together in a single memory that is branded into my soul.

By the end of the day we all smell like blood, dust and burnt hair. I love every second of the sounds, smells, and sore muscles. Again, these brandings held high in the Cascade Mountains are times that will never come again. I savor every taste. I am such a greenhorn cowgirl.

Standing quietly supporting all of the medicinal equipment is a white kitchen table. Sometime in the table's past life, it stood solidly in someone's kitchen holding breakfast for a cowboy. Supper and dinner are cleaned off its white surface. Now, the kitchen table stands in a corner of a dusty corral, holding the components of medicine for a ranch. The syringe needles, the shot-guns which inject the vaccinations quickly, the medicine bottles, the castrating knives, and assorted other things necessary for branding, now fill the table top. I would love to hear the stories of gatherings that this table has overheard while cowboys sat with their elbows on it.

How out-of-place the table stands now, serving its duties at a branding. No calf ever sits at this table. No horse backs over it. Nothing is toppled off the kitchen table in the calf-branding corral. The white kitchen table gradually fades into the soft grey color of the downed forest trees. The aging and sturdy table never topples in all the years of my branding at the Mill Mar Ranch.

CHAPTER 23
BRANDINGS & BOYS

I am invited to help with branding at the Mill Mar on a weekend. I help brand over 100 calves on Sunday. Our Sunday church is the branding yard. Many appeals to God are heard. The choir members are the mama cows bawling for their babies. The chorus members are the babies crying for the mama. The preacher is Chet Wolf yelling orders and laughing while he directs his congregation of helpers. I have a wonderful time.

I am famous for not wanting to give shots, so Chet assigns me the shot duty.

"Mercer! You give muci shots to the babies."

I don't even open my mouth to protest. I follow the chief's orders. I give over a hundred shots. I no longer worry about giving any cow or calf a shot.

The ranch children climb onto the bigger calves as the calf scrambles up from being roped and "doctored." The idea is to ride the calf. I never climb on, but the young kids certainly learn how to ride bucking calves. Great sport: no rules, no timer.

As Sarah grows older and moves into junior high school, I begin to gather boys. Sarah is a beauty. Not only is she a beauty, but she is smart. Actually Sarah is brilliant as we are to later learn with her school grades and test scores. Sarah is also boy-magnet.

I figure out the solution to boys. Better that I have 10 boys here than one boy. As soon as one boy "makes a move on Sarah," the other boys nimbly cut the "moving" boy away from her.

Sarah gathers 10 to 15 "brothers" around her. The boys are very protective of her. She enjoys their company at the ranch and totally ignores them at school. Somehow this arrangement works for everyone.

I feed the boys. We arrive at an agreement. The boys have to have at least a "C" grade to be here. I keep in contact with the teachers at school and Sarah tutors the boys that need help. I keep the boys busy with helping me ranch. I buy horses. Horses can be found at a reasonable price and the boys help train and ride the horses. I could not run this cattle ranch without the help of my "Lost Boys."

I am sure there is a hex sign on the post at the end of our driveway that says, "Will feed hungry, lost boys."

My first boys are two brothers, Danny and Kevin, who need a place to just hang out. Their dad brings them when he is on his way to work. They learn to ride here. The boys pick tons of small stones out of my riding arena and pastures. The rule is: "fill the five-gallon bucket with stones, then you can ride." The same rules apply to Sarah.

Suddenly, Sarah is no longer an only child. She had "fictive kin," and what rule goes for all goes for Sarah as well.

One morning I look out the bedroom window and see Sarah and the younger, borrowed brother "vaulting" on the broad back of the Morgan mare, Suzi. Kevin is sitting on Sarah's shoulders with his arms outstretched, and Sarah is holding his legs. Sarah is riding bareback on the steady old bay. The big mare is being lunged in a circle by a young girl. I hold my breath as Kevin does a perfect sliding dismount off Sarah's shoulders and onto Suzi's broad back.

I slip out the door and ask the kids to practice on softer ground.

I have lots of big ponies at this time. The youngest brother rides the ponies with our little toy poodle stuffed, like real toy, into the saddle bag. Sarah and the kids just play with the equines as I manage to extract work from the kids. This is a ranch and kids on farms and ranches are expected to work at real jobs.

One summer vacation, Sarah and another 13-year old classmate, Jenny, run Jenny's family dairy for five days while her mom and dad are away for a funeral. I check on the girls only once. They know what they are doing and successfully milk 50-head of cows twice-a-day for a week.

Sarah says, "I never thought I could tell which cow will kick me by looking at her teats."

After her experience on the dairy, Sarah becomes the "milk police." We never again waste a drop of milk on our ranch. Sarah also decides, at age 13, to become a non-meat eater, unless the meat comes from a cow that kicks her or charges her. So I tell her that the meat we eat always comes from the cow that kicked her or charged her.

One evening I go to an awards banquet for Sarah. She is in the top five-percent of her class. The school does a very nice job of honoring the children. I am very proud and honored to be there with her.

Chet Wolf discovers that Sarah is a whiz with numbers. He insists that she sit on the fence as he runs cattle through the shoots. Chet yells the numbers and the information about the cattle. Sarah dutifully records it all in the notebooks in her fine and clear, small handwriting. She never makes a mistake.

Chet always says, "Sarah comes with me."

One day while giving shots to calves, Sarah accidentally gives one of the darling young wranglers a worming shot. The cowboy backed into the needle just as Sarah was ready to "shoot" the calf. Nobody was hurt, but Sarah was mortified and never handled the needle again. Sarah would just as soon be helping Chet from the post or with Julia in the kitchen, cooking for the crew.

CHAPTER 24
FLYING

I have no idea why I thought I should buy an airplane and learn to fly. Flying sounds like a lot of fun. Here in the Pacific Northwest, almost 20 years ago, learning to fly was pretty easy. I take a couple of lessons from the guy at Medford airport. The husband of my riding friend, Paula, is a pilot in Shady Cove. He flies planes in Alaska. John knows a bunch of nice men, all of whom fly. John knows where there is a "dandy little Super Cub" for sale. The Super Cub is a 1947, rag-wing, tail-dragger, bright-yellow plane.

By now you have figured out that I am a bit impulsive. I am running a ranch single-handedly with the help of a group of lost boys. I am raising cattle, cutting hay, and am raising my daughter and also have a homeless girl living with us. I am OK on all fronts, except when I buy the plane.

One afternoon I picked Sarah up after school and she and I drive up to Shady Cove to fly. We use John's plane as he is a licensed pilot and has a plane that I fly.

Right now I have to tell you, I never fall in love with flying. If I had, I would be able to tell you everything about John's plane. I just remember that all three of us can ride in it.

We practice landings. I am getting better. I make two really good landings. Then off we fly to the top of Table Rock. I land the plane on top of the forbidden landing strip on Table Rock. Then we take off. We gain attitude instantly, to say the least, as there is a 1,000-foot drop over the edge of the Table Rock. What an experience, as my heart always beats fast with fear when I fly. John then flies us down over the Rogue River to look at bald eagles, herons and geese in their nests.

I fly for about a year with a licensed flight instructor. I'm just ok as a pilot. I can fly the plane, but the written test for getting my license is just too hard. My brain cannot wrap itself around the words. I cannot land at manned airports because I cannot talk and fly the plane at the same time (turns out that I cannot talk on a cell phone and drive a car or a truck at the same time either).

I fly in a storm. Fear comes white-hot and steaming through the sweating pores of my body as I pilot my small Super Cub through a dark and windy sky. The plane jumps from cloud to cloud. I fly in a storm. I land twice at Eagle Field as the storm progresses. John flies the plane home. I know the storm is bad when John says he will sit in the front seat. Another day, I land the plane in my hayfield. I am only a heartbeat away from my solo landing.

I hate flying. I think that I must overcome the fear. I do not feel cold fear. I feel white, hot fear.

I ask myself, "Carole? Why aren't you just content to needlepoint and knit? Why don't you bake cookies and read romance novels? No you have to learn how to drive horses and fly airplanes."

I keep flying. I manage my first solo. My fear of flying deepens. Then, on September 20, 1992, I walk away from a PERFECT dead stick landing. My friend's husband John and I have just taken off from my hayfield.

Fortunately, John is at the control stick when he says, "The engine just quit."

I heard him perfectly because it is VERY quiet without the motor turning.

What do I do at that moment? I SHUT-UP. I figure that John needs to totally concentrate on safely landing the plane. We barely clear the fence of a neighbor's field as we touch down on his freshly mowed hay.

Why does the engine quit? The engine block cracked. Bang! No compression.

The ground feels wonderful.

Everyone comes to see why the plane landed in the field. One neighbor runs me home and I come back with my tractor. We load the plane's motor in the back of a flatbed truck and John, who is certified to replace plane engines, repairs the engine.

"Well, Carole, you need to fly this plane out of the field. It is now fixed," says John happily.

I remind him that I threw up after the plane stopped and we crawled out of it and safely walked away from the plane.

"Nope," says I, "I am done."

I sell the plane and keep my log book. I haven't flown a small plane since I walked away from a dead stick landing.

I have, however, twice flown with horses to Europe, but that's another story.

CHAPTER 25
VOID

My entire world fell apart on May 24, 1997.

Sarah is now attending the University of California at Santa Cruz on a full scholarship. She loves to run as much as she loves to read, and on this day, my college sophomore is killed while out running at her college. She is hit by a speeding car, driven by a 19-year old, non-drinking, non-drug-using girl. Sarah is killed instantly.

I have shared brief experiences in Sarah's life up to this point, but her life is so much fuller than the stories from our ranch. Even after 16 years, my story-telling abilities cannot overcome my emotional devastation at the turn my life took on this day. Forgive me for turning to someone else's words to describe this desperate chapter in my life.

The following is a tribute to Sarah written by Kevin Taheny (for a special occasion several years later) that will help you better understand what a loss her death was to me, our friends, and community.

"I never had the pleasure of actually meeting Sarah Mercer. She had already died when I read the compiled documents and data about her. The following is what I learned about Sarah.

"Sarah's academic success included many honors. In high school she was an 'A' student. A National Merit Scholar and class salutarian. She was the editor of the school newspaper, lettered in track, and worked on her ranch to finance trips abroad. Sarah had completed enough high school units to graduate from her high school in her junior year. Instead of graduating ahead of her classmates, Sarah took and passed challenging advanced placement exams, without taking college courses, for college credit. Then Sarah went part-time to Southern Oregon State University during her senior year of high school while she attended her school at the same time.

"As brilliant a student as she was, her academic ability was only one facet of Sarah's extraordinary character which developed at her home. After reading copies of the letters from those who knew her: friends, classmates and teachers, they describe her as a wonderful person who has contributed to their lives. These letters contain references to "Lost Boys," skating ponds, horse rides, all a part of the once idyllic, small-town life that she and her mother shared on their ranch outside of Eagle Point, Oregon.

"What Sarah learned at home and in her small town was to care for people and to help her neighbors. Neighbors help each other in Eagle Point. Neighbors rely on one another. Country kids have real jobs and responsibilities on ranches. These kids are relied upon by their parents and neighbors to carry the work and the chores out. Sarah worked on the ranch. She would load hay and run tractors, feed cattle, and buck hay. For example, Sarah, then 13, and her 13-year-old neighbor, milked at least 50 head of cattle twice-a-day while the owners were out of town.

"The love of learning, the passion for excellence, was one of her remarkable gifts, but her real, great talents were much more than academics. Her concern for people was practical, not an academic interest in them. She would motivate those who needed it with some of the determination that she possessed in abundance. For example, there was one person she had met in high school who was drinking and living in his truck. Sarah got him to jog with her, stop drinking, and enter the U.S. Army. He still stops by the ranch to say 'Hello' to Sarah's mom.

"Sarah was a person who loved to have fun. She had a lovely smile, a brilliant mind and remarkable personal qualities. She was quiet, but popular with her teachers and acquaintances. Sarah was independent and applied for her own scholarships and used her own monies for travel and school. She was frugal. She would read and return her college textbooks within two weeks for the entire college bookstore refund. That action drove her roommate's nuts. Sarah bought her clothes from the thrift store. She was a bookworm and a rider who rode horses sidesaddle. Sarah had a boyfriend, scuba-dived, and she traveled to Egypt, Russia, Finland, Sweden, and France. She loved to go to school, to read, and to run. Sarah ran every day until a car hit her and killed her instantly.

"Money for the property on which this library is built has been given in loving memory of Sarah Ann Mercer and for the knowledge that she so loved in books."

Kevin A. Teheny, Esquire

CHAPTER 26
DARK DAYS

When Sarah was killed, I lost my past, my present and my future. I became very depressed. I almost became mortally depressed.

At my darkest moment, I stood on a chair in my barn, with a rope around my neck. I was one step from joining my child in death.

At that moment, my dogs Katie and Dolly came around the corner, sat down and looked up at me.

Seeing them, I could not finish my life in front of those dogs who had already been with me through so much. I kept my feet on the chair, removed the rope from around my neck, and stepped into life.

I had become agoraphobic. I could go almost nowhere. Just walking to the mailbox was a daily challenge. I *could* go to the library. I asked for every book on death that I could find. I consumed them. The librarians helped me. They found more books. They called me and told me that they had more books for me. They listened to me while I wept. They wept with me.

They didn't really know me, but every one of them stepped forward and helped me. Little did I understand the true meaning behind the group known as "The Friends of the Library."

One morning I accidentally came early to pick-up books at the library. A group of people were meeting at the library. They asked me to join them. This was my first introduction to the "Friends of the Library." Somehow, in the depressed fog of my mind, I understood from their meeting that Eagle Point needed a new library. I leaped up, went across the street, and withdrew a large sum of money from my bank account and tried to buy the old city hall.

Pat and John, from the meeting, were hot on my heels, trying to explain what was really needed, to a confused, severely-depressed woman who wanted more than anything to make a memorial to her dead daughter.

The good folk at the city hall wisely did not take my offer.

With that beginning, I began going to the Eagle Point Friends of the Library meetings. Somehow, I was asked to join a group in Medford, the Board of Directors of the Friends of the Library. I was able to go to Medford and met many new and fine people. Jackson County was in severe need of many new libraries.

Sarah and I owned a rental house in Medford. But Sarah was dead. I didn't need two houses. My future was gone with her death. I could just give the house to the Eagle Point Friends of the Library. And then we (notice I use "we" because I had now become a member of the Friends of the Library. I was no longer just "I.") could buy the lot down the street for the new library.

I still am not sure what all happened next (I was still in a depressed fog), but slowly, sometimes painfully, but surely, a plan began to grow. Every community wanted to build a new library, or at least expand the one they had.

Sounded good to me. Somewhere along the way in my depressed and confused mind, I wanted to raise a million dollars in Sarah's name.

A million dollars is a huge amount of money.

But *I* didn't raise a million dollars for Sarah. Something much better happened. The entire community, every community, every voter, got behind a huge ballot measure and raised *38-million dollars* to build *fourteen* new libraries for Jackson County.
I was only a very small part of raising this money.

There are many people who have picked-up and carried on when I gradually stopped going to the "Friends of the Library" meetings. People who helped to design the library, people who knew how to pick the colors for the interior, people who knew what would be a great library design.

I asked that Sarah's picture hang in the new Eagle Point library. Her memory book is archived in the library. The library is the one place I can go and see her, besides my house. I have accomplished what I needed to do as a parent of a dead child. I found a place for Sarah where she will have a past, a present, and a future.

Last night a woman said to me, "Sarah has become the child of our community. She has a place in our hearts."

Almost eight years after her death, I stand in this beautiful new building and say to everyone at the ceremony: "Thank you. Thank you all for coming here. I thank each person who helped to build this library, and every other library in Jackson County. I did not raise the million dollars for Sarah. *WE* raised $38,000,000 and we are building 14 new libraries. The Friends of the Library became my friends during a critical time of my life. I cannot turn a golden shovel of earth here. I want just a regular shovel. I am just a regular person with incredible friends, The Friends of the Library.

"How wonderful with the turning of this earth at Eagle Point, that we are building a new library rather than burying a life. Libraries connect us to the past, the present, and the future. Thank you all for giving me a past, a present, and a future, for giving the community a past, a present and a future. You are my friends, 'The Friends of the Library.'"

I lived through Sarah's death because building the libraries did happen that fast. When I got going on the committees, I would not quit until people said, "Yes." It is very hard to look at a crazy, grieving mother who has money in her pocket and wants to build a memorial library for her dead child, and say, "No." The entire county got behind the movement and we passed a huge bond issue to build not one new library in the county, but a new library in every town. They did not go up all at the same time, but the one in Eagle Point was first.

Most importantly, this library is no longer about Sarah and me. This library is about the community and a strong group of people. Last night, on my way home from another gathering at this library, I felt the weight of the death of my daughter lift from my shoulders. I could breathe again. For me, I made the right choice in creating a legacy for Sarah Mercer. The community's support and need gave me purpose. My purpose stands here for all of us.

I still battle the depression over Sarah's death, but I am very careful not to be seduced into suicide again. I dry heave. I vomit, but not as often. Not daily as I did in the beginning. I am still a bit agoraphobic. I have to force myself to leave the sanctuary of my ranch. Now I know I have to do that. The performance traveling I will finish this story with really helped. Now I recognize that I still have the agoraphobia, but I make myself go to the market to buy food. I still struggle, but I don't talk about the problems. I talk about my joys.

I got out of bed every morning to feed livestock and horses. I changed all the hand lines and wheel lines and I wept and wept and wept while I did the chores. Deep inside I knew I had to keep the ranch going. If I let it die, then I would also die. The ranch and the chores and the horses gave me huge purpose to live. The ranch still gives me purpose and fills my time well. The chores make me tired and being tired lets me sleep at night.

My dogs and horses give me joy. I love to teach and have horses that love to learn. I know just how fortunate I am.

I found I could not help gather the cattle. I could not take the pressure and the responsibility for racing through the mountains. One day Chet Wolf and the ranch manager came and picked me up to gather. We wound-up just going for a gentle trail ride. I could not run the horse, and my agoraphobia was over-whelming. I have never gathered cattle since my daughter's death. When the Wolf family formed a ranch in California and moved away, I was pretty much adrift.

One dear friend, Judy Belnap, would just sit me on her lap on a rocking chair and rock me like a baby while I cried. I have always been grateful to Judy for her kindness.

Another friend, and I did not know who it was in the beginning, became my secret pal. She left me a gift on each holiday with a note that said, "You are loved." On Mother's Day she revealed herself. She wishes to remain anonymous.

I rode the alleyway for the last time for the Cattlemen's Association sale. The Rogue Valley Auction Yard was sold the next week and torn down. I rode my mare Birdie. She was tired and so was I after the sale. I was sorrowful and relieved at the same time. I have a video of that last ride.

I still have huge sorrow about Sarah's death. I am no longer angry. Time helped the anger to go away. I have forgiven the driver of the car that hit and killed Sarah. I have learned that I have to set a high example of handling her death for her young friends who are left behind. They have looked to me for examples of how to live. They too still grieve, but life goes along. The friends of Sarah have now become my friends, and I am very fortunate to have learned not to hate and wallow in sorrow. I still miss my daughter deeply. There are no words for my sorrow.

The months of the year used to be months with special holidays that I enjoyed with Sarah. We never made huge events out of holidays. We celebrated them as we wished. Sometimes we even opened our Christmas presents several days early because we got tired of waiting for Christmas.

Now Sarah is dead. Killed by a speeding car while she was out doing what she loved. Holidays are different. I must manage Christmas carefully. I sometimes just pretend it doesn't happen. Other times I give carriage rides to all the neighbors and their families. September has come. With September come the changes of the seasons; cold nights, cool mornings and hot afternoons. I still wait for her school bus to drop her off after eight years of her graduating from high school, six years of her being dead. Sarah's love for books gave me an opportunity to donate funds to help build the new library and to honor Sarah at the same time. I hope Sarah's love for reading inspires others to create positive works out of great tragedy.

September is her birth month.

I am sad. I miss her.

Then I bought my black Morgan mares, sight unseen, on the first anniversary of Sarah's death. From that time on, I learned to set goals for a new beginning on each and every death date of my daughter. So on May 24th I plan for a new adventure and a positive outcome, and then I follow the joys.

Keep reading and see where I wind up.

CHAPTER 27
RIDING BACK TO LIFE

When my daughter was killed, I almost stopped carriage driving. I wanted to find another pair of horses to keep my brain going. A friend called and said that she saw a pair of 4-year old, black Morgan mares for sale in the *Capital Press* newspaper. They were in Idaho.

I called the number. The man who owned the mares was named George Valentine. I bought the mares over the phone, sight unseen, and wired him the money. He and his son, also George Valentine, delivered the mares in the back of a pick-up truck with a wooden, homemade frame you only see in comedy movies normally.

The mares arrived having eaten most of the wooden frame. He jumped them out of the truck and I led the mares into the pond pasture. They arrived on the first anniversary date of my Sarah's death.

I named one Valentine after my first black Morgan mare. The other was named Bobby after a friend's pony who had just died.

Those mares were WILD. Hot , hot and hot and WILD. They had shoes on their front feet and none on the back feet. My shoer came over and it took us five hours to get shoes on their back feet (a 30-minute job). I could hardly catch the mares. Now I had three pairs of mares. I had four bays and two blacks.

I started by teaching the black mares to be easily caught. Then I started to break them. I long-lined them for months. Then I saddled them up. Valentine bucked hard every time I saddled her. She bucked when I got on as well. One day I grabbed the reins hard before I got on and she was fine. The buck and the wild has always been there with Valentine. The wild is what gives her the beauty when I longline her in front of dear, *hot* but steady Bobby.

I rode these mares all over my pastures. I never gathered cattle in the mountains with them as I could not take the pressure of riding that hard. I was still very fragile from the death of my daughter.

Then one day a friend showed me how to hold the lines for a tandem ride-and-drive, with me riding one horse and driving the other one ahead of me. I was surprised. I already knew how to hold the lines. Tandem is the same as four-in-hand carriage.

I was not hooking Bobby and Valentine to the carriage or wagons at this time. They were very hot mares and still are very hot mares. They carry a fire in their hearts and in their feet and minds. I have learned to help them control their hot spirit and use that fire for their beauty. I never wanted to have them explode or burn themselves up.

I rode and drove them everywhere on my farm. I gathered cattle with them on the farm while I did the ride-and-drive. I practiced all the time.

A Morgan club stopped by to see them one day as I did the ride-and-drive. I was also invited to the Klamath Falls Packing Clinic to perform. I had to get a friend to drive me over to Klamath Falls. I was still too agoraphobic. I rode into that arena on the second anniversary of Sarah's death. The mares had never been off the ranch to perform. They were perfect. I got my first standing ovation.

I was then invited to go to the Horse Expo in Sacramento, California in June. I barely made it out of my driveway due to my agoraphobia. I cried all the way across the Siskiyou Mountains. I ran out of tears in Cottonwood, California.

I found my way thru Sacramento to the fairgrounds. I performed with a Morgan group in the afternoon and was well-received. I managed to get an evening slot that night for the big show. I rode into an arena of thousands of screaming people. The mares never missed a beat. We received a standing ovation, and I was hooked. The Dancing Morgans were on their way.

I drove my old, beat-up Ford truck and an old stock trailer to travel to other fairs and events. I stepped into a new world and slowly stepped out of my grief over Sarah's death. I owe my recovery from severe depression and agoraphobia to my two HOT black Morgan mares.

CHAPTER 28
A GOOD DAY

Today is a good day. Today arrived with the morning foggy and dreary. The trees dripped moisture onto the already soggy ground. The air was cold and damp. I had a difficult time getting the fire started.

Today started well. I walked out and called the mares in. They came in running, stopped, and each went into her stall to eat her waiting breakfast.

The day got better. I returned to the house for my second cup of coffee when the first load of firewood arrived. I helped my neighbor cowboy unload and stack a cord of oak. I went into the house afterward, swallowed an aspirin for my already hurting muscles, then the second pick-up load of wood arrived. This time the truck was filled with at least two cords of wood. I helped unload and stack the wood. Then I went into the house for more coffee and another aspirin.

I walked up to the barn and played "trick horses" with all the mares. Bobby is making the bow. She has it figured out. Only one more mare to go and that is Valentine. She will learn the bow too. I have to now remember all the tricks that they all know and what they do not know. I am trying to keep the lessons balanced. The trick-training reminds me of when I taught school and had to remember where all the kids were in all the lessons, all the time. Nothing like recreating what you love to do.

Somewhere this morning merged with some sun and then turned into afternoon. I have a long-lining lesson with a gal who brought a huge, beautiful 17-hand mare for training. The mare is perfect. The mare only needs a little tweaking, but she is perfect.

When the lesson is over, I haul mulch down to cover the open areas along the driveway so I will not have to water so much this summer. Winter work is the same as summer work. I guess that program makes some sense.

About that time my neighbors Brian and Kristy come along to feed their cows with Brian's nephew, Matt, riding on the back of the tractor. I jump up on the fender, with Kristy driving so we can "farm visit" while the men knock the flakes of hay off to feed the cows. Kristy and I have a nice visit. After they leave, I still have enough daylight, so I mow a small section of the pond pasture to keep the weeds even with the grass. I then come in for dinner of cold chicken and some vegetables. I have a good day.

Every day I get is a good day.

CHAPTER 29
JACK

The first time I met Jack was at the 2001 Western States Horse Expo in Sacramento, California.

On Thursday, May 2001, I drive to my friend Nancy's stable from my home in Eagle Point. I drive down to Sacramento for my first performance with my two black Morgan mares, the Dancing Morgans.

Friday morning I load up my Dancing Morgans and head to the Western States Horse Expo about five miles from Nancy's barn. I arrive and prepare to unload my mares. I open my trailer doors and there stands Jack, between my two mares. I can't believe what I see. We gaze deeply into each other's eyes. Where did this guy come from?

I have a stowaway in my trailer.

None of us move. Not the horses, not me, and not this guy. He is so handsome, with his huge, green eyes and his shinning carrot-orange hair.

I carefully step in and shut the trailer door. We are crowded in here, two mares, a nervous woman, and Jack. I can't resist. I have to touch this beautiful creature.

I reached forward and touch his hair.

He responds, "Meow!"

I pick him up and read his tag on his harness, "Jack." Jack is Nancy and her husband Tom's nine-year-old, orange-striped cat. Jack *loves* to go to horse shows. He has been to the Santa Barbara Morgan Show where he proudly sat on the box seat railing and meowed at the pigeons perched on the overhead wires. Jack said, "Meow, come down here pigeons and sit in the box seats so you can better see the horses."

"Meow," continues Jack, "I could even hold you in my mouth so you pigeons would not frighten the horses should you want to fly away."

Again, Jack says, "Meow!"

Five years later, Jack is still stowing away as he travels with Lucy, a schnauzer, Katie Mercer (a lab/skipperkee), Suzi Mercer (a Jack Russel terrier), Nancy (Jack's person and Carole Mercer's human friend), and Bobby and Valentine (The Dancing Morgan mares).

Jack manages to stow away and steal the hearts of the horse show world wherever he goes. Jack has remarkable talents for a cat. First of all, Jack walks on a leash. Secondly, Jack is the best, quickest, and quietest "door dodger" (a.k.a escape artist) of this entire bunch that travels together. Jack loves to explore, often sneaking off without Nancy's permission.

Jack disappears on Friday morning at Del Mar. We look everywhere for him. Nancy wanders the entire show grounds calling for her cat.

"Jack. Jack. Jack!" she calls.

Soon the entire show grounds are calling "Jack. Jack. Jack!"

Everyone knows Jack by now. The horse show people have been petting him for the last two days as Nancy and Jack walk around the grounds. Of course, Jack met many new friends.

Nancy's cell phone rings. The voice on the line says, "I have Jack. He is here at the Del Mar Fair Ground's maintenance shop. I called the number on his cat tag."

Nancy jumps into the truck and hurries to the maintenance yard and picks up Jack. Jack purrs into her ear. "See, here I am, stowed away with all these guys. Glad that I AWAYS wear my cat tag with your name and number! Meow!"

During the Dancing Morgan's performance at the "Night of the Horse," people in the audience ask me, as I and the mares dance by the stands, "Did you find Jack?"

Between the musical notes of the Blue Danube, I answer, "Yes, Jack called. He is safe with Nancy."

The crowd applauds for the Dancing Morgans, and of course for Jack's safe return.

CHAPTER 30
TRAVELS

If it is a Saturday, I must be somewhere!

Today the ol' red 1985 gas-eating Ford pick-up is following the flash of a huge, 2000 Dodge diesel truck zooming across the back roads of the Sacramento Valley. Both trucks are hauling Morgan horses back and forth, back and forth, back and forth, and then back, from the valley to the foothills. Nancy is at the wheel of the Dodge with a trailer load of stallions. One big, golden Morgan stallion and one mini-Paint stallion are close on Nancy's heels. That woman can haul horses.

Following far behind and usually lost in the vast expanse of

California's Sacramento Valley is me and my black mares. Nancy is the leader. She waits when I am left behind at all the red lights. Co-pilot Teresa even goes so far as to slow down a cement mixer that passes me and the trailer going up and up and up Highway 50 to Placerville. But that's another story!

For three days Nancy rode Sunny and I rode/drove the mares around the Wal-Mart parking lot. Teresa and Jackie were a part of this road show as they paraded the miniature stallion "Too Hot to Gamble" around the parking lot.

Now you are asking yourself, just what are these woman and horses doing in the Wal-Mart parking lot? Well, simple. We are helping to sell trucks for Thompson Auto and Trucks. What a sweet deal. The "Most Famous Morgan Stallion since Figure" and the "Dancing Morgans" are broadcast over the radio waves of the entire Sacramento area. People come to see the horses. People come to visit with Nancy and me. Friends come. People Nancy and I don't know come and visit. While visiting with the people we make lots of new friends.

Trucks and cars are test driven and sold. Then it is back down the foothills and the flatlands of Pleasant Grove. Teresa and her husband Greg house us, the hounds, and the horses. This group is added to their 23 miniature horses, two dogs, three puppies and an unknown number of cats and kittens. Greg cooks a different and wonderful dinner every night for four nights while our troop waits to move on to "Dressage in The Wine Country" (DWC).

I and my two dogs and two horses leave first for DWC. We find Santa Rosa and the fairgrounds. Nancy, Jackie, Teresa, and Kristy arrive the next day with help for me and the horses for our evening performance. My friend Bob also helps run errands.

The stalls are transformed into a showplace for the Dancing Morgans. The horses are brushed and groomed to perfection. Nancy is ever-ready with her camera. The show starts. What a show! Great riding! Great riders! Great vaulters! Great trick riders! A soprano on horseback too.

As I am warming up, a couple of cowboys wander over and introduce themselves; celebrity trainer Dennis Reis and the King of the Cowboys, pro-bull rider Ty Murry. They have come to see me ride, so I give the crowd my best. The mares are perfect. After the performance, Nancy gets a couple of nice pictures of two cowboys and one cowgirl at the black-tie event.

Nancy drives home to Malin, Oregon. I drive home to Eagle Point. Both of us rest for a week after our 15 days on the road.

CHAPTER 31
SEPTEMBER MORNING MEMORIES

This morning as I walk up to perform the morning barn chores, September morning memories strike me. September mornings that are lost to time. Never again will I get a call from Chet Wolf to be at Mill Mar Ranch at dark o'clock and be ready to ride. Chet and Terrie Wolf sold their ranch and have moved to Susanville to be closer to their son, his wife, and their grandsons.

Mill Mar Ranch has been sold to an unknown. The new cowboys are young and know their jobs. No old cowgirls need apply. They know *so* much about gathering cattle in the rugged Cascade Mountains that they have to call Randy Wolf, son of Chet and Terri, to help gather the cattle. Randy knows where the cattle hide and he knows where the hidden traps leak. Randy doesn't call me for help. He too is young and he *knows* where the cows hide.

I am lucky. I have ridden with the finest men and on my finest horses in the most rugged mountains, the Cascades. I have forgiven these mountains for not being the Sierras of my youth. I have grown to love these mountains for their youth. The time of riding for cattle with the Wolf clan will never come again. I was lucky. I rode with these men for ten years until Sarah's death.

After the accident I was too fragile to make the split-second moves and the decisions of safety for the others and me. I couldn't leave my ranch. I had lost the courage of life. By the time I recovered enough to ride for cattle again, cattle gathering had faded into other hands that don't know or care that I can ride.

The cold mornings remind me of school times and how Sarah walked to the bus stop at the end of the driveway and then would walk home in the hot afternoons. I was always so glad to see her. Those times ended when she left for college, never to return home. These September mornings come with a sadness of loss and mourning.

I have a carriage ride to do this morning. I don't want to take the ride with people who want too much. I know that I will enjoy it once I am finished, but I haven't even started yet.

Sarah would be 26 this September 30. She stays at 19. Her ashes lie in a box on my bookcase.

CHAPTER 32
HOMECOMING

I am home. The dogs are home. The horses are home. I think we are all glad to be home for the time being. Dancing season for 2003 seems finished.

I miss the dancing already. The final dance stage was the El Dorado County Fair Grounds in California. In two days we performed the dance seven times and did four long-lining clinics. I did it and can do it. The ol' red Ford pick-up is still running. I am still "camping" out of the stock trailer.

It is the end of September and the weather is still very hot. We zip up I-5 into southern Oregon in daytime temperatures of 105. I still must be crazy.

The dogs have figured out traveling. When we are away from home, if I pick-up my purse and make a move, they run for the pick-up. Dogs are so smart.

I figured out something else too. If a dog wants to do an activity or go somewhere, it shows up. People are the same way. If they want to do something, they show up. Good lesson for me to be tuned into.

I am busy trying to line up 2004. Life is now broken down into a series of where-we-go next. I am working on finding a new truck and a new living-quarter gooseneck trailer. I have put my ranch on the sales market hoping that someone with two suitcases full of money comes down the driveway to buy the ranch. Selling my ranch is a huge decision. I have waited six years since Sarah's death to sell. I am ready to move to a much smaller place. Thirty acres looks good. I want irrigation for the horses. I want to be able to just go.

Maybe next year I will try for the entire United States. That would be fun.

That would be crazy too. We will see.

CHAPTER 33
JUDGING WOOD

I live by myself. I have lived by myself too long. I can take care of myself too well.

Living alone is not necessarily good, but it's not all bad either. I have learned to fix fence, harness a team of horses, and hitch that team to·a wagon all by myself. I feed the cattle too and cook for myself. Too cheap to go out to dinner very often. Besides, it is no fun to dine out by yourself. At home I have the company of two hopeful dogs. I can hook my truck to the trailer, load the horses and dogs, and sashay down the road for thousands of miles all by myself. Sure, I get very lonely, but I guess I am just too picky to partner-up.

Winter came overnight here in Southern Oregon. We had six beautiful days of indian summer. Mother Nature turned from hot-as-hell summer to a six beautiful days of fall and then turned right into a winter wench. Now the temperature is cold-as-hell.

My ranch philosophy is *never* go anywhere empty-handed. I have jobs I save to do just while waiting for the vet. These are jobs that can start instantly and end in the beginning, middle, or just-about-done. These jobs keep my mind off the problem of what is waiting for the vet.

The biggest, unending winter job is heating the house with wood. I still live fairly primitively in the technological year of 2003. I pick up an armload of wood every time I come into the house. I have a red, wood stove that goes black-hot with heat. I set the fans to push the heat around and close all the doors to the rooms that are not in use. My bedroom door stays shut until I go to bed. Turning on the electric blanket is diabolically opposed to heating with wood, but the cost of a warm bed in a cold room is more than worth it. I keep the door closed all night, the window open, and the blanket on.

The Jack Russel that lives with me sleeps under the covers in the winter. The other dog sleeps downstairs, as she is too dignified to sleep with a person. Today, as I picked-up the stove wood from the wood pile outside, I realized I have developed a "wood eye." I know exactly how big the piece of wood is that will fit in the wood stove. I know if the split wood is too big and I won't be able to cram it into the stove. A remarkable ability for a woman to possess in the year 2003.

I am getting out the wood maul to fix the "too big pieces." At 56, I sometimes think I might be getting too old to split wood, but the old saying that you are twice warmed by splitting your own wood is exactly true. I also have noticed, riding through the woods, that wood breaks into pieces about the same size as the stove's fire bed. I personally think that the size of the stove's bed was ultimately determined by the size that wood naturally breaks. I mean the wood sticks that are about four to six inches in diameter. Just my observation, not necessarily true.

Yet when one considers that it has been women over the millennia who have kept the home fires burning, the size of the hearth has been determined by the size of the wood that a woman could gather by herself. A woman heating her home a million year ago determined the size of the wood that fits into my stove in 2003. My arms go out to her. The size is just right for me to carry all by myself.

While I tend my fire to stay warm, I also have to cook. I *can* cook. I cook some things once a week. I cook a chicken once a week. I eat off the carcass for the rest of the week. I eat lots of vegetables. Some vegetables I grow, the others come out of frozen bags purchased from the giant food store in town. I shop for groceries once or twice a month. I buy powdered milk and keep it in liquid form in a milk carton in the refrigerator.

My friends delight in opening my refrigerator door and pretending to be totally shocked at how little food is on the shelves. Right now there is a half-gallon of reconstituted milk and a covered container of cooked, brown rice.

I eat very simply and well. I work hard and my weight stays the same. I am not very strong anymore at 65 years old, but I am healthy and happy. I pay cash for the strength of others.

I will go out to dinner occasionally. I like good food, but cannot pay high prices for gourmet meals. I try to keep some parts of my life very simple.

As my appliances die, I do not replace them. I have not had a clothes dryer for at least 10 years. In the summer I hang the clothes outside. In the winter I have drying racks in the loft. I am single. This clothes drying method works for me. Sarah has been gone for some time. She used the dryer.

The microwave dies. I go without a microwave. I lived before a microwave and I can live now without a microwave.

In the winter when my wood stove burns all day, I cook on the stove. Cooking on the stove top is very easy and saves on the electric bill.

I do not buy the special box so that I can watch TV when the country changes from analog to digital. I have a very small-screen TV. I can watch videos or read. I have a library card and I read five to six books every two weeks.

This lifestyle works for me.

I get up at 4 A.M. in the summer and 5 A.M. in the winter. I drop dead into bed by 8 or 9 in the winter and by 10 P.M. in the summer. I use all the daylight that I can possibly muster in the winter or summer. I have chores to do all the time.

CHAPTER 34
SALE YARD

Today may be the very last time that I ever ride at the livestock sale yard. The yard is scheduled for demolition in the spring. I have ridden as an alley rider here off-and-on for 17 years.

Quarterly, on Mondays, I would ride for the Cattlemen's Association Sale. As I rode for the cattlemen, I watched several jet planes fly overhead. The yard is right next to the airport. The bawling of 500 cattle moving through pens, shoots, and alleys and back into pens drowns the sound of the jets outside. The single strand of electric cable wiring a single light bulb follows the huge beams of the barns.

I can't help it. I reflect on the lives I know working here. My friend, the livestock inspector, greets me from his wheelchair. Six years ago he was in a terrible automobile accident and has never walked again or ridden his horse. His wife still comes in and works in the office. Fred sits and visits with all the other people in the "lobby." I glance across at the alley. There goes the other retired brand inspector, riding his horse up and down that alley, moving cattle. His son died a couple of years ago from brain cancer. The young man left behind a widow and two children. Here I am, riding seven years after my daughter was killed. Another woman in the office has a young son of 26 who is paralyzed from a hospital mishap.

The man who is herding cattle towards me has a hook for his left hand. I have never met him, but I recognize his horse. It's his dad's horse. I rode for 10 years with his dad. Yes, that's the same horse. The man is named after his dad, but doesn't look like his father. He manages very well with his right hand and the hook. I work the gates. It's easier for my older horse and me.

Birdie, my horse, likes the sale yard, but this year she is really older. She gets tired after the first three hours and is glad to work the gates rather than bringing the cattle off the scales.

I have been here for 17 years. I know this job on horseback. I am here for seven hours. I am in shape and don't feel the effort. My horse does. She has gotten old. The young woman pushing cattle on foot was a babe-in-arms when I first started here. I remember her mother when she was pregnant with this very capable young helper.

Life goes on. I am lucky. I was able to have a unique taste of life here. Several men ask me if I am back in the cattle business. I think about being back in the cattle business.

"No," I answer, "I'm just here to help out."

I am the only woman riding a horse in the alley. I am lucky to know this job and to continue to be asked back to ride. The job goes very smoothly. Life goes on.

CHAPTER 35
PUDDLES

Twenty years ago, I became a cowboy and learned to gather wild cattle. Today I own a tame ox named "Puddles."

Puddles stands 5'6" at his back. I cannot see over his back when I am standing next to him. Puddles weighs in at approximately one ton. One ton equals 2,000 pounds. I weigh approximately 140 pounds. Puddles out-weighs me by a few pounds.

When Puddles does something naughty, you say in a firm voice, "No, no Puddles!" and shake a stick at him.

I rode him once when I bought him, but haven't had the courage to ride him at home. Besides, I don't have a saddle that fits him. I may not find that saddle.

I had dreams for Puddles before I bought him. I dreamed of having him dance with my Morgans as I traveled. I dreamed of making all sorts of programs for him to play in. I dreamed big dreams.

I now own an OX. Puddles is not only as big as an ox, but Puddles is an OX. Moving a one-ton ox to a horse expo is a huge undertaking. Puddles takes up two of the stall spaces in my trailer. I found that size deception on the way home from buying Puddles. Puddles really doesn't like to stay in stalls. Just where would he stay at a Horse Expo? Puddles likes to be able to see where he is. The stalls at the Horse Expos are often canvas, temporary tents. Envision a curious bull in a rip-able china shop.

Now just what was I thinking several weeks ago when I bought Puddles? I dreamed. I thought! I dared and I did.

Puddles is now at home with the Dancing Morgans. Puddle's job will be to stay and keep my other, non-dancing mare, Birdie company when I travel with the Dancing Morgans.

Puddles is art. Kinetic art. Come by and feed this gentle giant a cut-up apple, he prefers them that way. Give him a scratch on the neck. He loves it. Kick back and watch him eat grass. Enjoy this lovely, huge, sweet creature for who and what he is. It helps to be crazy in order to be an ox owner.

Puddles continues to grow and grow. He reaches 2,500 pounds. I cannot keep him. I put out the word that I have a tame ox for sale. I sell him to the perfect owner who wants a huge, tame steer for his guests to pet. Puddles is the right guy for the job. He loves to be petted while he gently eats an apple from your hand.

Puddles lives at his new home for two years and is 10 years old.

Yesterday I received a phone call. Puddles was ill and was put down. He now lies in a lovely meadow beneath a huge oak tree.

It helps to be crazy to love an ox.

CHAPTER 36
TRUCKS

I love trucks.

I never really had a pick-up truck until I bought my ranch. I love trucks but I can never remember what make they are or what year they were made. I just remember the color of the truck.

My first truck was blue and white. It died on the freeway from old age one fine day.

I replaced that truck with a great, rust-brown truck that I bought from a widow whose husband "only drove the truck on Sundays." That widow was a good talker. The rust- colored truck could barely pull its own weight, much less a loaded stock trailer. I sold it to a used car dealer for far less than I had paid.

I then limped around in an old, primer-painted, flatbed pick-up. I traded it in on the very nice, shiny, used, red Ford pick-up.

This truck had 4-wheel drive. I could get that truck stuck anyplace, even if I went through the mud first or last on gathering trips. The cowboys soon learned that they had to drive my rig thru the hard spots. I learned to warn them about my ability to get stuck no matter where I was in the line-up. They put up with me and my truck and always called me to come along and help gather cattle. The red Ford was good for the mountains and the ranch. It wasn't a freeway truck. The Ford was good as long as it did not have to travel very far or go very fast.

Knowing that the truck wasn't good on the freeways did not stop me when I started performing with the Dancing Morgans. I limped over the Cascade Mountain passes and coasted down into the San Joaquin Valley flats. Often the truck over-heated. I could not run the air conditioner in the hot, California valley, because the truck would overheat. As long as I chugged down the roads at 45 miles-an-hour, the truck mostly ran.

I had breakdown after breakdown. I was towing my old stock trailer with the two Dancing Morgans. I looked pretty much like a "goose in a new world." The important thing is that I beat my agoraphobia and went to the shows, the Expos, and danced with my mares.

The red Ford managed to get me to Pomona, California one weekend, but it sure didn't want me to get home. Coming up the grade on Interstate 5 out of Redding, California, I knew I was in real trouble. It was about noon when the clutch up and quit. I was stuck in second gear and the truck would barely run. I limped into a rest stop and used a pay phone to call AAA. I did not have a cell phone at that time.

The operator said she could tow the truck, but I would have to disconnect the horse trailer *and leave the horses.*

Sure. Like I am going to leave the horses and have the truck towed to some unknown repair shop. But she refused to send a tow truck because I had livestock.

I fell apart on the phone. I cried. I hardly ever cry. I was tired, scared, had a broken-down truck and I and the mares were stranded at a rest stop with a refusal for help.

I hung up on her.

I opened the side door to the trailer, sat down, and really had a major boohoo. All I could think about was that I wanted a man with a gun. So I called 911.

A lovely highway patrol man came to my rescue. *He* called a tow truck driver. I had 100 "free miles"on my AAA card. The tow truck driver and the patrolman both knew that I and my horses needed to get home. The tow truck driver asked me if I had a kitchen and bathroom in the trailer. He said if I did, the trailer would qualify as a recreational vehicle and he could tow it my 100 free miles. Neither he nor the highway patrol officer said anything about the horses.

Instantly, I "got it."

"Yup," said I, "it is a recreational vehicle."

The tow truck driver hauled me, the trailer, and the horses to Weed, California. That was the first 100 free miles. We stopped at the auction yard in Weed. The horses stayed overnight in the auction pens and I slept in the trailer.

The next morning the same tow truck driver showed up and hauled me the 100 miles to my place in Eagle Point. That 100 miles was *also* free, because I had 100 miles-a-day on my card.

I was so glad to be home.

A friend of mine came and looked at my truck's clutch. He said the truck could not keep going on the long trips.

I was scheduled to go to Lexington, Kentucky for Mother's Day. I was going to perform at the Kentucky Horse Park. I had ordered a real, living-quarters horse trailer, but the red truck could not make the trip.

I had the truck clutch fixed and sold the truck to a local shoer who was thrilled to have "Red." I then bought another truck.

This one was tan and black, so I called this truck "Bucky." Bucky is a good truck, but pulling the big, living-quarter trailer filled with hay and horses, Bucky had a hard time. I realized that if I was going to be on the road by myself or with one other person and the horses, I needed a BIG TRUCK.

I found a very good-priced Chevy Kodiak. I bought it. I hooked the trailer up and ran down the road. I could look the truckers right in-the-eye. The last thing they expected to see was a little old lady driving the big rig.

I loved my new set-up. The Chevy was an automatic. I was 43-feet of rig from front-to-back. I did not need a commercial driver's license (CDL), as the truck had a pick-up bed on it. If it had had a flat bed, then I would have had to get a CDL. Go figure.

I drove that rig all over the United States. I often went with my two mares and my two dogs. Sometimes Nancy came with me.

That set-up took me to the to the achievement of my dreams in 2010. I never had one bit of trouble with it. I just loved how easy traveling became. It was designed for long-haul trucking. It was a highway truck. No four-wheel drive. It had a compression brake for coming down hills. When I came off the Rocky Mountains into Salt Lake City, I never had to touch the foot brake once. The compression brake just held me steady.

The huge truck did have a drinking problem. She gulped down diesel, but I drove carefully and managed to average about 12-15 miles-per-gallon. I think that Chevy Kodiak was my favorite truck I've ever owned. I had a great sign on the back. It said "Silly Cowboy. This truck is mine."

When I came home from Kentucky in 2010, I sold the truck to a woman who was traveling the Quarter Horse show-circuit. I sold the trailer through a trailer sales place. I was finished traveling. I still miss the truck, but I have the fun of knowing that I put lots of happy miles behind me together with it.

CHAPTER 37
TRAVELING WITH 2 DOGS, 2 HORSES & 2 WOMEN

Now you know that I bought an OX on a whim. You already know that it helps to be crazy when you travel with two dogs, two horses and two women.

I have a "gig" in Arizona for the American Morgan Horse Association Convention this February. I'm from wet and wetter Oregon, so hauling down to sunny, dry Arizona in February sounds like a great idea to me. I contact my buddy Nancy and talk her into going with me, or was it the other way around?

I load the trailer in Eagle Point. Two dogs, two black dancing Morgan mares, and me. I load all the clothes, food, water, tack and hay that I will need. I slip over the ridge as the snow on the roads melts and arrive in Malin. We load one foal to be sold in Arizona. We load all of Nancy's "Magic Mountain Morgan Horse Club" booth and fundraiser stuff. We load all of Nancy's clothes, food, and "stuff," and we head out of Oregon on a beautiful sunny day.

We are on the road by high noon and headed for sunny California. We drive and drive and drive some more. We arrive in Simi Valley at 3 A.M. and sleep at Nancy's friend's place for about five hours. The mares are turned out to stretch and so is the foal.

Then we load up again and head for Phoenix, Arizona. We drive and drive, landing in Phoenix at 10 P.M. We are greeted at the barn where we have reservations by a huge sign that says, "NO DOGS." Well, we have two dogs. Have you ever tried to hide two dogs? Not easy. We are asked to leave. Nancy finds us a place to stay that will take in two mares, two dogs and two women in a huge trailer.

We get tickets to "Cavalia" and go to the performance. We love it.

Nancy and I meet all the young, wonderful riders. We invite them to come to my performance. They come. They love it. We all talk about horses, performances, costumes, spiking hair, and tricks of the trade. All-in-all a wonderful time is had by everyone, cast of "Cavalia" and cast of the "Dancing Morgans."

The next three days we spend at the convention meeting other Morgan lovers. Nancy has the best booth, featuring her stallion Farceur's Fool's Gold, as a fundraiser for Magic Mountain Morgan Horse Club. Nancy knows everyone and I meet everyone.

It rains hard every day in Arizona. I ride around with my umbrella up. The desert people have never seen anyone ride horses with an umbrella. I simply say, "I'm from Oregon."

Then they understand.

CHAPTER 38
GOING TO THE SADDLE MAKER'S SHOP

My day starts at 5:30 A.M. I leap up, quickly dress, and make the inevitable cup of coffee with cream and sugar. I drink candy in the early mornings, not black coffee. I am really jump-started. My two dogs, Katie and Suzie, hustle out the back door with me as we hurriedly stride to the awaiting pick-up truck and living quarter horse trailer.

Pictures for our horse entry to the Pasadena Rose Parade are scheduled for a 9 A.M. photo shoot in Malin, Oregon. Malin is a 120-mile drive away from Eagle Point. The horse trailer is parked facing out and down the road, ready to go. Everyone who drives a horse trailer knows "always park facing out." Bad things happen in the morning when you are in a hurry to leave with your load of horses. *Always* point the truck and trailer outwards.

I load Bobby and Valentine. They eat their breakfast of hay from the hay sacks. I am so prepared. I have loaded the dogs and myself and we leave at 6:15 in the morning.

Halfway to Malin, I think that I have forgotten my purse. Forgetting your purse is like leaving your identity on the back porch of your house. I sweat all the rest of the way to Nancy's barn. I drive very carefully. God help me if I get a ticket for anything. I have such a naturally guilty conscience. I am so not prepared.

The sky is colored grey and misty this morning. The trip is also wet and misty. The motorized unit climbs over the highway pass to

Klamath Falls with no problems. I love my truck and trailer. I have driven almost 10,000 miles behind this wheel in the past two years, performing with these beautiful Morgan mares.

I also can find myself almost anywhere. I can easily lose my purse. One trip I thought I had left it in the restroom. I was sitting on it.

I have a very small, black purse. Not a good purse, but easy to carry. I need to buy a bright pink purse to carry the little black purse. I own nothing that is hot pink.

I pull into Nancy's barn at 8:30 A.M. She is busy cleaning stalls. I unload my mares and put them into two clean and waiting stalls and pitch in helping Nancy with the daily morning chores. Of course we talk about the upcoming photo shoot. Of course rain is falling out of the gray and misty clouds overhead.

Nancy says, "We are cowgirls. We are going to go ahead with the photo shoot."

Nancy has her beautiful palomino stallion, Farceur's Fool's Gold, ready for the pictures.

"Sure," says I. "Riding in the rain in our parade outfits will be great practice for riding in the Rose Parade in the rain. Do we get to use umbrellas today?"

As I dress in my silver and blue sequin costume top, I find my purse nestled in one of the costume bags. I sing a song. "I found my purse. I found my purse." I do a happy dance. Such is the relief when you can re-establish your purse identity.

Sarah Baggs -neighbor, artist, photographer and friend- shows up with her expert eye and camera, complete with a plastic bag to protect the lens.

Sarah says, "Get out there in the field. I'll start shooting." She then explains, "The biggest problem is to keep the camera from focusing on the raindrops."

We put on our best smiles and our best parade wave. Sarah shoots. She gets just under 100 digital pictures. She goes home to put them on the computer. We must have them printed and in the mail today as our entry deadline is Monday the 9th and this is Friday the 6th. Somehow we always manage to get the job done, even in the rain.

We unsaddle and put the horses away. Off come the glittery parade clothes and they are hung up to dry before being put away. Hats are carefully placed so they will dry too. Man! It's a late, wet, Oregon spring this year. Nancy and I, and Nancy's small schnauzer, Lucy, pile into Nancy's truck. I leave my dogs in the heated office at Nancy's barn. We race over the Sarah's office. She has the pictures up on the computer. Her artistic eye picks the six best photos. She prints them. Nancy worries about her weight upon seeing the pictures. I worry about how old I look in the pictures. I am 58 and look every inch of every year. No plastic in my face, just lots of time.

The horse pictures look smashing. In my next life I am coming back as a beautiful horse. Sarah prints the pictures. We race 30 miles to Klamath Falls to the post office so we can overnight the photos to the parade officials in Pasadena. I run in with the envelopes and pay for the postage. One picture falls out before I can close the envelope. The woman behind the counter is so excited about the beauty of the horses. All the pictures come out and they are passed around to all the postal workers in the post office. The horses receive all the "oh's and ah's." Only in small towns where there are no lines in the post office can one share the contents of the entry envelope and receive the well wishes of the staff. The envelope is sealed and sent with many "good luck" wishes.

By now the clock shows 3 P.M. We stop for coffee and cookies. Coffee refuels our souls and cookies supply energy. Refueled by our healthy lunch, we are onto the next task: "shopping" at the 17th Horse Packing Clinic held at Klamath Fall Fairgrounds in Oregon. We briefly stop at the Morgan horse booth. The two women soldiering the booth are also eager to shop. I encourage them, "Go. Shop! It's early in the afternoon. No one will take anything. The booth will be ok." They leave their post unattended and we run into them several shopping stops later. They are having fun.

Nancy and I make quick rounds. We are not in a buying mood, but succumb to two rhinestone pins spelling, "Cowgirls." We must have the rhinestone cowgirls pins. We buy, pin "Cowgirls" in rhinestone upon our bosoms, and leave to pick-up wood shavings in Doris, California. We think the shavings mill closes at 4 P.M. It's already four but we persist. We arrive at 4:45 P.M. The shavings office is open, but it really closes at 3 P.M. on Fridays. The gal working in the office just stayed late to catch up on paperwork.

She says, "You are lucky. The guy in the back who loads shavings hasn't left yet."

Nancy drives around to the back of the shavings mill and the guy happily loads 26 bags of shavings into the truck. One more job done today.

We save the best stop for last. I always like this stop. Going to the saddle-maker's shop is almost a religious experience for me. We stop at the Doris saddle-maker's shop, Butte Saddle Maker. I only know the saddle-maker by "Conrad." The shop is small and is two rooms. One room is mainly for displaying beautifully handmade western saddles. The other room is lightly filled with western "stuff," dishes, glasses, spurs and books. We look around. My hands have to touch every saddle. The visit is like going to church and touching the relics and making a prayer.

Conrad is about our age (45-58 range). He isn't busy and is close to closing. No one here is in a hurry. The shop smells of leather, of dye, and of stories. Conrad starts the stories by asking, "So what have the two of you been up to now?"

"Do you really, really, really want to know?" say I.

Conrad sits down in his leather, custom-made director's chair. I plunk myself down in the other chair. Nancy props herself up against a display case. We are going to get down to the really serious business of telling really funny stories about our adventures. Conrad is curious about these two adventuresome women.

"You go first," he encourages us.

A little bit of encouragement is all we need.

"We played polo in Del Mar, California while we were there to perform with the Dancing Morgans at the Night of the Horse. It was the show's diamond jubilee," says Nancy excitedly. "Of course," she continues, "being old hands at traveling with horses arriving early to a show or performance is essential. By being early life opens its doors of adventure for us."

Nancy is right. I always insist upon leaving early for a performance. We might have a breakdown and I need to allow for more travel time. I like to get to the grounds several days early because the horses can rest from the trip and get to know the grounds. I *always* ride in the arena before I perform. I might be there several days before the show begins, but I must ride in the arena. I have to know the arena size and footing. Every arena is different, so I must allow for the differences from place-to-place. Also, by arriving early, Nancy and I make the opportunity to drive around the town we are staying in. Everywhere we go we have decided to do something new and wonderful.

"Look!" we shout in unison, "First lesson, FREE!"

There before our very eyes is a large sign in front of the beautifully groomed and manicured grounds. "First lesson free- Del Mar Polo Grounds."

Nancy swings the truck through the gates of the Del Mar Polo Grounds. Today is Tuesday. We sign up for a free polo lesson on Saturday morning. Of course Saturday morning is the morning of the "Night of the Horse" performance. Little matter. I'm only 58-years old and can still ride all day.

From Tuesday to Saturday our days have been filled with riding the grounds, dress rehearsal, and a live Friday morning television interview at 6 A.M. in full-costume. We were up at 4 A.M. in order to meet the timeline with groomed horses and me in full costume. Plus hunting for Jack, Nancy's cat. Actually we really use the early-arrival days well. We keep pretty busy.

Enter Saturday morning.

Our polo lesson is at ten o'clock. We arrive early to the polo field. We don't want the grey gelding. He bucks if you don't ride him just right. Nancy gets "Joker" and I get "Tess." Funny, Nancy's stallion is Farceur's Fool's Gold. Farceur means "Joker" in French. I just sold a mare named Tessa. Now horse people are not superstitious (ha, ha, ha!), we are just careful. Nancy and I decide that the names of the horses are a good omen.

Our mentor and teacher is Mark. His helper is Patty. Both people are incredible. Patty gets us dressed in helmets and hands us our mallets. I want a helmet with a face guard. I can ride with a broken arm taped up. I can ride with a broken leg casted and taped, but I can't smile without any teeth. Nancy's helmet is a tad large. She feels like "Edith Ann," whose hat always slips down over her eyes. The grooms, yes grooms, after all we are going to play polo, bring us our horses.

Up we go. Mark takes about a half an hour to explain and show us the rules of polo (polo rules are very important in polo, as I was to sadly discover once our "chucker" got going. A chucker lasts seven minutes. There are four people on a team. You try to hit the ball to the goal. You have one chance to hit the ball. You can't swing the mallet in front of the horse and etc. and etc. and etc. I get my horse and myself in trouble because I can't always remember the etc's.

Anyway, enough of my side-tracking and onto actually playing the game. The polo ponies really know what to do. My problem was that I wanted to ride the horse rather than let the horse do his job. GO STRAIGHT after you hit the ball and GET OUT OF THE WAY once someone else has hit the ball. I didn't get out of the way. I turned my horse into the ball and Tess got hit. Thank goodness that she wasn't hurt, but I certainly paid more attention to learning the etc's after that experience.

Nancy was on the opposite team. We galloped and trotted around like mad women and laughed. Polo is very fun and very exciting. We played for what seemed like hours. Our arms hurt from swinging the mallets and attempting to hit the ball. I cannot remember whose team actually won. After the lesson ended our ribs hurt too from laughing so much. (What do you mean? We only played for an hour?) We all shook hands and thanked each other for the game. The aspect of thanking each other for the game is sportsmanship and needs to be infused more in this day-and-age of expelling people from teams.

Now it is Conrad's turn to tell a story. He's a cowboy, so of course he has a cowboy polo story.

"One time (cowboy for, 'Once *upon* a time') when I was a young and wild pup, a bunch of us decided that we would play *cowboy polo.* Cowboy polo is played with western saddles, a couple of beers for energy, a broom, and some kinda ball. I think we used one of those balls you kick at school. Most of the ponies we were riding were just sorta broke. We used a mowed hayfield for the game.

"Man, we were tearing around that field having a grand ol' time. Pretty soon my ol' dad shows up and wants to get in the game too."

Conrad pauses with the ease of a really experienced storyteller. He goes on with the cowboy polo game.

"Well, my dad is a pretty good cowboy, but he is old compared to all us young bucks. We couldn't believe him. He could stand in the stirrups and really hit that ball. I think he made more goals than any of us.

"Well," continues Conrad. "After awhile we were pretty much played out. My ol' dad got off his horse and was moving pretty slow."

Conrad smiles and again pauses. Conrad is a master storyteller.

Conrad says, "I was a good kid when it came to my dad, so I walked over to unsaddle his horse. I couldn't believe what he had done. My ol' dad had tied his stirrups together under that horse's belly. Why, he had hobbled those stirrups! Those anchored stirrups were why he could stand up and hit that ball! My ol' dad was hard to beat."

I decide I will remember that ol' age and treachery wins over youth and inexperience in cowboy polo every time. Nancy laughs. I smile. I love saddle shops and cowboy and horse story-telling.

Nancy says, "Carole stole the show at the 'Night of the Horse' in Del Mar."

Nancy turns to me and says, "Tell Conrad what happened."

I say, "You tell Nancy. You tell."

Personally I like to hear the story, not just tell the story.

Nancy starts, "The Dancing Morgans stole the show at the Night of the Horse in Del Mar. Her tandem ride-and-drive raised the audience to their feet when the demonstration blended into a bridle-less musical kur and then back to a bridleless ride-and-drive. She was so nervous out there with Valentine. She didn't hear anything."

Nancy takes a breath. She begins the story again. "When the mares and Carole re-entered the arena with the cowboy cutters, the audience leaned forward wondering what she was gong to do next. The cattle began to move and Carole's lead mare, Valentine, leaped into action followed by Carole on Bobby. The Dancing Morgans are cutting cattle on long-lines. The crowd went wild." Nancy pauses. She too is an expert storyteller. "During the grand finale, the crowd roared as the Morgan mares danced around the arena to the drum beat of applause. We really have a good time on the road!"

Nancy drives back to her barn. We unload the shavings. I load my mares and drive home to Eagle Point. I pull into the barn around nine that night. I unload and feed my mares. I think to myself, as I feed the dogs and myself, "Full day. Tomorrow I have to buy a hot pink purse."

I buy a hot pink purse and can now spot it anywhere. I am *so* prepared.

CHAPTER 39
DREAMS VS. FANTASY VS. REALITY

In March 2005, I am watching a program on PBS when a notice appears about a "Texas Ranch House Re-enactment."

Like Santa, I fly from my seat and race to the computer and look up "Texas Ranch House.'" I fill out the application faster than you can say "On Comet! On Cupid! On Donner! On Blitzen!"

My application to be on the Texas Ranch House PBS reality show whisks through cyber space and lands in the piles and piles and piles of other applications. I have to wait until June to either hear from, or not hear from, PBS television.

I am *so* sure I am going. I have a plan. I am going to befriend two young cowboys and have them buy me two little steers. Those young guys are going to halter break those steers and teach them to come when called. Then we will teach those steers to swim, so we will have the lead steers for the cattle drive, which is to take place at the end of the program. By owning the swimming steers, those boys, steers, and I can lead the cattle drive. Man, I am *so* prepared to go to Texas! I wanted to go so badly.

I go to the library and read *everything* about Texas in 1868. I read books on southern cooking. I read books on trapping and cooking wild animals. I read the entire "Foxfire" series of books. I read and read. I am so ready to go to Texas.

I am ok on the ranching part, because I have been running my ranch here for 20 years. (Strike one.)

I can work cows from horseback or on foot. (Strike two)

I can hook horses to a wagon and drive the wagon. (strike three)

I have the everyday ranch stuff down pat.

I am so sure I am going to Texas. I pay all household and ranch bills four months in advance. I round up back-up help for my ranch and I am ready to cancel my Dancing Morgan programs the instant that I hear from Texas.

Like a guy who you really want to call you, Texas never calls.

I am so disappointed. I am so prepared. I have done a crash course on 1868.

"Texas Ranch House" went on without me. And I went on without Texas. I hayed. My hired man quit. I ran the wheel line and hand lines and all the flood irrigation all summer, all by myself. I had an Oregon Ranch House experience, right here at home. I mowed and clipped the fields. I hired the hay to be put up, all 40 tons of it. I ran the Oregon Ranch House for the summer of 2005. I have the horses and I have the tame steer. I just missed the cattle drive. I went camping with the horses and my friend Nancy and her stallion. We were at horse camp pumping water with a hand pump when I look at Nancy and say, "I am *so* glad I am not in Texas. I would have been pumping water all summer. I am only on the third pump down and the third pump up, and I am glad I didn't go to Texas."

Nancy laughs at me.

I reply, "But by sugar, I was ready to go to Texas. I would have known what to do."

Nancy answers, "Knowing what to do is why you didn't get to go. You were over-qualified."

"Oh! I never thought of being *over*-qualified. I guess I have trouble with the concept of being over-qualified. I want someone who knows what to do in a problem situation."

We pump the buckets full of water and that night, we cook our dinner in the comfortable living-quarters trailer, go to sleep, make coffee in the morning with a propane stove, take a hot shower, and use the potty. It is all thanks to the comfortable living-quarters trailer. But a part of me still wants to go to Texas 1868. I love an adventure.

I went on the road and danced with my Dancing Morgans as planned. Life went right on by without my going to Texas. I rediscover a previously known truth. There is a distinct difference between a dream and a fantasy. Dreams can come true. Fantasies have a script that you write in your head and they don't come true. Reality, of course, is the best of all dreams and of all fantasies. Some dreams do come true, and the great and small adventures that you never thought of come right down your road of life.

I guess reality is the reason that I didn't go to Texas. I dreamed, I fantasized, I dared, and I didn't go to Texas. Still, had Texas called, I would have loved to go to Texas in the summer of 2005. I would have loved every minute of the adventure.

CHAPTER 40
BEND, OREGON SHOW

The summer of 2005 rushes in full-bloom on the ranch. The late spring rains come just in time and the grass in the hayfield is taller than me. The pasture grass is tall from the lack of cattle this year and my green lawn dressage court must be mowed weekly. Still, we are running out of irrigation water here in Eagle Point. The late spring rains brought no moisture to the snow pack in the southern Cascades. Snow pack equals money-in-the-bank for farmers. My 20-years of ranching pay off. I know how to carefully balance every drop of water here on the ranch and how vital every drop already is. My days are long and monotonous. I am restless. My ranch is for sale. I am ready for a CHANGE. I love my beautiful ranch, but my painting here is done. The beautiful ranch hangs in perfectly-framed fences and wonderful mature trees border the frame.

Nancy calls. "Do you want to go to Bend to the regional Morgan horse show?"

For a moment I am stunned. "To the Morgan horse show? Are we going to be showing horses? We don't show horses. Why are we going to the show?" I ask.

"Silly," replies Nancy. Nancy is always very kind to me when I don't "get" something. Five years ago when she "discovered me" doing my ride-and-drive performance in Klamath Falls and encouraged me to take the performance to the Western States Horse Expo, I was literally a "goose in the new world." Nancy had to show me how to work the motion-activated sink in the restroom. I had lived on the ranch for so many years that I didn't know that the water turned on automatically. Nancy still knows that I "don't always get it right away."

"Silly," she says again. "We can just go and watch the show and see what is going on."

"You mean that we'd just go someplace without two or three horses, three dogs and your cat? You mean that we won't spend a week packing the 35-foot living-quarter gooseneck horse trailer and pack the truck with feed for two weeks on the road?" I am stunned. "You mean that we would just go someplace like regular people and just watch horses and not beat ourselves to death having too much fun?" I can hardly believe what Nancy is proposing.

"Do you want to come?" she patiently asks again.

"Sure," says I. "I'm game to just go to the Morgan horse show in Bend."

"Meet Sandy and me in Chiloquin. We can leave your truck at Barbara's place and drive up in Sandy's car together."

"You mean that we are going someplace in a *car*? A regular car? No trucks, no trailers, no horses, no cats, no dogs?" I have never in the past 20 years gone many places in just a car. "Wow! This sounds like a real trip."

We plan to meet at 9 A.M. on Friday morning. I get up early to turn horses out for their morning grazing. I move sets of water before I bring in the horses and take a shower so I'll be clean for the "car ride."

I drink my candy coffee (coffee very heavy on cream and sweetener), and I climb into my truck for the 90-minute ride to Chiloquin. I live in an extraordinarily beautiful place. The mountains are on my side, the far side is green and lush. As the Ford truck climbs the grade over the pass, I drive through almost old-growth forest and drop down into the Klamath Basin. I love this drive as I make my way across to Ft. Klamath. I cross the Wood River and see vast, green acres filled with cattle. I love the ranching and the cattle and the difficult way of life that comes with ranching. I remember once when I drove over here for something (just what I was doing here, I have long forgotten) and was delightfully delayed by cowboys moving vast herds of cattle from one field to the other. It was all I could do to NOT jump out of the truck, unload my horses and help them. Those cowboys didn't need my help, but I surely would have loved to be in the thick of that trail drive. Sweet memory.

I meet Nancy and Sandy at the appointed spot. I park my truck and get into the car. The car. A real car. A vehicle that doesn't pull a horse trailer, that just transports people down the road to a destination. I am relieved.

I remembered my pink purse and Nancy has her little schnauzer dog Lucy. We are NOT without an animal.

Nancy says, "Lucy wanted to come and I couldn't get her out of the car."

"Like she wouldn't mind you," says I.

I say "Hi" to Sandy, a photographer from Sacramento who is a friend of ours. We visit for the couple of hours car ride to Bend. We talk about people and horses and horses and people. The car rides comfortably. Lucy sleeps in the back seat with me. Amazing. Just to ride in a car.

We get to Bend at the horse show lunch-break. We hunt up coffee and horse show expensive-food for lunch. We eat and then hunt up friends and visit. Nancy has provided us with great t-shirts emblazoned with her stallion's logo. My t-shirt has Farceur's Fool's Gold's picture on it. People stop me and ask me about the horse galloping across my chest. I brag about Sonny and Nancy pulls out terrific pictures of Sonny taken at Western States Horse Expo. Trainer Lynn Anderson is riding the stallion and both horse and rider are enjoying themselves. Everyone loves the pictures and Horse Expo stories.

The trainers are hard at work with their clients and preparing for the classes. Visiting is quick and on the run. We decide to shop. I find beautiful "bling" for my ride-and-drive wardrobe. I buy it. Perfect. Then we discover that almost every gal at the show is walking around with a great hairdo. I have to try on the "false pony tail." I am smitten. I am silver haired by nature and the silver ponytail is perfect. I plunk it on my head and swing my new 'do down the barn aisle. A horse show is the perfect place for a fake ponytail.

Today's trip is a day trip. We have to leave. We are again starving so we make a Starbucks coffee stop for Nancy and a food stop for Sandy and me. We stop at Safeway. As I am going into Safeway, my silver pony tail jiggles loose, so I just sweep it off my head (very short hair is hard to attach to a ponytail) and stuff it into my jeans pocket. I ruffle my short hair and again look darling. We get our foodstuff and go.

The coffee and snacks don't hold us very long. We stop in a small café in a small town (both shall remain nameless in order to protect the innocent). Sandy orders fish. No fish. Sandy and Nancy both order chicken-fried steak. I order clam chowder. Plates of food arrive. The food is terrible. The chicken-fried steaks were flattened in the road. The gravy is cold and the mashed potatoes are goop. My clam chowder is paste.

Sandy is from California. She's mad. Nancy and I are from Oregon, we live in small towns and know the code. Don't create a problem. You may need a tow truck 15 miles down the road from here, and the café waitress may be the tow truck driver's wife. News of "rude" travels instantly in a small town.

We keep Sandy hushed up. We take some time and then I ask for a take out container. A different waitress brings the box. I artfully arrange the chicken-fried steak in the take out box. In goes the chicken, in goes the mashed potatoes; I make a well in the mashed potatoes. In goes the corn in the potato's well. Close goes the box.

We pay with a smile and the waitress asks, "How was dinner?"

I reply with a smile, "Great!" (Remember, I have been broken down many times before and a nice tow-truck driver is the difference between comfort and major discomfort.)

Sandy and Nancy drop me off at my truck and they go on home. I return to my ranch at nine o'clock in the evening. Beautiful day. I change my clothes, put on my rubber boots, get the flashlight and change the sets of irrigation pipes.

I can only hope that Nancy's husband enjoyed the chicken-fried steak they brought home. At least we didn't need a tow truck driver.

CHAPTER 41
FROSTY MORN

Frost lays smoothly everywhere this November morning.

I look out my bedroom window when I awake. My look is my daily barometer of work duty.

Summer looks mean moving water because the heat of yesterday still is lingering at 5 A.M. the next morning. Move-the-water is the first rule of the day after a quick cup of coffee and dressing in shorts.

Frost on a November morning means a lingering cup of coffee and several layers of clothes before I walk out the door to work.

I walk to work. Every morning I walk out my front door and immediately I am at work. Working on a ranch has its pluses and minuses. I have never made a tally on the ledger of life. Some days I fear that the minuses would out weigh the pluses. I am never sure where to put, "I love my job" on the ledger. There is no category in the tax register for loving the job. Of course there is also the moment when I breathe out the words, "I hate this job!" No place on the ledger for "hate" either.

This morning I take a scalding cup of coffee with my layers of clothes bundled on my body. The coffee is for internal heat. The coat, vest, turtleneck, scarf and missing hat are for exterior heat.

I open the barn doors and put hay out in the paddock for the mares. Then the dogs and I troop out to bring in the horses. The morning is cold, sunny, foggy and frosty all at once. I follow the clear movements of the horses' hoofprints and muzzles in the grass. As the mares graze, the warm breath from their noses lightly melts the frost. Their hoofprints follow the muzzles and further melt the frost. Perfect paths of the whereabouts of the mares.

The dogs and I quietly bring them in. Bringing in the mares is a wonderful ritual here. I believe they are warmer turned out at night so they can move and graze all night. The movement keeps them warm, as does the grazing. Grazing and digestion provides the fuel for warmth during the night.

Turning out the horses at night is the old way of caring for them. During the times when people actually used horses for a living and real jobs, horses and people worked during the day. The horses were turned out at night to rest and graze. This method worked in the past and works for me now. I feel that turning the horses out at night is better than keeping them in a stall all night with a large feeding (a bonfire), that is quickly dispersed and then the heat is lost for the rest of the night. The mares do not stand still all night and therefore do not require blankets to keep warm. I feel moving is much better than standing in a cold stall after eating an evening meal.

On a frosty morning, tracking the movements of mares grazing is an "I love my job" moment. Their coats are sheared velvet in order to keep warm. Later, when I use them to work, we start out velvet and return satin because the hair lays smooth and slick from their temperature increase due to their working in the fields.

I love the mornings where we all go from velvet to satin.

CHAPTER 42
COWGIRLING-UP THROUGH EUROPE

Nancy and I "Cowgirl-Up" through Europe in November and December of 2005. The trip consists of taking the Morgan stallions Farceur's Fool's Gold, Juvat, and a six-month-old Morgan filly to new owners in Sweden and Austria. Farceur's Fools' Gold (a.k.a. Sonny) will soon live in Sweden. Juvat (a.k.a. Jake) and the cremello filly head to Austria.

Just how did the finest bloodlines that the Morgan horse world has to offer wind up in Sweden and Austria rather than staying here in the United States?

Well, the story is as long as the journey to Europe.

Sonny is a horse that belongs to everyone. He is a fine representative of the true Morgan horse. Not only is Sonny exceptionally beautiful, but Sonny represents the versatility of the Morgan. Even with the aura of Sonny's extremely stunning looks, this horse never loses his ability to be a Morgan. Sonny is a showman in his looks, personality, and ability. Sonny does it all. Plus he is an outstanding breeding stallion.

Juvat is equally as talented as Sonny. His conformation is classic Morgan, but with the added dimension of height. Juvat stands just under 16-hands tall. Juvat also exemplifies the versatility of the Morgan breed. He rides English, western, saddle seat, and drives. His sons and daughters have the stamp of Juvat. They look just like their father.

The trip starts in Malin, Oregon when Nancy and Tom decide to change their lives. They go out of the Morgan horse-breeding business. They own two of the best examples of classical Morgan stallions in the United States. These stallions are sent to Europe to preserve and maintain classical Morgan bloodlines. Sven Anderssen of Harby Morgans in Sweden buys Sunny. Regina Wagner in Austria buys Jake.

Selling the horses is the difficult part. Transporting the horses to Europe is the adventurous part. The trip becomes the adventure and thus the name of "Cowgirling Up." We will travel 16,000 miles with only two plane reservations. One reservation is for the plane trip to Amsterdam from Los Angles, and the other reservation is the plane trip from Amsterdam back to Los Angeles. What happens in between is up to us.

We depart Oregon on November 12 just ahead of a snowstorm. We must leave before we are trapped in Oregon and miss the plane out of L.A. on the 16th of November. We drive 16-hours straight to L.A. The two stallions and filly are in the trailer and, due to the quarantine regulations, cannot be unloaded. The doors of the horse trailer are sealed with official clips that can only be undone by the U.S.D.A. vet in L.A.

We arrive in L.A. in the wee hours of Monday morning. Following the directions off the freeway, we find ourselves in front of the *locked* "Jet Pets" driveway. Remember always, this trip is a "Cowgirl Trip."

We set-up camp where we can, and we are in the middle of L.A., so we set-up in front of the locked Jet Pets gate. It is 2 A.M. and we have a trailer full of stallions and one filly camped-out on the streets of L.A. We make our camp in the living-quarters trailer. I opt to sleep in my clothes in order to answer the expected knock on the trailer's front-door. Of course I don't want to be in my cowgirl-print pajamas to answer a policeman's queries as to why we are illegally parked on the streets of L.A. Thank goodness we are cow-girling up and are not in a panic. We sleep four hours, then jump up and are ready to drive through the Jet Pets gates at 6 A.M.

At 8 A.M. the gates open.

We drive through the gates and then wait until 10 A.M., when the horses are finally vetted by the USDA quarantine vet. The horses pass the import tests and are unloaded and placed in new quarantine stalls. Jet Pets is a two-acre business located right next to the L.A. airport. The airport runway is about 700-yards north of Jet Pets. Several rows of pre-fabricated, easy-to-wash-and-disinfect stalls stand ready for the horses. Tucked away from the stalls are various other outbuildings for a variety of other animals, from primates to elephants. Quarantine areas are very strict. We are not permitted to lead the horses into the stalls and are not allowed not to come into the barn. We feel very strange not being able to pat the horses a temporary "good-bye."

The flight is uneventful, but upon arrival in Amsterdam, Nancy at one point grabs the European contact man by the shirt collar in order to facilitate the paperwork so the horses can continue to their final destinations of Sweden and Austria. Nancy never stops smiling.

We watch as Jake and Creamy load into a special van with two full stalls. Regina has arranged for comfortable transportation to Austria for her new Morgans. Nancy and I then climb into the cab of the 18-wheeler that transports Sonny to Sweden. The two cab drivers are great horsemen and don't smoke. The drive lasts 20-hours. The truck passes through Germany and Denmark in the dark, stormy night. The roads are slick with ice and snow and rain. Sonny's truck takes the ferry across the Baltic Sea. Everyone in the truck arrives in Sweden as the light of morning dawns.

Eskilutna, Sweden looks like home for Sonny. This area of Sweden is very much like south-middle Oregon. Farceur's Fool's Gold has come home to Sweden. Sonny's new family has built him a brand new barn and wonderful, big outdoor paddocks. He is left in the best of hands.

Nancy and I stay in the private homes of the new owners. We stay three days teaching the new owners everything we can about Sonny. During this time, these cowgirls meet new friends and visit Anne Erikkia who trains Morgans in Sweden. The cowgirls walk in the old barns of Sweden. These barns are the cathedrals of horse people. The beauty and antiquity of the barns humbles these cowgirls. One old barn courtyard is softly bathed in the pale, yellow light of a street light. I can hear the sounds of the courtyard from 100-years ago. The sounds are muffled by the slow drifting of new, falling snow. I hope to return to Sweden with my Dancing Morgans to perform at the Stockholm International Horse Show next year.

It's time to leave. Amongst tears of parting and tears of joy of new ownership, the cowgirls board the train to Stockholm. From Stockholm we fly to Vienna, Austria where we stay with Regina Wagner and her family. Regina lives in the small Austrian village of Pommersdorf. Pommersdorf lies about an hour-and-a -half outside of Vienna.

Jake and Creamy settle into their new home. Jake is turned out with his band of Morgan broodmares. He feels instantly at home. Creamy is welcome too. Each stallion is placed in the best home according to the personality of the horse. Sonny loves his private stall and paddock. Jake loves his band of Morgan broodmares. Again, these two cowgirls stay with the horse owner's family. Nancy gives several lessons on western saddle-fitting to all the interested Austrians. The cowgirls visit the Spanish Riding School in Vienna. I make the journey to Shoenborn Palace to see the carriage collection. The cowgirls tour and visit barns and meet new Austrian friends. I fall in love with Austria and Vienna. Not knowing when I will return, but I will return soon.

Time to go again. Again tears of parting and tears of joy of new ownership. The cowgirls fly to Portugal to ride the Lusitano stallions at Morgado Lusitano. We ride, we laugh, we sight-see. We leave for home.

All-in-all, these two cowgirls have traveled 16,000-miles in three weeks. The stallions are left in the best of new hands that understand the importance of classical Morgan conformation, ability, mentality and beauty. Europe now has the world's finest Morgan stallions, Farceur Fool's Gold and Juvat. The cowgirls, Nancy and Carole, now have the best memories of "Cowgirling Up" through Europe. The job is done and done well, cowgirl style, with laughter, tears, joy, and new friends.

CHAPTER 43
VET VISIT

I drive over to pick-up some medicine from my vet this snowy, cold December 27 morning. When I arrive there is a cowboy and his son with their old dog that has been attacked by another dog. The old dog is lying on the tailgate of the cowboy's truck and a full-scale operating-room surgery is occurring. I stand back while the vet and the two cowboys, deftly as surgeons, stitch the anesthetized old dog back together.

It never ceases to amaze me that these rough-and-tumble men of the west are so adept at sewing.

CHAPTER 44
ENJOYING A PERFECT SUNDAY DRIVE

Last Sunday the weather broke. The incessant rain stopped and the reluctant sun trickled out between the clouds for several glorious hours. The Pacific Northwest is experiencing one of the wettest winters in recent years. I hook my two black Morgan mares, Bobby and Valentine, to my wagonette and go for a Sunday drive. I load up my lab-skipperke cross, Katie. The dog proudly sits up front on the groom's seat next to me. My Jack Russell, Suzi, snuggles down under the lap robe on the front floor of the carriage.

I love to drive. I just drive my mares for the pure joy of driving. These mares are well-broke. The traffic doesn't bother them. We don't bother the small amount of traffic this Sunday morning. The winter air is crisp and cool. The mares love to trot down the road. Their eight-footed hoof-falls are one sound. Each mare is in perfect harmony with the other. I drive in perfect harmony with the mares. The dogs are just glad to come along for the ride. I enjoy having the company of the dogs. My hands play the musical instrument of the horse's mouth. They make sweet melody together as they trot down the county roads of southern Oregon.

The few cars that pass are full of careful automobile drivers. The people in the cars smile and wave. I tip my whip and smile in return. The mares never miss a beat. Neither do I.

The snow-frosted Cascade Mountains shimmer in and out of the foggy clouds that drift above them. The cold sun peers out from the overhead, snow laden clouds for brief moments during the ride. I step back 100 years. The horses and dogs share the instant of transposition in this time warp. Time is peaceful and quiet for an hour. Then a car passes, and time changes to once again the present day. The moment is not forgotten. The moment is to be shared.

I tucked my spares kit, extra halters and raincoat into the boot of the carriage just in case I might need anything. I *always* carry the extra stuff. I have never needed the emergency equipment, but best that I carry what I might need. One never knows when a person and horses might need the halters.

I have my hat, warm wool jacket and lap robe. I am warm and comfortable in the chilly sunlight. The temperature is perfect for the mares, cool enough that they don't overheat.

I drive over to a neighboring farm and back. The roundtrip lasts about two hours. I come home and unhook the mares. They stand whilst I wipe down the harness. I always wipe the harness down while it is on the horses. The harness is always clean for the next trip. I wash off the carriage wheels and brush down the mares and turn them out for a good roll.

The melody of being in tune with the mares, the cool sun, and the happy dogs is reason enough to drive down the country roads on a Sunday afternoon in January. I drive, not for the ribbons, not for the competitions, not for the admiring looks of the passersby, but because of the pure joy of driving in perfect harmony with my beautiful Morgan mares and sharing the day with my two little dog-passengers. Sometimes people are so busy competing and driving extreme sports that they forget to just enjoy a beautiful Sunday drive.

CHAPTER 45
DANCING MORGANS IN WYOMING

Making the journey to Wyoming takes 50 years and 3,000 miles to achieve the dreams of Carole L. Mercer's childhood.

The huge horse trailer is packed with hay and tack for the Dancing Morgans. Water buckets, more tack, clothes for me, food, sleeping gear and all the other "stuff" necessary for a 3,000-mile roundtrip adventure. I load the two black Morgans mares, Bobby and Valentine, into the trailer. They settle right in for the long trip. The huge Chevy Kodiak diesel truck is loaded with dog beds, ice chests filled with food for the road, and maps.

I pick up the two dogs, Katie the black lab/skipperke and Suzi the Jack Russell and gently toss them in the back seat of the truck. The seat is too high for the dogs to jump into from the ground. The dogs are expert travelers. They have been across the United States to the Kentucky Horse Park with me and The Dancing Morgans. In fact the two dogs have been to most of the places the Morgan mares and I have danced. They too settle down for this trip.

The horses, dogs and one human crew are departing from Oregon for Wyoming. The mares are booked for their performance with the "Buffalo Bill Wild West Show" in Sheridan, Wyoming on June 23, 2006. This trip is an extra-special trip, because I grew up just outside of Sheridan at Fort McKenzie. I have not been to Sheridan for more than 25 years, and I have some unfinished dreams waiting for me.

The first night on the road is spent in the small town of Madras,

Oregon. The horses are turned out in a corral at the fairgrounds and the dogs and I make camp in the Exiss Living Quarter's trailer. Three-hundred miles are under the wheels of the truck and trailer. I drive the rig up the Columbia River Gorge between the Oregon and Washington state line. I turn the big rig east onto Highway 12 towards Montana. The crew is retracing the eastward journey of Lewis and Clark. Serendipity steps in. The dogs and the horses and I are two days ahead of the Lewis and Clark reenactment. The Dancing Morgans stay the second night in Lolo, Montana at the very hot springs where Lewis and Clark camped upon their return journey to Washington D.C.

In the morning, I saddle the mares and actually ride, with the dogs faithfully following me, on the Lewis and Clark trail. I ride west in the Bitterroot Mountains of Idaho and Montana for several hours, then turn east on the Nez Pierce trail. The Dancing Morgans have now walked in the very path of Lewis and Clark and the Nez Pierce Indians.

We return to the truck and trailer, load dogs and horses, and pull out once again to the highway. By late afternoon we arrive in Three Forks, Montana. I stop at the local saddle store and asked the young saddle-maker, "Do you know where I can camp with a truck, trailer, two horses and two dogs?"

The young man gives me directions to the local KOA campground where the kind owner takes "the crew" to a spot overlooking the rivers. He tells me that this spot may be an actual campground where Lewis and Clark camped 200 years ago.

As the sun sets over the western Rockies, I marvel at my good luck. Twice "the crew" has camped in the very spots where Lewis and Clark stayed on their eastern return-trip across the United States. The crickets chirp, the wind blows, the rivers run, the horses nicker, and I listen to the same sounds that filled the Montana nights 200 years ago.

Morning comes with the usual cup of coffee, brewed on the stove in the trailer. The horses eat their breakfast while I cook eggs and then feed the dogs their food. The dishes are washed. The dogs are loaded and the horses are loaded. The huge rig pulls out and heads east for Sheridan.

It seems so strange to go east in order to wind up in the very western town of Sheridan, Wyoming. The rig pulls into the Sheridan rodeo grounds around 3 P.M. The mares are unloaded and put into the barren corrals. The dogs check out the fairgrounds, but know to come when called. I make a shade tent for the mares and put up a tarp for a windbreak. A huge thunder, lightening and wind storm rolls into the fair grounds. Lightening flashes. The thunder rolls as I rapidly unhook the truck from the trailer and load the dogs into the truck. We move away from the large light pole and wait out the fierce afternoon storm. The mares stand under the canvas shelter that madly flaps in the wind. The storm passes and the setting sun welcomes the crew to the Sheridan Rodeo Grounds.

I spend one day exploring my childhood town. I know my way around the town, but have never driven a car through it. Now I navigate the huge truck though the city streets. I find a parking place and enjoy visiting King Ropes, a giant western store and museum where I donate an artifact of a western coat made for my mother by a saddle-maker long ago in Sheridan. With the donation are pictures of me and the Dancing Morgans. Look for us when you visit King Ropes in Sheridan.

I spend the rest of the day going through stores in Sheridan.

Sunday I find myself at a polo match in Big Horn, Wyoming. The Big Horn Equestrian Facility harbors one of the very finest world-class polo fields. The Big Horn Mountains form a magnificent backdrop to the excellent polo games played here.

As I sit in the back of the truck, a fellow approaches. The man says, "You have quite a pink purse there."

"Yes, I can never lose this purse and if I do all I have to do is ask people, 'Have you seen my pink purse?' Someone always points the purse out."

The fellow invites me to sit with him as he photographs the polo match. I sit on the ground with Jon Hanson as he takes pictures of the horses and players. Jon works at the Tongue River Red Angus Ranch just 12-miles outside of Sheridan.

I ask, "Do you know anywhere I could camp with my horses? I am having another little Morgan mare delivered to the fairgrounds three days after the Buffalo Bill Wild West Show and I need a place other than the fairgrounds to camp."

Jon has an idea, but replies, "You will need to come out and talk to my boss. I can't make the decision."

We exchange phone numbers. It turns out that they are both planning to go to the Buffalo Bill Wild West Ball at the Sheridan Inn, on the following Friday night before the Wild West show. Jon promises me a dance.

The Wild West Show is still several days away. I hook-up truck and trailer and load dogs and horses. I point the rig up, up, up, the Big Horn Mountains and drive 50 miles to a place called Bear Lodge, Wyoming. There, the end of my dream born 50-years ago takes place.

All of my equestrian life I have dreamed of riding my very own horse in the Big Horn Mountains. In my childhood, my parents had built a summer cabin on a dirt road down Big Willow Creek. I had always wanted to ride my horse down that road. I saddle-up Valentine and lead Bobby and ride toward Big Willow Creek, one mile away. In the 50 years since I had been to this place, the high-mountain meadows have changed for the better. The wild flowers are abundant. There are fences where there were none before. The meadows and high alpine trees are healthy. The mountains have changed for the better. The forage is healthier. The dream is more spectacular than I remember.

The dogs faithfully follow me as I open the gate and walk the horses through it to the dirt road on Big Willow Creek. The dream is happening.

Suddenly five beautiful deer jump out of the willows down by the creek. The mares look. The well-trained dogs stay with me and the horses. We walk down the dusty road. Wildflowers paint Monet pictures on the landscape. The dream is better than a dream. The dream blends into reality. The dogs, horses and I see moose. Never have there been moose along the creek. The crew now see's six moose. Not one, not two, but six moose.

Slowly we savor the journey. Step-by-step, the childhood memories of this road awaken. Then, there appears the log summer-home that my father and mother built more than 60 years ago. Yes, the cabin looks smaller now than it did when I was a child. Things from the past *do* shrink. I can see that small children still play in the small trickle of a creek by the cabin. I remember the stones in the rock wall behind the cabin. Everything looks the same, but wonderfully different from the back of a beautiful Morgan horse.

We ride on to the end of the road and then turn back and become part of the Monet painting. One cabin along the road is occupied. A man named Jim comes out and invites me in for an iced tea. The horses are put in the corral around the cabin. Jim's wife, Bertie, is coming in tonight. Jim invites me to bring the truck and trailer down the road and stay the night in their front yard. The horses can stay in the corral. I ride back to Bear Lodge, load dogs and horses, and drive as delicately as possible down the dirt road to the cabin.

Bertie arrives and we become fast friends. As I listen to Bertie's story, I discover that Bertie and her sister saved this mountain-top and helped establish healthy riparian areas along the creek. I am staying with the very woman who transformed the damaged canvas of the mountain meadows into a Monet painting. It was only natural for Bertie to help paint the canvass. Bertie is a fine artist. Her name is Bertie Cox and she makes wonderful things out of rawhide.

The next day I ride up the mountains and watch a herd of 60-70 elk bugle and watch my black mares. The elk are across the valley on a mountainside. We ride back to the cabin and then across another hillside. We see 16 deer in all. The mountains are teeming with wildlife. We see more moose. There is no longer a need to keep count of all the animals. The dogs, the horses and I blend into the mountain painting of livestock, wildlife and wild flowers.

The dream of 50 years is fulfilled. After two incredible days of riding in the Little Big Horn Mountains, I load up and drive down, down, down the mountain road back to the Sheridan Rodeo Grounds. The Wild West Show program starts tomorrow.

It is Friday night. I dress in a red Victorian dress for the ball. The two chuck wagon drivers say they would like to go to the ball. We all meet at the Sheridan Inn and walk in the grand procession together.

"Nothing like finding yourself with a chuck wagon driver on each arm!" I think, as I am introduced to the actor playing Buffalo Bill.

Very soon I meet up with Jon and we sit together at a table at the ball. The ball is wonderful and I get my dance with Jon. After the ball, he escorts me around to the nightlife of Sheridan. At the Mint Bar (what a great cowboy bar!), everyone admires the red dress and asks Jon, "How was the ball?" It is a small town, and everyone knows what is going on in town.

Saturday morning comes early. One hundred young riders and their horses have arrived at the fairgrounds. Everyone is getting ready for the big parade in town. The police send an escort to the fairgrounds and I ride my horses with the stage coach driver, the trick rider, and the 100 young people who all help make up the cast for the Buffalo Bill Wild West Show.

The parade is huge. It starts at the Sheridan Inn where Buffalo Bill used to sit on the porch and judge the talent for his show. The parade goes through town and then winds its way back to the Sheridan Inn. The police escort the Wild West Show back to the fairgrounds for the evening show.

The show begins with the stage coach carrying in the dignitaries. Soon it is time for the Dancing Morgans to perform. The mares waltz into the arena. The audience loves the act. The Dancing Morgans are so unusual and beautiful to watch. The mares and I receives a standing ovation as we leave. The show ends with all the stars signing autographs on a Wild West Show Poster. The evening is a success, not only for the Dancing Morgans, but for the entire cast.

The next morning I drive my truck to the Tongue River Red Angus Ranch. I talk to Forest, the owner, and he kindly agrees to let me camp with the horses and dogs down by the river in a wonderfully private place, the wintering grounds for the Red Angus Bulls, the "bull grounds."

I return to the fairgrounds and take down the horses' canvas tent, the windbreak tarp, load the horses and dogs up, and off we all go to the Tongue River Red Angus Ranch.

The camp is located in a huge cottonwood grove on an oxbow of the Tongue River. There are five acres of shade trees and grass for the mares. There is also a huge bullpen for the horses to stay at night. I call the place "Cottonwood Camp." The camp site is perfect. The horses are so happy to be in a large area that is shady and cool after five days at the windy fairgrounds. The dogs, Katie and Suzi are thrilled to have logs to hunt under, and I am so happy to be in a clean, safe place, waiting for the new mare.

Dale, the ranch foreman, comes by and says that he will show me where I can ride on the ranch. We haul water up to the cattle in a ranch pick-up truck. Dale explains the road to me. Later that day, I take the horses and ride on some of the 1,800 acres of the ranch. The day is cool enough to enjoy the ranch.

The next day, I ride in the big John Deer tractor, baling hay. Jon drives the tractor and explains how the bales are made. The bales are huge compared to the ones that I make at home in Oregon. Everything here on this ranch takes special equipment. At home, everything has to be "woman size" because I run my own ranch.

On day three, Dale asks me, "Can those fancy horses work cattle?"

"Of course the mares can work cattle, they are Morgans and

Morgans can do it all."

I help Jon move the bulls from one pasture to the other. I ride Bobby in the first field and then change to Valentine in the second field. The day is very hot. Thank goodness for my really big cowgirl hat. The horses are perfect and Jon is great on his ATV. What a combination, the Dancing Morgans and an ATV, moving bulls on a ranch in Wyoming. What a perfect addition to the dreams of coming home to Wyoming.

The next day my young mare arrives. I take one day to teach her to lead and to load safely into the trailer. The mare is three-years old and has never been handled. Her registered name is Two Eagle Wildfire, and I call her "Dolly" because she is so smart and so sweet. After one easy day, Dolly can lead safely and load into the trailer. Thank goodness I spend that day with the mare. The next morning as I finish loading the mares into the trailer, I slip on a rock and break my left foot.

There is only one thing to do. I leave my cowboy boot on for a cast, stop and say, "Goodbye Jon, and thanks for the great place to stay!" Then I drive two, 14-hour days home to Oregon. After all, I am a "cowgirl" and can really "Cowgirl-up" when things get tough! This broken foot in a cowboy boot is tough!

I get home and unload the horses. Then I have to take it easy for my foot to heal. So I spend four weeks sitting in a chair in my arena getting to know Dolly and teaching Dolly tricks. Dolly is learning wonderful tricks. So far she can bow, give me a kiss and a hug, and say "thank you" to the audience.

CHAPTER 46
THE STORM

I wait for the storm. Today is July 23. We have no rain since April 1. The neighbor installed a huge water gun. The sound covers the gentle click and swish of my rain birds on my wheel line. The gun shoots out an enormous amount of water. The water looks like sleek whales leaping out of the ocean, only to disappear into the parched earth. The gun has been firing water for ten days.

My electrical motor is down by Antelope Creek. The neighbor doesn't use an electrical motor. He pumps the whales with a giant diesel-engine. My quiet sounds of summer have changed forever.

I wait for the storm. The sky, dark with thunderheads, sits on the heavy, hot air of the baked-earth. The thunder sounds like the hooves of horses on dry land, racing ever faster and closer from the lashes of lightening cracking before the sound of their hooves rolls past.

I wait for the storm. The water gun will help my ground. Once released from the banks of the creek, water flows downhill. My fields lie below the gun. The water will help keep my fields wet. The smell of the whale water is like the dry ground when the rain hits. The odor is arid and moist. The whales of water continue to leap out of the gun.

The water in Antelope creek drops two inches when the gun turns on. If I were a hydraulic engineer, I would know the amount of water pressure pulsing out of the gun. I am not. My measured and experienced eye tells me the creek drops two inches in a matter of moments after the gun explodes with its bullets of water.

I wait for the storm. The gun does not shoot at night. I don't know if the other neighbor complained. The diesel engine sits right across the creek from the other neighbor's new home, not more than 20-feet away. The noise must be shattering.

One day I will know what has happened. I will run into a couple of men who will be talking. One of them will ask me about the neighbor's new gun. I will reply that I can see it and hear it pumping great volumes of water out of the creek. One man will know exactly how much water pressure the gun shoots. He will know the details of the skirmish between neighbors that men know and that I will now know.

I wait for the storm. The clouds might bring much-needed rain. The lightening and thunder bring fire to the countryside that has been without rain for four months. If we are lucky, the rain will extinguish the lightening fires. If not, tomorrow and the weeks to follow, the sky will be thick and terrible with black and gray clouds of forest smoke.

I wait for the storm. The gun keeps shooting leaping whales of water.

CHAPTER 47
NIGHTGOWN GATHERING OF BLACK HORSES

My summer of 2006 has been filled with adventure, to say the very least after traveling to and from Wyoming. I then spend four weeks limping around the best I can with the stress-fractured foot in a soft cast.

I get Dolly halter-broke and broke to lead. I manage to start trick-training Dolly as well. Much of this new horse training consists of me sitting in my covered arena with Dolly. The two of us just hang out together and bond very nicely.

One morning I don't feel too well. I take my temperature. At 11 A.M. the thermometer reads 99° f. One hour later I know I am slipping rapidly. My temperature is 104° and my thinking is really poor. Poor thinking leads to stumbling into the pick-up and driving to the doctor's. I have a raging case of strep throat and an ear infection in both ears. The nurse says, "You need a shot of antibiotics right now."

I, the woman who can vaccinate 100 cows in a day, still faint at the sight of a needle pointed my way. I say, "Let me lie down. If I faint, just give me the shot while I am out."

Bang! Shot given.

I slowly drive home and collapse into my armchair. My neighbor happens by. Kristy walks in and takes one look at me and says, "Oh my gosh! What's wrong with you?"

Long story short, Kristy goes to the pharmacy and gets my prescription of antibiotics and does farm chores for me for two days. I slowly recover from the ear infections and strep throat. I feel better after ten days of antibiotics.

I get better.

Then one morning I wake-up and have a huge sinus infection, plus my ears are inflamed again. Another trip to the doctor, more, different antibiotics, I get better. (For all the herb-people out there, I believe in modern medicine. I believe that people have been dying for thousands of years before modern medicine. You can do as you please. I take the antibiotics.)

I recover from this round of infections. I feel better. The horses are being ridden and bang! I get bronchial pneumonia. Back to the doctor's, a different series of antibiotics. I am going to bed early and napping most afternoons. I am slowly getting better.

Then one night, I am lying in bed at 9 o'clock. I hear the pitter-patter of mare's hooves trotting down the driveway. Faster than the breeze-driven leaves, I (dressed in nightie, muck shoes and a jean jacket) grab a sack of apples, jump on the ATV known as the "Timber Puppy," and follow the black mares down Alta Vista Road.

The mares always go in one direction to one neighbor's house. This neighbor has an excellent apple tree in her driveway. The mares got out two weeks earlier when Nancy and the young cowboys were visiting. Nancy and I received a call from the neighbor, "You have a bunch of brown and black horses in my yard."

Nancy and I had done this very round-up once before, a couple of years ago, so the cowgirl team knew just what to do then, and this time too.

Only on this night, I am on my own. No Nancy. I grab some halters, jump on the ATV, and drive over to the neighbors. Sure enough, there are the four black mares, happily eating apples.

The neighbor laughs and says, "Is your friend here again from Klamath Falls?"

"Nope," I reply, "I have a new mare that knows how to open the gates. I will change the closure on the gates tonight."

Picture this sight: There is a quarter moon faintly lighting the heavens. I am on an ATV, leading four dark horses home in the dark, and I am wearing a nightie, a jean jacket, muck boots, and no glasses. I cannot see without my glasses. The mares have never followed the ATV before. The drive home is a little jerky. It's not easy to keep your thumb on the throttle while leading two horses with your right hand. The left hand is steering and leading two horses as well. Good thing the antibiotics are working well on the pneumonia. What fun to be nightgown-gathering black horses on a warm summer evening while recovering from bronchial pneumonia!

Life is good at the home of the Dancing Morgans.

I never lost my "Cowgirl Card." The horses all came home with me. I fixed the gate that night.

There seem to be a series of escapes on the Rolling Wheel Ranch since the arrival of a certain black mare named "Prize." She is the master locksmith.

CHAPTER 48
PAJAMA ROUND-UP

I know better. I really do know better. Last night things were strange. Who knows why or if there even is really a "why?"

The horses are restless and I can't sleep, so I read the night away. Saturday night, sleepless in Eagle Point, a good book in hand at 3 A.M.

Finally I can feel the small hours of the morning begin to change. The owls make their last, hooting cries. The coyotes yip on their way back to their dens. The morning air turns very moist. Fall fog is forming in this last hour before dawn.

I give sleep one last, half-hearted try. It is, of course, now Sunday morning. A morning that I could rest and sleep in.

Sleep will not come.

The horses are still restless. I keep hearing them pace in the paddock, then become quiet. Never a good sequence: noise, then quiet, with livestock.

I crawl out of bed. It is 6 A.M. Still very dark.

I make a fire and put on a pot of hot water for instant coffee. I long to have the Sunday paper to read. I decide to commit a cardinal sin on a ranch, I decide to walk up to the mailbox in my slippers and cowboy pajamas.

Let me describe the cowboy pajamas. I have a red flannel shirt with cowboys and bucking horses darting all over the shirt. The bottoms are cozy, red flannel pajama bottoms. Nothing stylish, just warm. I need my red coat too as the fog is forming this fall morning.

Out the back door I go. I look up and see the horses in the pasture. They are not supposed to be in the pasture.

Ah, now I know why it got so quiet all of sudden. "One" of them had picked the gate lock and opened the pasture gate sometime last night. Prize is the "prize" lock-picker.

I walked out and herd them in my lively pajamas. They are so silly. They run and run and run in the corral.

I say aloud, "The time has come. I have to put corner panels in the paddock so no one horse can trap another and hurt themselves. I've needed to do that for 20-years and this morning is the morning."

I walk up and get the Sunday paper. I come home. The horses are still racing around. Silly girls.

I change out of the pajamas and into work clothes. No easy Sunday morning for me.

I move the horses into their stalls. I unplug the hot-wire charger. I take down the necessary hot wire. Drag the panels over, place them, fasten them to the fence and then redo the hot-wire.

Naturally I have to trim the cypress trees too, because the branches are starting to touch the hot wire.

Then I tend to the knocked-down gate. I take it off the hinges, haul it down to the hayfield for a temporary (for the *next* 20 years) panel, and haul the gate-panel up to replace the broken gate.

It is now 11:30 A.M. Sunday paper still unread.

I come in, have breakfast/lunch/brunch-a Sunday brunch-how delightful! Cold meatloaf and green beans. I then ride the mares. I take two at a time and ride the 140-acre pasture. The fog has lifted and fall is in her warm, sunny glory.

I have been working with Dolly teaching her to drive. Today I have the cart shafts in the tug straps on her harness and she pulls the very light training cart with the tugs. She is being such a good girl.

The Sunday paper is finally read at 4:30 P.M. with the company of an early dinner. Life here is once again very good. After 20 years, I have fixed the gates and fences.

CHAPTER 49
EULOGY TO BIRDIE

Here is a poem I wrote when my mare Birdie died. My old dog Dolly died last summer, before Bird.

Birdie died last night.
The last night in August.
She colicked and died
Painlessly at the vet's.
Last evening I saw,
For a fleeting moment,
My old Dolly dog,
Long dead, waiting
In her ancient age
Under the old oak
By the barn, for Birdie.
Dolly brought
Her old friend, Birdie,
 To new trails once again.

CHAPTER 50
THE PRESENT PASSED THIS SUMMER

The present passed this summer. Old man Gerry Black died. His library of knowledge burned down with his death.

I studied under his harsh, knowing ways with horses. I was his legs and his arms with the horses. He was my will and the law as he softly shouted instructions about how to handle the wild, 2,000 pound horse in the small corral.

"Get over," he'd softly call. "Get over now! You'll be crushed if you don't learn where to be."

Gerry trained my mare Birdie. Harsh. Firm. Too harsh for her one day, as she turned and struck him. She broke his ribs. He saw the fire in her eyes and never again was so rough with her.

They both died this summer. Gerry, old, died in a retirement home. Past his prime by years and years. Birdie died of colic in the vet's clinic. She died without pain, with the magic of kindness. They both left me this fall. They left me with memories. And with the sadness of knowing their greatness that is gone.

They went to join in a heaven, if there is a heaven, to be a team again. Driver and horse now pulling the stars across firmaments. My daughter is there in the wagon with them. Grudgingly riding for my sake. She would rather be reading, but this night she rides in the wagon. For old time's sake and for Gerry, Birdie, and for me, because the wagon ride is important for me. And Sarah is a good daughter.

My old dog Dolly and the other dead dog, Popsie, are lying in the back, their tails softly wagging, glad for the ride.

I'm sure my dear, dead friend Mymy sits on the seat with them. Or she is riding Billy Buckskin shotgun. Fred is there, watching cattle for missed brands. Bay joined the team this summer like Birdie-colic. Birdie, the bay, is on the right. Bay, the bay, is on the left. My perfect bay team. Sarah, Gerry, Fred, Mymy and my dogs are all laughing across the skies.

The wind is their laughter. The thunder is their hooves. The rain is my tears.

CHAPTER 51
TALKING TO BUCK

I called Buck this morning. I called him to let him know that the memorial service for Jerry Black was being held this day at 1 P.M.

"No," says Buck, "it is on October the 29th. Not today."

"You are so right!" says I. "I am so wrong."

Buck laughs, relieved that the younger woman, younger by 30 years, was wrong and admitted the wrong.

Buck and I met through the old man, Gerry Black. Buck had a horse or two down at Jerry's place. These two men once used the oldest iron disk plow and tractor that I have ever seen to plow and harrow an old, dried field. They fought with each other: the men, the old iron, the old tractor and Old Mother Nature, to get the fall plowing done. They got the job done and the friendship lasted.

Buck and I are going to the memorial service. I am going to see the last of the old men here. I want to listen to their stories. I want to hear the stories one last time before their libraries disintegrate with their deaths.

I say to Buck. "I don't go to the funerals or memorial services because I cry."

Buck is one of the toughest men I know. One of the men who could gather wild horses from the top of Pilot Rock to Mt. Shasta replied, "So do I. Stand next to me and we can cry together."

Buck didn't come to the service. He can't walk anymore and can't get across the swinging bridge that is his last link to the outside world.

I went. I cried for both Buck and me.

CHAPTER 52
THE FLICKER FEATHER

The flicker feather
Lay in the arena sand,
Face up-orange and black.
I meant to pick it up.
I was too busy.
The next time I walked by
It still was orange and
Face up.
I meant to pick it up.
Once again, I passed
The flicker feather,
Now face down.
Thought I,
"Best pick it up now
Or it will be gone."
The bright orange and black
Of the Flicker feather
In my breast pocket,
It brings a quiet joy back
Into my heart.
I walk to my four
Black mares that nicker their greetings.

CHAPTER 53
THE GRATITUDE OF CALVES

In the background of my early morning mind, I can hear the dogs barking. The clock's hands point to 5:45 A.M. Outside is dark and cold. Very cold. 12° F above zero to be exact. I lovingly ask the dogs to stop barking. "Shut up!" I yell from the warm, cozy comfort of my winter bed. The dogs stop barking.

My brain sinks back into the seductive morning sleep. The dogs start right up again. I calmly encourage them to stop barking. "Shut up, you stupid dogs." I rarely talk to my dogs this way, but outside is very cold and all I want to do is turn over and go back to sleep.

My mind sinks back, then my brain shoots out of sleep. The doorbell is ringing. The dogs are barking. Oh, God, someone is ringing the door bell. The door bell is *never* good. When the doorbell rings (and it is ringing again as I am bolting into my bathrobe and racing down the stairs) there is always someone I don't know at the front door. Everyone who knows me knocks on the back door or barges right into the house.

Ring. Barking dogs.

There stands a young man ready to go to construction work. He smiles as he looks at a bleary-eyed old woman in her bathrobe.

"I'm sorry to wake you up, but I think your horses are out."

My mind is still upstairs, lusting for the warmth of the bed, but the brain is in gear.

"Do you know anything about horses, and where are they?" my brain asks.

"Oh, they are right at the crest of the hill grazing on the side of the road. I know a little about horses," he replies.

I know I am in good hands. A good cowboy will always say, "Oh, I know little about horses." A person who knows nothing would have to convince himself and you that he is just the person you need at "o" dark thirty in the morning.

"Please go out and hold them," says the brain part of me.

I dash upstairs and put on my winter layers as fast as I can. I grab my hat and heavy coat as I dash out the back door and run up to the barn. Man, the cold air smashes into my sleepy mind and the mind suddenly joins the brain with jolt. I throw open the shop door and by some sort of Tuesday morning miracle the four-wheeler starts right up. I grab four halters and race down the freezing driveway to the road.

The young man has perfectly stopped the mares. As I walk up to them, the mares *giggle* and race by me.

"I'm not much help here am I?" I say to my new young friend.

He just gives me the age-old smile of a cowboy that has been had by livestock in the early mornings too.

Again I walk up to the mares. This time they stand. I slip on their halters just as the neighbor drives up. He is on his way to work and blocks the horses with his truck as I climb on the four wheeler and, taking the lead ropes from the neighbor, start home. I ask the young man his name. "Jason," he says.

"Jason, please stop by on your way home from work today."

He later shows up at 5 P.M.. I give him $20. Young cowboys dressed as construction workers can always use $20. He thanks me and off he goes down the snowy driveway. I have a new friend.

The time is now a freezing 6:20 A.M. I drive off with four horses in tow. Prize has managed to open a gate, again. Any time I don't put the extra snap on the gate, she opens it. I left off the snap last night, because when the temperature is below freezing it takes me a minute or two longer to open the snap. But no more. There are no shortcuts.

I feed the mares in their stalls, go out and get the newspaper. Come home, stoke the fire, start the coffee and begin my day. The early morning roundup is not part of my usual routine. Later I run into Eagle Point and mail a package. The sky is heavy with snow. Just as I pull my truck into the carport, the snow begins. In three hours, four inches of snow lie on the frozen ground. I worry about the twin calves that were born yesterday into Brian and Kristy's cow herd in my lower field. I have a vested interest in the cows. First of all, I so admire Brian and Kristy for embarking on this farming/ranching endeavor, and secondly, I watched the twins being born from my deck. I wander down to the field. I can find only one calf in the field. I call Brian and Kristy and leave a message on their phones.

I am getting snowed upon. The frozen ground under my feet is too slick for my sleigh. No sleigh rides in this snow storm. I watch as my near neighbor Lily slowly drives down the driveway to her little house. Good. Lily is home safe. The icy roads are treacherous. The dogs and I climb back up the hill to the house.

Presently the snow lessens, so I take my camera to record the day. As I am taking pictures, I hear Brian's big Ford tractor chugging down the ice-covered Alta Vista Road. I take his picture and then beg to help feed the cattle. He agrees. I climb onto the back of the tractor on the stacked hay bales. Off we chug. I am in heaven. Snow, tractor, hay bales, young Brian, and someone else's cows to worry about.

I open the gate and Brian chugs through the gate. I am busy snapping pictures. Brian and I change places. He feeds and I drive. While I am driving, I am looking for the black, calf dots on the field. We don't see them. After dropping the feed we chug around the field. Brian spots one calf. He picks it up and we haul it to the mother. The baby is really hungry and cold. I walk the field and Brian sets off on the tractor and finds the second twin on the opposite side of the field, far, far, far from the first calf. We had driven right by it. He picks it up and settles down on the back of the tractor.

"I think this calf is peeing on me. It's warm and wet!" says Brian, with a huge smile.

Both calves have been found in the snow and hungrily reunite with their mother, who is delighted to see both babies at once. I take pictures of the memories. Brian and Kristy's memories.

Kristy has magically appeared at the top of the hill. She has been learning more about computer spreadsheets. I tell her that I have pictures of Brian. He is getting cold from the wet experience with the calf. I ask Kristy to come in and I make her a disk of the day's events. Kristy is thrilled.

Little do Brian or Kristy know how much I loved this day. Just once again did I get to feed cattle on my lower field and look for calves. Just once again to touch the life I truly love and enjoy, but have chosen to no longer follow. That life is too much for me by myself, but this snowy day I got to help. I stop by Lily's house to let her know that both calves were found. She asks if I would like to come for dinner.

"Yes. Give me half an hour to feed my mares."

I place feed out in the field and turn the horses out. I'll clean the stalls in the morning. I have a nice hot dinner waiting. What a perfect country day.

CHAPTER 54
FLATBED POINT

In August, Nancy and I finally make time to go horse camping. We meet at Four Mile Lake in the Cascade Mountains. We settle the horses and pitch our separate tents side-by-side.

I have to explain, the "tents" are really our living-quarter horse trailers. Both of us have agreed that the comforts of a hot shower and a soft bed are just too necessary at our age. So pitching the tents consists of me backing my horse trailer into the campsite and Nancy doing the same with her trailer. We have gotten older and wiser; we sleep and live in comfort when we camp.

Camping is so wonderful. Four Mile Lake is a jewel in the Cascades. It is midway between both of our ranches, easy to get to, and has miles of wilderness trails. As soon as the trailers and horses are set-up, Nancy and I decide we need to go for a ride.

Nancy brought two Morgan horses, as did I. She has Rusty, a gelding that is a tried-and-true trail horse. Nancy also has Ricky, another gelding, who is a lovely, green broke, arena horse. I have Dolly, a newly turned four-year-old mare that has not been horse camping, and Prize, a seven-year-old mare that I am taking out for the first time. Both mares have been ridden mostly on my ranch trails. So we have three green horses and one veteran.

Off we go in our mountain riding outfits. I wear a huge, sombrero-type western hat because of skin problems on my face. I really wear an umbrella-style hat and always ride either in my dressage saddle or my sidesaddle. This afternoon I am riding in the dressage saddle. Nancy is decked out in shorts with a beach towel slung over her western saddle for comfort.

We find a nicely-marked trail that is called Ridge Trail. It looks good and winds gently up a forested hillside. The trail never becomes terribly steep in grade, but gradually, ever so gradually, becomes more and more treacherous. On the west side of the trail the hillside turns straight up to heaven, and on the east side of the trail the mountain is falling right down to hell. The trail has grown narrower and narrower. We are stuck before we know what is happening. We *cannot* turn around. I am leading the way riding Dolly while ponying Prize behind us. Nancy is on Rusty, ponying Ricky.

Usually we joke and laugh a lot while riding. We enjoy the vista and the pure joy of riding our horses. We both like trail riding and love putting careful miles on horses. Today we grow strangely quiet. We are on a dangerous trail with no way to turn back.

Where we are going is an unknown factor for two very experienced horsewomen and trail riders. Nancy is always the optimist. Suddenly the forest canopy lightens and she calls out in the wooded stillness, "I bet we will pop out of here and have a great view in about two seconds."

Pop out we do. We pop out on a ridge that is the size of a flatbed pick-up truck. Three sides of the space drop down over 1,000 feet. (I know this because I checked the contour map when I got home.) We can see Highway 140 stretched out below us, running straight east for miles. The cars are smaller than ants. Three green horses, one seasoned horse, and two woman who are absolutely terrified of heights have popped out onto a suicidal drop-off.

I have to step off the horse onto firm ground. My vertigo is so overwhelming that I will fall off Dolly. Nancy shouts encouragement.

"Get back on stupid!"

Of course she is right. I leap back onto Dolly's back and watch as Nancy expertly turns her two horses around and heads back into the forest. I do the same. We ride in not "dead" silence but "grateful-to-be-alive" silence for about 20 minutes. When the ground around us gradually flattens out we squeak out a conversation.

"That was really scary," I squeak. I am startled at the fear in my own voice.

Nancy replies, "That was really stupid." Her voice squeaks too.

A half and hour more of silent riding and we try to joke our way back into a normal voice.

"That trail should have a warning posted, 'NO HORSES…YOU WILL FALL OFF THE CLIFF AND DIE,'" my voice sounds almost normal.

"Thank goodness we can ride," is all that Nancy says.

CHAPTER 55
A SQUIRREL IN THE BEDROOM

My neighbor came home today from the first in a series of breast cancer chemotherapy treatments. Last night we played around with a gold scarf that I gave her and a small, red-haired hairpiece I had on hand. We played a light-hearted but serious game of dress-up. We wrapped the scarf around her head and clipped the hairpiece on the scarf and said how beautiful she looked. We were trying on how she would look with no hair from the chemo. Perhaps she could and would look beautiful.

I took my neighbor to the hospital this morning for her second series of chemo for the breast cancer. I left a message on her phone so when she came home there was a friendly voice rather than an empty line. I left a bouquet of homegrown flowers as well and an uplifting message on her e-mail. Her church friend brought her home.

When they returned, there was a squirrel in the bedroom. My neighbor's snow white Bichon Frise dogs were beside themselves with glee, hunting the squirrel. Poor neighbor, now we three women (and my dogs as well) have a hunting project. I move the breakables off the chest-of-drawers where the squirrel is hiding. I am in bare feet. I know this is going to be a "kill" job on the squirrel, not a remove and rescue job. I need my dogs. They hunt, capture and kill squirrels when we ride fences. They know how to kill cleanly and quickly. Not a pretty picture in a very beautiful bedroom. Just last week this squirrel was captured in the same bedroom and released outdoors. Two times is enough, squirrel needs to be removed permanently.

The two women are very nice. They wait quietly. They both know that this is a kill hunt with no room for hysterics. Just remove the squirrel, slowly. I move the chest. I call my dog Suzi, a Jack Russel. She knows her job. She has the heritage of a vermin killer. She moves in and catches the squirrel, dispatches it, and takes it outside. Thank God the squirrel never runs over my bare feet.

My neighbor turns down her covers and crawls into bed to rest for her fight against breast cancer and chemo. The church friend leaves for the evening. Mission complete, I go home and finish my evening chores.

CHAPTER 56
EUROPE THE SECOND TIME AROUND

I am standing in the dark, cold fog on the tarmac of the San Francisco Airport. The month is late November. I find myself once again as a groom for three Morgan horses that are being transported to Europe.

This trip it is just me with Nancy's horses. There are two mares and a yearling. The Cargolux jumbo jet dwarfs everything around it. I can see at least 50 feet up is the cockpit.

I have been shadowed by my female security agent for several hours. My backpack has been searched and loaded into the jet. I have no idea where it has been placed. I am assured that the backpack will be returned to me upon landing. I am permitted to carry my leather briefcase holding my passport and the documents necessary to admit the horses into Europe. One horse is going to Sweden and the other two will go to Austria. I will go with the horses to Austria.

I climb up the folding ladder into the cockpit of the jet. I walk into a large room that looks very much like a living room. There are three rows of first class seats on each side of the room. The pilots' cabin is open to the room. Tucked on one side is the restroom and on the other side is a small kitchen. The kitchen has a microwave and a refrigerator. There is also a coffee machine.

The six pilots introduce themselves to me. They are all European and young. To me they look like they are between 12- and 15- years old, but when we get to know each other, I find out that they are actually between 28 to 40 years old. They are all old hands at flying the Cargolux jet.

We get ready to taxi down the runway. I climb down the stairs into the cargo hold of the plane. I need to stand with the horses when we take off and when we land. The cargo hold has several huge semi-trucks and trailers parked in it. There are cars, huge containers, and of course, there is the box with the three horses. The horse box is like a three-horse abreast trailer. There is a space for me to stand in the front of the box so I can feed and water the horses. At take off I stand in the front part of this trailer. If I am calm, then the horses will be calm.

People ask me if the horses are tranquilized and if I carry a gun so I can shoot one it the horse should get out of the box. Neither is needed. I don't tell the horses that we are *flying,* so they don't worry. And it stands to reason, if security will not let me have my backpack, certainly they would not let me carry a gun to shoot horses.

I have no book to read on the trip. The book is in my backpack and I did not know that I would be separated from my backpack. When I return to the cabin, one of the young pilots asks me, "Coffee, Madame?"

Wow! Old lady cowgirl is being served by pilots with a demitasse china cup!

He explains that there is food in the refrigerator and I can heat it up in the microwave. I decide not to push the red button on the microwave. Too scary-I blow-up something. They are all so funny and they heat up the food for me.

I fold down the three seats so I can sleep. A couple of pilots retire to the bunk beds in the other room. We settle down for our flight. When I wake up, I use the one-and-only restroom on the plane. This restroom stays spotlessly clean the entire flight. All seven of us on the plane are well-raised and cultured. I have never used a restroom on a plane that stays clean all the way across the United States and then across the Atlantic Ocean. I am invited to sit in the cockpit of the jet. They all love that I had a Super Cub and used to fly. I have no desire to fly the jet, nor do they offer.

We land with no problems in Luxembourg. I am immediately met by a security guard and he hands me my backpack. He speaks only Portuguese and French. I speak a few words of French and can pantomime in any language. He figures out I am with the horses and takes me arm-in-arm through the bowels of the Luxemburg cargo terminal. We race through warehouses filled with people moving huge boxes and cargo trucks moving more huge boxes. He never lets go of my arm.

Suddenly we arrive at a very large garage door. He presses a button and voila, the horses are there, standing in big box stalls.

My friend Christian appears by one of the stalls. I know Christian and his wife Sabine from my last trip to Europe. Christian has arranged to stay in the hotel next to the airport. He has a truck and two-horse trailer to haul me and the two the horses to Pommesdorf, Austria. The van man for the foal going to Sweden gets the horse papers from me that night and loads the foal for the trip to Sweden.

Christian and I eat breakfast very early. We have a 12-hour drive in front of us. We start in the morning dark and arrive in the dark, 12 hours later in Austria. By now I have lost all knowledge of the time or date. It is winter and I am in Europe, heading to Austria.

We deliver the two horses to the family that has purchased them. I go home with Christian and see my dear friend Sabine. I spend about a week with them. They are so good to me. They both work during the day, and so I walk from one small village to the next. The villages are only a couple of miles apart, so it is easy to walk. People are very friendly and surprised that an American cowgirl would walk so much. My German is rusty. I understand more than I can speak. Lots of pantomiming takes place on those village pathways.

We go to many great places. On the weekend, Christian and Sabine take me to see an abandoned castle. We can climb all over it. We go to the amethyst mine and then we see a wonderful Christmas parade as well.

I have arranged to take some driving lessons in Bavaria. The

villagers helped decide which hotel by the train station will be good
for me, and then Sabine and one of the village "chief men" drive me
into Vienna to stay. He takes us for a guided tour of Vienna, as he used
to work in that beautiful city. I take them to dinner at a Christmas
bazaar and order hotdogs in German. It is wonderful.

They leave me at my hotel. Sabine and I part with many hugs and
some tears as well. I am staying in a foreign city all by myself. I sleep
like a total log.

The next morning I walk a half block to the train station. I say to
myself, "You are not in Oregon, Carole." I am very nervous about
making the right connection to Salzburg. I find the correct platform
and climb on a lovely train that pulls out of the station exactly on
time.

I check every stop to see if I am in Salzburg. I am so afraid I will
miss my connections that I can barely enjoy the train trip. The
countryside is cloaked in snow and cold. The train is clean and
pleasant.

When I arrive in Salzburg, I disembark and wait at a small station
for the train that will carry me into Bavaria. I board a small train right
out of 1920. The cars are old and quaint.They are very clean, and very
empty. Out of 15 cars, I am only one of about ten passengers. I am
carried into the darkening evening as it begins to snow. I watch the
mountain turn into an absolute fairy land. Evergreen trees are bowing
down, covered by light, perfect snowflakes. I sit in the warm, old-
fashioned railroad car and feel transported backwards in time as this
little train climbs the mountains.

I am met at the train station by the gentleman who is to give me
driving lessons. Upon meeting me and collecting the money owed to
him for the upcoming lessons, he is most pleasant. We for my food
supplies and then drive through the morning to his small farm in the
Bavarian Alps. My lodging is on a small dairy farm in a cottage built
for tourists. My lessons are to start the next morning. I sleep well and
can hardly wait to begin.

The gentleman who picked me up at the train station turns into a
cruel and evil taskmaster the moment the lessons begin. He is rude
and believes that I knew nothing. He yells and curses no matter what I
do. I had told him that I drive. He cannot believe that I have ever even
touched a horse. In true military fashion, he wants to tear me down
and rebuild me to his, and only his, way of driving. By day three I

have had enough of being yelled at. Now I am in pretty much of a predicament. I am in a foreign country where I speak no German. I am out in the country where there is no transportation, and I have paid in full and have no chance of recovering my money.

So I lie.

I say, "Herr Nimmits. I am a journalist. I came to write an article for my magazine. You are mean and harsh and a terrible teacher. I will not take lessons anymore. I will be a paying guest and you will treat me as such. I will go out into the countryside twice a day. You will drive me in a coach pulled by your four horses. I will be treated like the famous journalist that I am."

Oh my gosh! He buys my line!

He totally changes. I go out twice a day in the coach with four mares pulling us thru the snowy woods. The Japanese tourist buses stop and take pictures. Herr Nimmits takes me to dinner every night. I love being a journalist. When my six days are finished, he takes me to the train station. He very happily asks me what magazine I write for. I smile and say that I will not write an article for the magazine when I had been so poorly treated. I turn and get on the train that speeds me towards Luxemburg, and ultimately towards home.

Trains in Europe are wonderful. The train has a "kindercar" designed for families traveling with children. Perfect for the rest of us. Quiet, clean, and rapid travel. I sit next to a lovely woman who speaks perfect Queen's English. She is so interested to meet a "cowgirl" from Oregon. We visit most pleasantly for the rest of the trip.

I arrive in Luxemburg, hail a cab, and go to the airport hotel. I get a room and sleep the night.

My plane home is scheduled to leave the next day at 9 P.M. I get up in the morning and take a bus into Luxemburg. I love that small city. It has the entirety of Europe. There is a castle. There are all the best shops from Paris. And you can walk the city in a couple of hours and not get lost.

I wander around most of the day. I then catch a bus back to the hotel, check out of the hotel, go to the airport, and catch the Cargolux jumbo jet for San Francisco. I am just a passenger this time. The young pilots are as nice as the first group. I have a book in hand this time. I read until I am ready to turn down the seats and go to sleep.

I wake up as we land in San Francisco. It is night and pouring rain. I am dropped off in the terminal. The airport is totally empty. I make my way to the car rental place, rent a car at midnight, and start to drive home in a huge storm. I make it to Eureka, California at 5 A.M. The highway over the mountains is closed. I call a friend, who lives in Eureka, to come and have breakfast with me. We visit until 10 A.M. when Interstate 5 over the Siskiyou Mountains opens. I then get in line with all the truckers and slowly drive over the pass into the Rouge River Valley and to *home*. I have been gone for three long weeks. There were days when I was the only person in the world who knew where I was: behind horses, on a train, or in a plane.

I am so glad to be home. My dogs are delighted. My horses whinny to me. What a trip. I would not have changed a thing, including suddenly becoming a journalist.

Am I going to be a horse flight groom again? Who knows? Right now I am just glad to be home and to sleep in my own bed.

CHAPTER 57
TIME WARP

This morning was a very long time ago. Actually this morning started last night with a midnight midwifery on a cow and calf. The cow belongs to Brian and Kristy and was having problems. I loaned Brian and Kristy my four-wheeler and I was the gate girl (too dark for a horse-no headlights).

Ahhhh! The joys of being the age of a grandmother, I get to work the gates and not chase an about-to-be mother cow though the cold, wet, night blackness.

And the chase did happen. From where I was standing at the gate, the lights of the four-wheelers looked like a crazy dance of fireflies. Brian and Kristy manage to get the cow into my horse stalls. With the help of the buckaroo and buckarette (who live in my front apartment), they pull the backwards calf out, who manages to be born alive. Hurray for the midnight riders and the currently breathing calf!

I started the day normally, with a hundred variations.

CHAPTER 58
DAVE'S HORSE

We talked this afternoon. About Dave's horse. His yellow horse, the palomino that he loves. The horse colicked and is at the vet's awaiting surgery.

Dave asks, "What do you think?"

"I think surgery is a waste with colic." I pause. "Usually they will colic again and die within six months to a year after surgery." I pause again. "Recovery is slow and painful. I believe in the kindness of modern medicine. What you do is up to you."

Dave leaves.

Lilly my neighbor and I go to the diner. Mother Nature dumps gallons of water on the ground. I can see the Antelope River rising on my way home. I have a message from Dave when I return. He put the horse down. I can hear his tears in his voice.

I check the river. We are going to loose the irrigation pump to the rising river if we leave it by the river.

I call Dave. I listen to his voice. They saved the horse from a painful death with the kindness of modern medicine. Dave's horse is dead. I need Dave's help. Dave needs my help.

Dave comes with his friend Brandon. Two strong, young men in the middle of the night. To help an old woman. I need these men.

We talk about death in the dark, rainy hayfield. There is life after death, the life after death that is for the living.

My dead, golden-haired daughter meets the golden palomino horse at the gate into the pastures of Heaven. She says to the horse, "I know Dave. I'll take care of you here." She pats him on his neck and the horse follows her to Heaven.

CHAPTER 59
UNDER AN ALMOST FULL MOON

I find that I have come full circle in almost 25 years of living on my ranch. On the summer's birth of a new year, June 21, 2008, I am in my hayfield, picking up hay. Actually *I* am not picking up the hay. I am driving the hay truck pulling the flatbed trailer. Two men are picking up their hay from my leased hayfield.

Dave has leased my field. I have known Dave for almost 25 years. He was just 19 when I first met him. Now he is in his very early 40s. Sarah was just 19 when she was killed. I will never know her at 40.

Dave is enthusiastic. He carries great energy but also worries.

"I couldn't sleep the last couple of nights worrying about the hay," he says.

I am relieved. I don't have to worry about the hay. I have passed the worry-baton to Dave's strong hands. I have graduated in the classes of hay work to driving the hay truck. I no longer worry about the tons of hay and the thousands of dollars lying in the field.

Mother Nature is busy playing with us. She started early this morning by arranging her backdrop for our hay gathering. Our field is not the only field that Mother Nature is playing with. My neighbors, the Stanleys, have their field down. And the ranch across Highway 140 has their field down. I can see their field from my field.

Mother Nature begins this summer of 2008 by gathering up thunderheads and adjusting her morning lighting by tossing around lightening bolts.

The hay in the field has been cut and raked. Our question is, "Do we dare bale the field?" Hay cut-and-raked isn't much bothered by rain if the sun comes back out. We can rake and re-dry un-baled hay. Baled hay *is* lost if Mother Nature tosses water on the bales. The hay gets moldy and spoils. The hay in the bales cannot dry out.

The men decide to begin baling. And so bale they do. Dave arrives with his hay-hauling truck and Dave's right-hand man Brandon arrives with his truck. I volunteer to drive one truck while the men buck and stack. Finally I have the *easy* job. I just drive the truck and trailer around the field close up by the bales.

One man walks along the flatbed, picks up the bale, tosses the 100-pound (man's) bale onto the flatbed trailer and the other man stacks the bale on the trailer. Twenty-five years ago when I first bucked bales and stacked them, I cried for days afterwards. I was so tired. Today I sit behind the steering wheel of Dave's truck and enjoy the drive.

At one point, Dave rushes up to the window.

"Do you have pliers?"

I am wearing my ever-present Leatherman (a granddaddy of a tool set in one knife). I hand Dave my pliers on a knife. He pulls part of a rattlesnake body from one of the bales. Brandon smiles and says, "I am scared to death of snakes."

We go on picking up bales. I can hardly believe that this cowboy who I have watched get bucked-off HARD onto the ground so easily admits to being afraid of snakes.

I get to work with a non-competitive team of men from time-to-time. I like being part of the team. I fit into my new part of this hay team. I just drive the truck. The men load 115-pound bales onto the truck. I am buying this load from my own field. Up the hill and into the barn goes the hay. The men unload and re-stack it into my barn. The job is easy when we have a good team. My little dog Suzi rides in the truck with me. She is not safe to roam in the hale field when all the equipment is running. Next we switch to Brandon's truck and trailer. The rain storm looks heavier and heavier. Now we are racing to pick up the hay while Mother Nature continues to play her summer games with us. "Will I rain on you? Or will I not rain on you?"

FULL-CIRCLE

CHAPTER 60
THE WORLD IS MY STAGE

My life has been a long story of ups, downs and crashes. I have made myself and created myself, but one dream is still beyond my grasp. It started with a little girl dreaming of being a rodeo princess on a tired-old horse in Wyoming. It grows into wanting to ride and share my Dancing Morgans with an audience of horse people who truly understand their training, athletes and history. This audience can only be found in one place.

I start the full-circle journey to the *Alltech Fédération Equestre Internationale (FEI) World Equestrienne Games* (WEG) in 2010. Held in a different nation every other year and showcasing the best horses from the worlds of jumping, dressage, reining and carriage driving, this year it is in the good old United States.

This will be the largest horse event *ever* held in the United States, and it is the *first* time the World Equestrian Games have been held in the U.S.

The horses that will compete range from the occasional "saved from the slaughter-house" quality to the more typical $100,000 blue-blood with generations of carefully selected champions in their very expensive pedigree. It will draw local horse-lovers and captains of industry alike.

Every horse-oriented eye in the *world* will be watching. The Games are to take place at the Kentucky Horse Park in Lexington, Kentucky. And I plan to take part in these Games. Me, Carole L. Mercer, and my Dancing Morgans. *We* are going to go to these games.

I begin my plan to be part of the show in 2008. First I need to make an application. I try to download the application for the WEG celebrity performers. While most horses will be taking part in competitions that they must qualify for, just like the Olympics, a select group of horses and their riders will attend to educate visitors in between events, to entertain at the ceremonies, and to showcase the best that the United States has to offer. Sharing my Dancing Morgans with these people is my dream.

But I cannot download the internet application.

A supportive friend who lives in Tennessee downloads the application, prints it, and mails the 15-page document to me. The application sits on the top of my desk and gradually sifts to the bottom of the paper pile until I can make time to do it properly.

One day I decide to open the application. In one heart-stopping moment, I see the due date has passed. I call the phone number listed and the remarkable woman on the other end says, "If you can get the application in by 10:30 A.M. tomorrow, we will be selecting participants then."

I grab everything required for the application process. Everything in my Dancing Morgan resume portfolio is stuffed in a market bag full of news clippings, videos, CDs, actual photos, and my checkbook. I race to Kinko's with my supplies and make a WEG application portfolio. I send off the panic-finished application Fed Ex overnight. Then I call the woman at the Kentucky Horse Park the next morning. She actually received the packet and personally takes it to the meeting.

The day goes by and nothing. I hear nothing for the next month. I call the Horse Park. No one knows anything.

September passes.

Halloween passes.

Thanksgiving and then Christmas fly by.

The New Year of 2009 rolls in. Nothing. No news. Nothing happens. I am afraid to call Kentucky. I don't like no news, but I certainly dislike bad news. I keep reminding myself that, "no news is good news."

Then one morning in early February, an e-mail appears on my computer screen from "Equine Village."

I almost delete the e-mail, as I have no idea who Equine Village is or why they would be sending me an e-mail. But I open the e-mail.

What to my wondering eyes should appear, but a note stating that *"all WEG Equine Village participants should send more information"?*

I call the number listed in the e-mail and begin the first of many phone calls. The Dancing Morgans have been *accepted* to perform at the Alltech FEI WEG 2010 Equine Village!

"Yippee! Yippee! Yippee!" I shout to the dogs and the hayfields.

I am really excited.

I can hardly believe that my Dancing Morgans have been accepted to perform at such an amazing venue.

In the meantime, I apply to the Morgan Idol program that has been created to identify and support Morgans qualified to be breed ambassadors for the American Morgan Horse breed at this international event.

After going through a very long process for the Morgan Idol Program, my Dancing Morgans are rejected by AMHA, with a brief explanation stating that the mares are not something the Equestrian Games would like to have at the Equine Village.

Fortunately the WEG selection committee felt otherwise, and has already chosen us as one of only ten ambassadors to represent the world of horses at the games.

I am so excited. Part of the early acceptance criteria is that I can tell no one that I am going until I receive the official Alltech FEI WEG 2010 announcement. I can hardly keep the swell of joy contained within my soul. I long to shout "Yippee" so the whole world can celebrate with me in hearing that The Dancing Morgans *and* Carole L. Mercer are chosen to be part of the Equine Village performers.

But wait I must. I wait four long months. The official announcement form arrives.

The mares and I are really going to Lexington, Kentucky.

At first I was going to be at the games to perform for the last four days, but whomever organizes the events places me in the first four days. We are to be at the Kentucky Horse Park from September 25-28.

Now I have about a year to raise the money needed to get the horses and me to Kentucky. I ponder about finding a sponsor, but make a critical and positive decision. I realize I want to represent the United States, the *people* of the United States who have supported me so much in my musical rides and seminars. So I decide to plan a grassroots movement.

I plan to sell a mile of travel to people for $5. I have 3,000 postcards printed with my official picture on the front of the card. The back of the card is complete with a map of the trip. The map line starts in Eagle Point, Oregon, and ends in Lexington, Kentucky. The distance is 2,700 miles from point-to-point, one way only. Not only do I have to get us to Kentucky, I also have to raise enough money to get us back home. Leaving the ranch has been so difficult ever since I lost Sarah, and after this momentous and very public occasion, I want to be able to come home when we are done.

I start my fundraising. I put up a Pay Pal account on my website. Actually I have the guy who runs my web site do all the important computer work. I can ride-and-drive horses, but working a computer, even for basic programs, is a huge effort for me.

People begin to rally around my campaign. Many articles are written about my going to the games. Money starts to trickle in to the *WEG 2010* fund. I work really hard too. I sell a horse so I can put that money into the fund. I cut back on everything. I move from the main ranch house into the hired man's house. I sell family antiques so I can add to the fund. I eat less food so I can add to the fund. The mile money continues to trickle into the Pay Pal account. I continue to save every penny, nickel, dime and dollar. I buy nothing that I do not need.

I am also frantically trying to find a place to stay with the truck and trailer in Kentucky so that the mares will be close to me. I make many phone calls and lots of e-mails. I am phoning blind, making cold calls to stables close to the Horse Park. The standard answer at the other end of the line goes as follows: "I am so sorry. If you had called two (or 10-8-7-6, you get the idea) days ago, we might have had room for you. We just rented the barns out to the (French-Spanish-Swedish-Arab-take your pick) team at $300 dollars a day, *per horse*."

If you have never boarded a horse, it is useful to know that $300 typically covers staying at a small barn, for one month.

There is no room in the inns and certainly no stalls in the stables. Everything is totally snapped up. In desperation, I call a local man, Stan, who has contacts in Lexington, Kentucky. Stan knows the brother of a guy who might have a place.

I call the brother, John, who has a thick southern drawl. I think John is "Don" for the longest time.

But yes, he has a place that might work. We settle on a price. I send him a contract and half the money. To make a very long, complicated story shorter and sweeter, John's driveway is too steep for my truck and trailer to drive up. But, my hero John finds me the perfect spot, right next door to his farm.

The Dancing Morgans wind up at the Pine Ridge and Thompson Thoroughbred Farm in Paris, Kentucky. We have a place to stay. My truck, horse trailer, living quarters, two beautiful Morgan mares, and myself, have a home with a tree-shaded, grassy paddock to rest up for two days before I take them into the Horse Park. I have a place to keep the trailer for at least 12 days while we are in the Horse Park. I am thrilled and so relieved. Owner Dustin Thompson even has a washer and dryer in the barn. Life is perfect!

I am ahead of myself here in the story. I haven't even explained our trip yet. You can see how relieved I am to have found a perfect home-away-from-home for the horses when we get there.

The bills for going to WEG mount up. I pay as I go. I can afford no debts. I walk everywhere on the ranch to save fuel money. The B*uy 5 Miles* money continues to trickle into the Pay Pal account. I figure I need between $15,000 and $20,000 to cover ALL bare bone expenses to travel to and come home from WEG. Fuel, stabling while traveling, stabling for horses while at WEG, rent for trailer space while traveling and while staying in Kentucky, all cost money. So do the food expenses and the laundry expenses. I bring as much feed and bedding for the horses from home as can be wedged into the front box stall in the trailer.

I fill an ice chest in the truck to keep my food to save money while traveling.

I am so set. I have raised enough money to get to WEG. I have to be very careful with the money as I have no room for extra expenditures. I have no room for errors. I plan right down to the last penny.

Just before departure day, my friend Nancy, who almost always travels with me to performances, drops a huge bomb in my lap. At the very last moment, she decides that she cannot go. While she has her personal reasons, it is enough that I feel totally betrayed, and our long friendship does not survive her choice of letting me down at my greatest moment of need.

I reach out to another longtime friend, Linda. I have known Linda since she was 15 and I was in my mid-30s. We have kept in touch all these years. When I first e-mailed Linda that I was going to WEG, she offered to come. I explain that the WEG trip is a two-person trip and Nancy has already agreed to come on the last of our great road trips together. Now I call Linda in person and explain that everything has changed.

I say, "Linda, Nancy has decided not to come. Do you still want to come with me to Kentucky?"

"Yes! Yes! Yes!" shouts Linda over the phone.

"I have to call the people at WEG and have them send you the homeland security form so you can be on the registry and get in as my groom," I explain.

"Yes! Yes! Yes!" shouts Linda.

I call Kentucky. Linda has an eight-hour deadline to complete the security form and to be approved for entering the WEG grounds as my groom.

If we have even one glitch on Linda's Homeland Security Clearance electronic paper work, I will go to Alltech FEI WEG 2010 by myself. I know I can travel this road alone, as I had driven to the Kentucky Horse Park five years ago. I went then with four horses and two dogs. What a very long trip that was. I am not looking forward to making the Kentucky trip again by myself.

I wait for the day to pass. The next morning I receive an e-mail from the staff at WEG. Linda secures her Homeland Security clearance. I have a traveling partner. True, we don't know each other very well anymore, but I have a partner to come with me. And I now have my own personal vet.

Once again, I utter softly the single word, "Yippee!"

Linda receives her clearance and the enormity of our project begins to settle in on her. We have two weeks to get Linda's veterinary business put on hold and get ourselves organized.

Linda plans to arrive the day before we leave. We are leaving on September 10 I want to travel no more than six or seven hours a day. I want to be sure that the Dancing Morgans will not be too tired when they arrive in Kentucky. I plan for two layover days for two different time periods for the horses and for me. Now that Nancy is not coming, I will be doing ALL of the driving myself. Linda does not have the driving experience to handle the huge truck and trailer that I use on long-distance trips.

This trip is a huge trip. While I am driving, all of our lives depend upon my driving skills. I hold four lives in my hands all the way to Kentucky. I am more than up to the challenge. My entire life's skills all come into play on this trip.

Linda arrives. She wants to go look at a flock of sheep in Grants Pass. I take her to look at the sheep. I know that we are going to look at trash sheep, but go we must. I have to give something to Linda too. If she wants to look at sheep, we'll go look at sheep.

Indeed, the sheep are inbred "trash" sheep. I don't even get out of the truck as the farm-setting is filthy.

Linda wisely decides she is not interested in this flock of sheep. We are done looking at sheep. Tomorrow we start the trip of a lifetime.

CHAPTER 61
DAY ONE

We load and pack every last, little thing into the truck and trailer. I am still sure that I am going to the moon.

Linda must eat gluten-free food, and I must not eat any sugar. If you have ever dealt with dietary restrictions on a long road trip, you'll have an idea what challenges this creates with mostly junk food choices at every stop. We are the "odd couple."

My friends wave goodbye. We pull out of the driveway at 8:30 A.M. on September 10, 2010.

Our first-day goal is Susanville, California and the Wolf Ranch. Linda is the navigator. Thank goodness for the navigator. I still get lost so easily. I have zero sense of direction. *No* concept of direction as a matter of fact. When I am without a navigator, I write out the directions for my travels every day and post them on the steering wheel. I do not own a GPS. I need to purchase one, but I choose to spend the GPS money for fuel.

We talk the entire way to Susanville. Linda is still shy in her late-40s. I hopefully am not as bossy as I was when Linda was 15. We are working at the relationship that we must establish for a positive trip together across the United States. More than anything, I must keep my positive, healthy state-of-mind for the upcoming performances at WEG.

Sometimes people will tell me that I am "compulsive–obsessive" about this project. I prefer to think of myself as *passionate and motivated.*

I must get and keep Linda in this same "passionate and motivated" frame-of-mind. I hope to manage all of our mind-frames: horses, Linda's, and my mine. We have to maintain being positive to arrive in a refreshed and successful position. We are stepping into the largest horse event in the entire world. I can have no flaws.

Small mistakes, not getting lost, and lots of laugher, is what we must maintain on this trip.

We successfully arrive in Susanville, California and manage to only get lost once finding the gateposts to the Wolf Ranch.

CHAPTER 62
THE WOLF RANCH

I have known Terry and Chet Wolf for many years. After at least ten years of gathering with them, they moved to Susanville, California, about a year after my Sarah was killed. I manage to keep a strong thread of connection with them after they relocate.

The Wolf Ranch is a family ranch. Their son Brian, his wife Michelle, and their two young boys also live at the ranch. Each family has their own home. They raise bucking bulls for rodeo and everyone has an outside job as well. Chet works at the state prison in the kitchen. Terry works for a dentist. Michelle works for the Five Dot Ranch. Brian is the agricultural teacher for the Junior College in Susanville. They all work, all the time, as they also run a very large cattle operation plus raising the bulls.

I arrive with the Dancing Morgans and Linda, and I are immediately pressed (not really pressed, but given the opportunity) to move some cattle around. What fun. I love this family. I always enjoy working cattle with them. They are experts. I listen and do what I am told to do. I ride one mare and pony the other beside me.

Chet and Linda are on the four-wheeler and Linda films the event. Chet goes just fast enough to thrill Linda, but not so fast that she cannot film.

That night, Terry makes dinner. In true ranching style, Terry cooks and usually feeds anywhere from 2 to 12 people. Not only does she cook dinner for anyone who shows up, she also does ranch breakfast for everyone. Remember, Terry also works at a day job full time. She is well-respected and is the absolute hub of this ranching operation.

I manage to explain that coming to visit is very hard for me. This family floods my memories with thoughts of Sarah. I have constructed my life to avoid what I miss most after losing Sarah-having a family. I miss her so much. Terry understands, and we both weep a few tears. I promise to try hard to visit this important family in my life as often as I can.

On the morning before we leave, Terry takes Linda and me on a trail ride over their ranch. This morning's ride is perfect. Three women, who love to ride, amble across the high desert of upper California. The ranch nestles in the valley of Susanville. We ride for a couple of hours in the bright morning sunshine. The horses are glad for their night in the freedom of the corrals and the morning ride.

CHAPTER 63
OFF TO ELKO

The next day we load the horses and ourselves up. Linda, The Dancing Morgans, and I start for Elko, Nevada, our next destination on our journey to the WEG.

We have a direct line to Elko and a fast highway under our truck's big motor and tires. I drive the Nevada speed limit of 75 m.p.h. I am ever-conscious of the shortening daylight hours of September. I drive well, but I cannot see well enough to drive at night. Period. Night driving for me is dangerous. I find myself hurrying toward Elko.

Linda adjusts slowly to life on the road. Our road trip is complicated by the huge rig plus two horses. Our trip is very much like living on a ship. Everything must stay ship-shape and we must get going early in the morning. I like to put six or seven hours of road time on each day. Usually that time is equal to 300 miles. We need to factor in fuel stops as well.

Fuelling the big rig is a carefully managed Chinese fire drill. I fuel up at the BIG truck stops. The Chevy Kodiak is designed to use truck-stop fuel nozzles, and I love being able to pull right in. I am startled to find out that Linda has never stopped at truck stops before. She gains a roadtrip education.

I send her inside with the debit card. I pump the diesel fuel. The fuel pours into the tank at 30 gallons-per-minute. We must stop twice a day to fuel up, and I always like to start my day with a full fuel tank. I never like to get below a half a tank. Rarely do I travel down to a ¾ empty tank. I have too much responsibility in my hands. The very last problem I need is to run out of fuel on Interstate 80. Running out of fuel is easily prevented. I just monitor my fuel gauge. When the gauge runs on half, I stop and fill up the tank.

Linda must cross in front of the roaring, grumbling line of trucks to enter the cashier stations in the truck stops. The noise, the shaking of the ground, and the ever-present "maleness" of the truck stops intimidates her. Linda is still new on this adventure. Linda masters her intimidation. She crosses the truck lines and becomes a top hand at spending the money on the debit card. Linda and I watch every penny spent on this card. We need every dime of the money raised to complete our trip.

I call into the casher from the pump phone. The casher starts the pump. I pump the fuel. Linda pays the cashier, runs the gauntlet of trucks, truckers and noise, jumps into the Kodiak, and off we rumble eastward down Interstate 80 towards our daily goal.

We pull off I-80 into the Elko, Nevada fairgrounds. I have stayed in Elko before and magically my brain remembers where and how to get into the fairgrounds. Upon our entrance we happen upon Eitan and Debbie Beth-Halachmy of Cowboy Dressage fame. Their truck is broken-down and Debbie is ill. Eitan was ill, but is barely feeling better. They are traveling towards the same goal. They too are going to WEG as Morgan ambassadors.

I ask, "Is there anything I can do?"

"No," replies Eitan. "The man will come in the morning to repair the truck." He is very dejected. There is no glory in being ill or broken-down on a road trip to Kentucky, and Kentucky is still a long way away.

Eitan asks, "Do you have your stops planned?"

I answer, "Yes and no. I am going to wing this trip. Linda has a smart phone and she is a smart navigator. Tomorrow, we are going to the Golden Spike Event Center in Ogden, Utah and then to someplace in Wyoming. I have no stops scheduled after Ogden."

"Why are you going out of your way to Ogden?" he asks.

"Because I can," I reply. "The Golden Spike Center is perfect for us and the way I travel."

Eitan is silent, a rarity for his lively personality. He really does not feel well.

My rig is parked by the corrals and a light post on the other side of the rodeo arena. I unload the horses into the big corral and put out feed and water for them. They are always the first ones out of the trailer. But the feed and water are always in the corral before the mares walk in. The mares know the travel routine. They get out and eat and drink while I turn the truck around and set-up our camp.

Setting-up camp in the trailer's living quarters is simple. I get the long, electrical trailer cord out of the rope bag. I keep the cord in the round lariat bag. The bag is the perfect container, but designed for coiled ropes. My rope bag is BRIGHT PURPLE. I always know where I store the bag in my tack room.

I plug us into the outlet on the wooden electrical pole. I explore the grounds while the mares eat. Linda rests in the trailer. She is tired after her first day out. This is a huge undertaking.

I discover the local high school rodeo team in another arena. They finish their rodeo practice and hold a barbeque. I am an old hand at road trips. I introduce myself and am quickly invited to a yummy dinner. I bring an extra plate to Linda. The food revives both of us.

We saddle up the mares. Linda always rides Bobby, and I always ride Valentine. There is no "schooling" of the mares. I just want them to stay in shape, both mentally and physically.

Riding over to the arena, I show the kids how to do my event. They are excited. Everyone gets a postcard and pin. They hope I come back. I think I will. I keep the card of their adult sponsor and will call this winter to line-up a clinic for next year. But next year is miles away. I focus on going to WEG. I must always husband and focus my energy.

We load the mares up bright and early and drive into Elko. As we motor out of the fairgrounds we see the mechanic's truck working on Eitan's truck.

I exchange cell phone numbers with them and say, "Call us if you get in trouble."

As I pull out of the Elko Fair Grounds, the front tires of my truck find the one muddy place. I almost become *stuck* in a medium-size mud puddle. Only the fear of calling a costly tow truck to pull me out of a mud puddle causes me to quickly think and back slowly out of the puddle. True story! We almost sink into a puddle at Elko.

Linda and I find a great parking place in the town of Elko. We walk to a small market to buy ice. No ice. A big street party on the weekend consumed all the ice in town and no one has ice. We have no ice either. Oh well. Ice can be found later at a truck stop.

Out next stop in Elko is the famous tack store, J.M. Capriola's. This store contains a museum full of old, quality tack. The saddles, bits, spurs and bridles radiate the past history of Nevada's Great Basin.

We finger stuff. I dream of the vanished west. Here in the small western town of Elko lingers a grand bit of the past. I hate to leave the town. My future awaits me in Kentucky.

Linda sports a new hat. She wears a Great Basin, flat brim, white, straw hat out of the store. The hat makes a new woman out of Linda. She looks smashing in the hat and blossoms under its brim. Linda is leaning to "cowgirl up." That hat makes the woman.

CHAPTER 64
ELKO TO OGDEN

Interstate 80 lies like a ribbon in front of my eyes. I drive 75 m.p.h. If I edge up to 80, I can feel the big rig start to shake and slip out of my control. I stay at 75. Linda is the film crew. She is an artist and decides to film for one minute at 12:30 P.M. where ever we are at that time. We look forward to our minute-a-day.

Linda films a burgeoning forest fire climbing and clawing its way up a mountain top. We watch from Interstate 80 and draw closer and then pass the fire on our south side. Passing life unfolds in front of our eyes. We sit in our "space capsule" and look out. We watch the world flow by like the pictures flickering on a screen of a TV set. The windows of the truck separate us from the landscape. Many times I find myself uttering, "The pioneers walked this route. What tough people they were." I remain impressed with the rugged migration of the pioneers.

Usually I maintain a journal on a trip. I am so focused on driving during this trip that my journal lies clean and untouched. I count on the film to be my journal.

We cross the high basins of Nevada. I stop at the truck stops and fill the fuel tank of the truck. The truck's gaping tank must never be hungry for fuel. I spend lots of money per minute when you calculate 30 gallons a minute at almost $3.50 a gallon. Phew.

Every time I fill the tank, I say, "Thank you" for every $5 donated, and I mean it. "THANK YOU!"

We snicker as we read the Nevada State Highway signs that state: "Prison. Do not pick up hitchhikers."

We don't pick up hitchhikers. The fact that I drive a pick-up doesn't mean I pick-up hitchhikers, nor ever do I pick-up hitchhikers. Never, never, never.

All too often, a cowboy will come smiling up and offer to trade his horse for my pick-up truck. I simply ask him to read the sign on the back window of the Chevy Kodiak. The sign in the back window states: "Silly Cowboy. This pick-up is mine. Cowgirl-up."

We cross the Salt Flats of Utah. We roll into Salt Lake City and see the Great Salt Lake. We enjoy our lesson in geography of the West. The West is full of empty space.

Golden Spike Event Center is perfect. Getting to the Center consists of meandering down a rat maze of detour signs. Thank goodness I can back this rig up and turn around when necessary.

When you are traveling with me, I have no concept of direction, and that means that occasionally I get into positions where I must back-up in order to turn around and reach the turn I missed. The left turn is now the right turn. All the left and right turns that are now reversed make turning a monstrous mess for me. I am so dyslexic. I do know up from down, but left and right have no meaning in my vocabulary. Not only are left and right not in my vocabulary, left and right are not in my directional mind.

Fortunately, on this trip I have Linda. She holds some sort of magic phone in her hand that shows us as a blue dot moving down the road. Sometimes Linda watches the dot more than she watches for the road signs.

I yell, "Linda! Stop watching the dot and watch for the exit sign. Linda! Linda? Linda!" That blinking blue dot mesmerizes Linda, but we never miss an exit. Not yet anyway.

We pull into the Golden Spike Event Center early enough to settle ourselves and the horses. The Center sits at the base of the open granite walls of the Rocky Mountains. The horses enjoy a roll in their new surroundings. I wash the truck and trailer. We saddle up and ride around the race track. The center of the track is a cross country jumping course. On the north side of the track lies 20-acres of baseball and soccer fields. The fields hold many children playing soccer and adults playing baseball. Linda rides Bobby. Bobby loves the noise coming from the soccer fields. Her ears go forward and she is ready to dance into the arena for an audience. No arena for Bobby here. She looks back at the scorer field with confusion as we ride by. She is ready to dance. We once again find ourselves in a perfect rest spot. I sleep well this night.

CHAPTER 65
DAY 4

We load-up and head up the Rocky Mountains. I love my truck. I drive a huge Chevy Kodiak truck complete with a 4500 Duramax Diesel and an Allison transmission. The truck is a two-by-four. These words mean I do not have four-wheel drive, just rear-wheel power. Not having four-wheel drive is why I almost got stuck in the mud puddle at Elko, Nevada. I know, in my heart of hearts, I can become stuck with a four-wheel drive truck as well. But if I need a four-wheel drive for a road trip on highways, I should not be driving. I have air brakes and an air ride. However, many of my woman friends complain that the truck rides like a truck. This Chevy Kodiak is so big, I look the semi-truck drivers in the eye when they drive past my window. The last thing the truck drivers expect to see is a little ol' cowgirl and a young cowgirl driving along the Interstate pulling a 30-foot horse trailer. We get many horn honks and thumbs-up along the trip. I just smile and wave and keep looking down the road.

I love this Chevy. The truck pulls us right up the mountains. Up, up, up we travel. We slip into Wyoming. Again we study the vastness of the West. The miles roll and roll ever eastward.

We fly by the seat of the truck. I guess where we will stay in Wyoming. We are actually ahead of schedule. In Rock Springs we buy fuel and Chinese food. I think we should stay at the Terry Bison Ranch just outside of Cheyenne. I once holed-up at the Bison Ranch in a terrible May blizzard about five years ago. The mares stayed in the camel barn with the camels.

Linda finds the ranch number on her smart phone. She dials on my phone as I have a hands-free device. Linda's comfort zone does not include talking to strangers, and I lack the ability to use a smart phone. Between Linda's smart phone, her smart brain, and my ability to talk to anyone, anytime, anyplace, we form the perfect road team.

"Hello? Hello!" I yell. The road noise and the poor connection overwhelm my calm, quiet voice. "Do you have room for a truck, trailer, two horses and two women?" I shout.

The voice on the phone states, "You have to use stalls and we are full-up in the camp site."

I respond. "I don't need stalls and we are totally self-contained. I think you have a rodeo ground where we can turn out the horses. We can park down at the rodeo ground."

"I have to check with the boss," says the voice on the phone.

"I'll call you back in 20 minutes. We are four hours out and will arrive around 3:30 or 4 P.M.."

We move forward 30 miles. Twenty minutes pass. Linda calls Terry Bison Ranch.

"Did you find out from the boss if we can stay?" I plead.

"No. I haven't had a chance yet."

"Please check. We must have a place to stay as we are headed for World Equestrian Games."

Little do I know that these words "World Equestrian Games" will unlock all of our future overnight lodgings. I learn to explain our travel mission from Wyoming onto Kentucky.

Linda dials the Bison Ranch number again in an hour.

I talk to the voice on the other end of the phone. I now know I am talking to Stephanie. She replies, "Come on in to the office when you get here. We will have you all set-up and ready-to-go. You can park down by the rodeo grounds and turn the horses out in the arena."

I let out a huge breath. Tonight we will stay at the Terry Bison Ranch just outside of Cheyenne, Wyoming.

We pull in, sign in, and off-load the mares into the rodeo arena. A cowboy named Randy comes up to talk with us.

Linda meets and sees what she thinks is her first REAL WYOMING COWBOY. He chews tobacco, he limps, and he is missing some teeth. His neatly-pressed clothes are into their fourth or fifth consecutive day of being worn. Randy's body is 50-years of being worn out.

"Where are you going with those Morgans?" asks Randy, as he looks at the magnetic sign on the truck. The sign is a picture of me on the Dancing Morgans, complete with the Equine Village logo.

"I am taking them to the World Equestrian Games."

"Sounds like a big deal," says Randy. He continues, "I wanted to be a million-dollar bull rider. I rodeoed a lot. Rode them bulls. Never made it. I sure tried. It's nice to meet somebody who has made it to the big time."

I look at Randy's eyes. There in the mists of time lingers the hunger for fame and fortune. He is not jealous of my success. He just wants me to know that he tried for the "big ride." He does not feel that he failed. He knows that because he tried for that one bull ride of fame and fortune, that there was no failure in trying.

I thank him for sharing his story. Life is all about the stories on the journey. People are filled with stories. I am learning to listen and enjoy the stories.

That evening I perform a small ride and drive for a couple of the cowboys who work at the bison ranch. As I ride, four camels amble by. My mares never miss a beat. The cowboys don't miss the beat either. After watching the ride-and-drive, they understand why I am going to WEG 2010.

We wander into the Bison Ranch souvenir store. There stands a stuffed, saddled bison and a large, saddled jack-a-lope. A jack-a-lope is a very large "cross" between a jack rabbit and an antelope. This jack-a-lope has elk antlers. We totally jump into the saddles and laugh and mug for our own cameras. We don't go anywhere, but have the rides of our lives on theses two huge, stuffed, saddled animals.

Later, Linda and I wash our dirty clothes at the laundromat. Coin-operated machines suck up the quarters. The nice result of clean, fresh clothes is worth the cost of the washing machines. I use the campground shower as well. I have my towel. Linda was not expecting to get a shower on this outing, and she does not want to walk a mile back to the trailer to retrieve her towel. Linda turns cowgirl. She counts her body parts that need drying and pulls the appropriate number of paper towels out of the dispenser. Linda "cowgirl-ups" to opportunity and walks out clean and dry.

We sleep well in Wyoming. The coyotes howl outside of our trailer. I howl back. They howl. I howl. They leave. I go to sleep.

We leave in the morning for Nebraska. N-E-B-R-A-S-K-A stretches out before us. The horizon rarely varies. Long, low, flat, and the prairies go forever. Again, I think of the pioneers who have walked this route that I am taking at 75-miles an hour. I am pulling the trailer with my priceless horses in back, not the horses pulling a wagon filled with me and my meagre pioneer possessions. 150- years of passing time changes the order of the destination and the order of the equines. Linda and her smart phone locate the Heartland Fair Grounds in Grand Island, Nebraska. She dials the number.

I begin "Hi, I am Carole Mercer and the Dancing Morgans. We are going to the World Equestrian Games and need a place to stay tonight."

The man's voice on the phone gives directions. Linda writes them down. Four hours later we pull into the gates of the Hartland Fair Grounds.

Once again, the fairgrounds are huge, new, and beautiful. We ride on the race track, and then put the horses out in a huge arena. In the distance we hear the train as it speeds by. The train whistles. I don't whistle back. Sadly, I can't whistle. Once again we sleep well.

The horses are fed and watered while we eat our breakfast. Eating for Linda and I is difficult. Neither one of us like to cook. I eat no sugar and she eats no gluten. We slowly figure out meals. Rice cakes with cream cheese, topped with grapes. What we eat is not memorable. We just eat to live, not live to eat.

The horses are loaded, the truck is fueled, and we roll down the road. Linda finds fair grounds in Davenport, Ohio. She dials the number.

I begin to talk. "Hi, I am Carole Mercer and the Dancing Morgans. We are on our way to the World Equestrian Games and need a place to stay tonight."

I am talking to Bob Fox, manager of the small fairgrounds in Davenport, Ohio. Bob is wonderful. He meets us at the gate on a small electric scooter. We follow him to a small arena and a flat spot to park the truck. Bob says, "No charge. Our way of supporting you on your way to WEG."

I thank him. At every stop we give gifts. I purchased small bags of stone ground flour from my local four mill in Eagle Point. I also have some lovely jewelry from my earlier days of selling stuff in my booth when I went to horse expos. At every overnight stop, we give away the Butte Mill Flour, the jewelry and the official Dancing Morgans postcard. We thank everyone at every overnight stop. I feel I represent the United States when I am at WEG. I represent everyone who donated $5 for every mile to carry us across this really big country. I also just want to say "thank you." "Thank you" feels really good to say. I am so grateful to be on this journey. "Thank you" just flows off my lips. I sincerely mean "thank you."

We leave Davenport, Ohio. Fuel tank filled, we roll down the road. We turn south. We head to Indianapolis. For two terrifying hours we travel at speeds too fast for the rough roads that take us through this busy city.

At one point, Linda says softly, "Carole, do you know that you have less than two inches on each side of the truck?"

"Better an inch than no space at all," I shoot back with a tight smile, but just barely.

The roads are filled with pot holes, construction and detours. Huge trucks pin us between them on both sides and in front and back. The road noise is deafening. I cannot make even a blink mistake. I am so tense and I know I must relax. I pretend I am driving a marathon course with a four-in-hand. Not only am I driving a marathon course with a four-in-hand, but I am in a chuck wagon race as well. I can feel the sweat trickle down my back. I sit straight up in my truck seat. I consciously think about breathing. This stretch of highway is the worst drive I have.

Slowly we edge out of Indianapolis. We barely joke, but joke we must to clear the tension in the air.

Linda guides us to Hamilton, Ohio where we have plans to spend a two-day layover before we go into Kentucky. The horses need to rest and so do I.

We meet the Creightons. Kathy and Ed Creighton turn out to be the best hosts ever. Ed built two, brand new wooden stalls for my mares' arrival. In front of the stalls is a sweet paddock where the mares can just loaf. Ten yards from the paddock and brand new stalls is a hook-up for the trailer. The perfect spot for us and for the horses. As I offload the mares and lead them into their perfect paddock, I whisper into their ears, "Do *not* chew or lick *one* brand-new board on *any* one of these stalls. If you are going to poop, poop outside in the paddock."

CHAPTER 66
CREIGHTONS

The mares remain perfect during their stay at the 200-year old Creighton farm. They lay down in the paddock, eat in the paddock, and poop in the paddock. The mares are just so glad to have a rest after the trip through Indianapolis.

Linda and I need a couple of layover days as well. Little do we know that we just landed in paradise.

Kathy and Ed are wonderful people. They both love history and know so much about their area. They are not only the perfect hosts, but the perfect tour guides.

Ed cooks really good food. After five days of our "healthy" road-food, Ed's breakfasts, lunches and dinners taste like heaven. Linda and I need some T.L.C. and Kathy and Ed take care of us. Then they chauffeur us to all of the interesting historical sights.

We visit old villages built of logs, then off to a town called Minamora. We ride the horse drawn canal boat. On the way back to Creighton's farm, we stop at an old chapel and Linda speaks from the pulpit and from her heart as her voice resonates throughout the old chapel. She recites her own poem on smoke. We all get goose bumps.

The next day we run down to Kentucky to check out where we are staying. Thank goodness that John Fritch understands that the Kodiak has slick tires and cannot pull the trailer up the hill to his house. He arranges for us to stay at the Pine Ridge Thoroughbred Farm in Paris,

Kentucky. Pine Ridge shares a back property fence with John's farm. Dustin, the farm manager, turns out to be another excellent tour guide of the Kentucky area.

After the visit to Pine Ridge, we head onto the Kentucky Horse Park. The games are not in session yet. The Kentucky Horse Park is closed to the public. Security is pretty open. Ed is very well known at the Park for his volunteer work, so we waltz in on Ed's notoriety, and Ed proceeds to give us the grand tour.

We start at the Morgan Pavilion. The building is a glorious light-filled shell. The potential of the building is stunning, but the doors will remain closed until the building is complete.

I see where the mares will stay. They have nice stalls with a good roof over their heads. I am relieved.

I take a wonderful picture of Ed standing next to the historical information sign by the big barn. Ed's great-uncle John Creighton built and owned this barn on the historical Kentucky Horse Park. Ed's family roots run deep in this Kentucky and Ohio soil.

We depart the horse park. Linda and I plan to drive down the next day and make one more layover for the mares before we come into the park on September 24.

Linda and her smartphone guide me back to Pine Ridge Farm. This move brings us two days closer to actually entering the Kentucky Horse Park. I realize I am only two days out from being at the WEG. The opportunity of a lifetime is here. I am going to be at the 2010 World Equestrian Games.

CHAPTER 67
PINE RIDGE FARM

Dustin appears from his apartment as we pull into our allotted space at Pine Ridge Farm. I can see in Dustin's unimpressed eyes that I have about 45-seconds to make friends.

I laugh and say, "Let me put these mares in that paddock first." The grass in the paddock is short and brown. Kentucky is in the middle of a drought. I am lucky that the grass is short and brown. My mares need to keep their performance weight and not run the chance of foundering on lush Kentucky grass.

I pop them out of the trailer and lead them to the paddock. The paddock is perfect. Shade trees, fresh water, and space to roll and move around.

I come back and thank Dustin and immediately pay him. I want to stay here. Dustin's eyes change. Polite woman. Polite horses. Woman who prepays the board bill. Dustin's eyes speak volumes. I know we will be fine here and so does Dustin.

The two wonderfully important items to make our stay easy is a washer and dryer that we can use and a toilet. All of these amenities are on the other side of the downstairs breezeway (aisle) in the barn. Linda and I have found cowgirl heaven.

I unhook and level the trailer. I need to make the drive to the Horse Park so I can find my way to the Park and back later with the horses and trailer. We are 19 miles away. Our drive takes 40 minutes one way. 80 minutes for the twice-a-day run to-and-from the park. I do not like that I am so far from my horses once they are in the Park, but I can do nothing about the rule of "NO OVERNIGHT" trailers at the Park barns. I have never left my mares when I travel. This change in my travel plans worries me. The mares are always reassured that if the trailer is around, I am never far away.

Linda and I pick up our gate passes and the passes for John Fritch and his daughter, Ashley. John and Ashley are on the homeland security roster along with Linda and me.

Linda and I feel so excited. We immediately put the lanyards around our necks and admire the passes.

"We are in," I say. "We are really in. I am really going to perform at the Equestrian Games." I hardly believe that I am here, early, but here, at the park.

The Horse Park is ablaze with frantic activity. Workmen sling hammers and saws buzz. Fancy tents spring up like white mushrooms. I never have been to such a large event. "Oh yes," I think, "WEG is the largest horse event in the *world*."

Linda and I cruise the grounds. The magnetic signs proclaiming our status as the "Dancing Morgans" allow us to drive all around the grounds. We will be unable to "cruise" in the truck once the games begin and the grounds are under Homeland Security lockdown.

Convinced that I can find my way to the Horse Park and back to Pine Ridge Farms, we stop at a market to refresh our food supplies. I constantly wear my huge Dancing Morgans belt buckle. Whenever someone comments on the buckle, I hand them a card and say, "I am Carole Mercer and I own the Dancing Morgans. We are performing at the Games."

People love the cards. I am thrilled to hand them out and gather quite a following from just doing local business.

Two days of rest works wonders for us. Linda and I ride the mares down the local road. We sleep well at night.

CHAPTER 68
THE HORSE PARK

Finally the 23rd of September arrives. John Fritch and Ashley come by at 6 A.M. to help drive us into the Park. We arrive before our set time. The early arrival is no problem as there is no waiting line yet at the entrance of the Park.

We have all the correct documentation to pass Homeland Security. The veterinarian checks all the paperwork. We wind our way through the narrow and twisting lanes to Barn 1 and fill the stalls with wood shavings. I off-load the mares into the stalls. Bobby is very nervous about being alone in her stall. She paces and paces.

Naturally, trainer Pat Parelli has a stallion that has been placed behind us and sets up a racket to impress the mares. His beguiling snorts and nickers don't help Bobby. I make sure that our tack room is placed behind his stall to help buffer his commotion.

Like a Chinese fire drill, John, Ashley, Linda and I set-up the tackroom. The tackroom needs time to be organized, but we must get the truck and trailer in-and-out of the road quickly as other participants with their vehicles are waiting for us to move.

Bobby panics as we pull out. I always leave the trailer in front of the stalls. Bobby is sure that I am abandoning her. I feel the same way. I never leave them alone on a trip. I worry about her.

The day comes in hot and the night follows the heat. I make a pallet on the hard Kentucky ground and sleep outside of my trailer at Pine Ridge. My cell phone rings at 11:30 P.M. The voice on the other end is the night guard at the Kentucky Horse Park. He says, "You have a black Morgan mare here that is very upset."

My blood freezes. "Put her in with the other mare. She is not used being away from me," I say to him.

He states, "I have to check with my supervisor, but she's my daughter. There should be no problem. I will call you right back."

My blood stays frozen in the hot night. I wait, wide-awake, for an eternity of 11 minutes. My phone rings. The voice says, "I put the mare in with the other mare. She settled right down. The supervisor said I could move the horse."

I say, "Thank you. Who are you?"

He says, "Dale."

I reply, "Thank you so very much Dale. I am so grateful." I *am* grateful to Dale. He let me know and did all the right things. I hate not being next to the mares. I *could* sneak in and sleep in the tack room. I know that several other barns have their grooms on the premises. But the logistics for me are too difficult.

I rouse Linda at 5 A.M. The park opens at 7 A.M. I get her going in 15 minutes. We are at the gate early at 6:00 but they let us in. We park in our designated parking lot, a 100-acre pasture *two miles* from Barn 1. I am in a huge hurry to get to the mares and we start walking. We soon figure out that we should hitchhike on one of the many golf carts buzzing around on the grounds. We flag a guy down. We step into the cart and plead, "Please take us to Barn 1. I have a mare that is not doing well."

The driver generously takes us to the front of the barn. We jump out, hand him cards and jewelry, and thank him profusely.

We love our excellent mode of transportation. The golf carts rent for $75 a day. Too expensive for Linda and I, but our thumbs are free. I won't pick-up hitchhikers on the road, but here we quickly become expert at thumbing rides.

I check out Bobby. She is fine, and happy to be stalled with Valentine. The 12' x 12' stall is crowded with both of them in it. I walk around and see that other performers have dismantled the stall walls so horses can see each other or be together, and I ask the day manager if I can take down part of the wall between Bobby and Valentine. He is more than willing to make the mares comfortable. I take out the wrench that I always carry in my pink purse. We take down half the wall. Later I simply remove the rest of the wall so the mares can move around freely and be close together.

I saddle- Valentine and lead Bobby. We go on a riding tour of the Park. I make sure the mares go everywhere and see everything. We even slip into the huge, main outdoor arena where the main competitions are held. What fun. We will not be performing in that arena, but I ride in it just the same.

Once I am on horseback, I can go anywhere except the competitor's stall area and the cross-country fields. With horses from every continent and their own varieties of germs and viruses, the horse-health security is tight. The event promoters want no one to bring any horse across the invisible contamination barriers. I, of course, honor those simple and wise requests. I ride in this picturesque setting for two hours each morning and two hours each afternoon.

While I ride, Linda explores the grounds. She manages to go everywhere. She is a vet and the "vet card" opens doors for her. She meets everyone. Linda sees everything. I just ride. We both know just how lucky we are to actually be at the Park on this occasion.

When I leave the Park that night, Bobby is okay. She is with Valentine and knows that I will return every day. Horses and especially Morgans are so smart. We overlook just how smart they are. I know I will always have these two mares. We are a team.

When I make my outside bed again at Pine Ridge Farms, I sleep through the night. No phone call from Dale. Bobby is safe. Dale is an old thoroughbred racetrack man. He knows horses and keeps an experienced eye on my Morgans.

I leave a "Thank You" note for Dale at the supervisor's desk and then write a note to the supervisor thanking her for the excellent job that Dale does notifying me and following through with Bobby. I leave the mares in great hands every night when I leave the Park. I hate leaving the mares, but I must.

I will follow the same procedure every day. Linda and I get to the Performer Parking lot at 7 A.M. We greet all the parking people.

"Good morning! Good morning! Good morning!" we holler out the rolled-down windows of the Kodiak.

Soon all the parking people know us and call back. "It's the cowgirls with the Morgans."

We also holler, "Goodnight! Goodnight! Goodnight!" as we leave. We receive the same "Goodnight" chorus as we bump out of that 100-acre parking lot.

By day two at the still-closed park, Linda and I are expert hitch hikers. One morning we jump into a highway patrolman's Gator. Officer John says, as we stick out our thumbs, "If you can get *into* the back of the Gator, then I can give you a ride."

You should see his surprised expression as two gals instantly swing up into the back of the Gator.

We hand him cards and jewelry for his wife and little girls. Officer John waves every time he sees us.

The next time I need a ride, I flag down a golf cart. I hand out the card and the jewelry and strike up a great conversation.

"I am Carole Mercer with the Dancing Morgans. I am so thrilled to be here at the Horse Park. Everything and everyone is just wonderful. Who are you?

"I am John Nicholson. I am the head of the Horse Park."

I continue to tell him just how wonderful everything is and how excited I am to have been chosen by WEG to be an Equine Village participant. John delivers me right to the front door of Barn 1.

I begin the routine that I follow the next five days. Each night I feed the mares heavily so they have something to do all night on their own. When I arrive each morning at 7:30, I take them out of the stall and tie them up. I clean the stall and re-bed it deeply. I brought all of my own shavings. I make sure the stall has at least 18-24" of clean shavings. The mares are standing on asphalt under the shavings and I hate that the foundation of the stalls is so hard. I use as much of the shavings as I can to cushion their feet and legs. I believe the deeper the shavings, the better for my horses' legs. I brought fifteen bags of shavings. My horses are going to be as comfortable as possible during their stay at WEG.

I brush the mares from tip-to-toe. I saddle up one or the other. I always take turns when I ride one and pony one. They are both comfortable with the ride-and-pony arrangement. We head down to the front gates and smile and greet the visitors as they come into the Horse Park for the WEG. We are the only performers who decide to be "greeters at the gate." I hand out hundreds of my cards. People ask me about the Morgan breed. They ask me about my lovely mares. They ask me for directions. Unbeknownst to me, Linda has taken it upon herself to carry the direction folders and she is handing directions out to all the visitors as she hands out my postcards as well.

Without trying, we create a full house every time we perform. Everyone knows about the Dancing Morgans from our visit at the gate and they want to see us dance.

After an hour of meet-and-greet, I take the mares for a lovely ride over the pathways and roads of the Kentucky Horse Park. We are out for at least three hours every morning of our days at the park.

When I have a demonstration or a lecture, I factor in the time to ready myself and the horses. If we are not performing or giving a demo, I am either riding or hand-grazing my mares. In the daylight hours I want my mares out of the stalls as much as possible.

Linda checks out everything and goes everywhere. We touch base via cell phone. She always shows up for my performances or demonstrations. Linda is always camera-ready.

We trade stories of our independent adventures. Linda manages to get free tickets to the events and to see them. Linda is becoming a master of event-seeing.

I just enjoy watching the performers. I am not much interested in the competitions. I want to learn everything I can from the trick riders, trick trainers and the reining trainers.

I am totally enjoying the rare atmosphere of the Games. I don't care that there is not enough food handy. I don't care if everything is too expensive. I am having such an incredible experience just to be part of the Equine Village participants that I have come to enjoy the event. And enjoy I do.

September 25 dawns warm and bright. Today I ride my first performance at the Alltech FEI WEG 2010.

I will open the educational lecture series for the games and I am the first person to speak in the lecture hall. I speak to a crowd of about 30 people at 11 A.M. The first-step of the last, personal event for me is taken. I am very well-received. Everyone gets a piece of free jewelry and my postcard, and they love it when I say, "Here is a piece of jewelry and a postcard. These are the only two things that you will get for free at the Games."

Then I am ready to ride again at 2 P.M. The stands are filled with about 500 people. Even more people watch from the fence behind the stands.

Wayne Williams the announcer reads our introduction.

The music begins and I ride the Dancing Morgans into the empty arena before the packed seats. We receive a standing ovation. I have 30 minutes for a meet-and-greet session afterwards. The mares stand perfectly as people ply me with questions. The second step towards our final dance is taken. The Dancing Morgans and Carole L. Mercer are performing at the Alltech FEI 2010 World Equestrian Games. My dream is true. My dream is now and it is here.

Tonight is the Opening Ceremony for the Games. I purchased spectator tickets in January. Linda and I have great seats.

I almost make us late, as I thought that the event started at 7:30, so I am dawdling around at 6:45 P.M. Linda finally looks at me and says, "We have to run. We are going to be late."

We try to snag rides to the Ceremonies in the golf carts. They are all too full or too busy. We really run and just make it to our seats.Thank goodness for Linda and her sense of time!

The Opening Ceremony begins. I am actually at the Alltech FEI WEG 2010. I weep when the athletes begin their walk around the arena. I am not watching this ceremony on a TV set. I am here. The United States national anthem plays. The Kentucky anthem plays. We all stand. The flags of every country pass by. Different areas of the stands wave the flags for their country and cheers go up as the riders and drivers walk by. The air fills with pride and *energy*. The energy hangs in the atmosphere during the entire time that I stay at the Games.

An American Indian opens the Games with prayers. Then the performers for the opening ceremonies give us a great show.

I strike up a conversation with the Spanish-speaking family sitting next to me. Their 7-year old daughter is one of the hundreds of children dancing in the arena during the ceremonies. At the end of the ceremony, the mother is looking for her daughter. In the midst of all the cheering they see each other. The child sees her mother in the thousands of people in the stands. I say to the mother, "Stand up! Shout! Wave!"

The mother stands up and shouts her daughter's name. They make the connection. In a split second, over the audience's roar of cheers, mother and daughter make a connection. They see and hear each other only as a mother and daughter can at that moment.

I miss Sarah. My loss is always with me. I weep for the joy of the mother next to me, and for the sorrow of my loss. The emotional ceremony closes.

Unknown to me, while he was taking part in the breed presentations of the ceremony, my friend Eitan Beth-Halachmy suffered a fatal heart attack as he left the arena and tumbled from his horse, dead.

As he rode past during the ceremony, I had commented to Linda, "His ride is flat. Something is wrong."

Again, unknown to me, Eitan is revived with emergency CPR and rushed to the University of Kentucky Hospital. Miraculously, he recuperates and continues to ride and teach his elegant Cowboy Dressage as I write today. All my blessings go to Eitan as he continues his journey in the horse world and bringing Cowboy Dressage to riders.

I know that my plan to stop performing after WEG is good for me. I know that I am at the top of my game, and I want to stop at the top of my game. There is no glory in an obituary.

Linda and I hitch a ride back to Barn 1. The departing traffic out of the huge parking lots will take hours to disperse.

I want to check my mares. I toss them more hay and fill their water buckets. I press my postcard into the resisting hand of actor and horseman William Shatner. His tries to refuse the card. I tell him, "Here, take this. Check it out. You might like it."

Linda and I then catch a ride in a gator with a nice husband/wife team. The husband turns out to be the commander of the Kentucky Highway Patrol. I figure out that the Kentucky Highway Patrol units all drive Gators.

They are a delightful couple. She tells him how to drive. Women are so universal with their help (I call it coaching). The Commander is so good-natured. We hand them my card and lavish jewelry upon the wife. We discover that she drives a Ford F350 4x4. I tell her about the monster truck I own and drive.

The Commander makes a quick turn. Everywhere we go, the Highway Patrolmen are saluting him. Linda and I spy Officer John. We wave and holler at him, "Hi Officer John! Hi Officer John!"

Officer John is busy saluting the Commander, but he gives us a smile and quietly waves the non-saluting left hand.

The Commander and his wife slip us down the security path. There exists an armory of vehicles and large truck-trailers. There are also dog units. Linda states brightly, "I am a vet and have worked on security dogs."

Both the commander and his wife are impressed with their hitchhikers. They take us as far as they can go in the Gator. We can just see the top of my truck across the sea of vehicles still left in the lot.

Linda and I hike the last quarter of a mile to the top of the hill where the truck is parked. The sea of autos slowly trickles out of this huge, pasture parking lot. We push the seats back and nap in the truck for an hour. The soft crunching of wheels driving past on the gravel stops. The road out of the parking lot is now moving freely.

I start the truck's diesel motor and creep into the slowly flowing line of cars. We are greeted by the cheers of the parking staff.

"Goodnight ladies from Oregon! Goodnight Cowgirls!" These people spend their entire day at the parking lot. It is now 1 A.M., September 24. The lot has been moving since 6 A.M., September 23. We finally arrive back at Pine Ridge at 1:30 A.M..

My mental alarm goes off a few hours later at 5:30 A.M. I take a shower, get dressed, make my coffee and rouse Linda. I need to get going. The second day at the Horse Park is about to begin. I need to be at Barn 1 to feed, water, and clean stalls. We have the 20-mile drive to make.

"Let's go. Time to get up."

Poor Linda. She would like to crawl out of bed, but knows that we have no time for the luxury of a slow cup of coffee.

I pack an assortment of food. The cost of food in the park is astronomical. We go through security at the front gate and they check our purses, but not our bodies. We have given out cards and jewelry to security already. They all remember us. We pack water bottles, apples, cheese, and snacks under our clothes. We go into the gates fat and lumpy, and come out each night remarkably "slimmed" by our day's work. It works every day. We need to eat, but just cannot afford the $17 chicken sandwiches every day. We unload our food into the cooler that we brought in with the horses. The horse park has huge ice machines, so we pack the cooler with free ice. We eat well and affordably.

Today is the official day two of the Alltech FEI WEG 2010. I check my mares, clean the stalls, saddle them up and start our morning ride. We meet and greet again. I haven't had much sleep. We got to the horse trailer late and left at the earliest hour possible. I offer to fill the clinic space for Eitan.

I do a great long-lining clinic at 11 A.M. in place of Eitan's Cowboy Dressage. I am not Eitan, but am certainly able to put on an hour long clinic. The mares get to stand and watch. Linda helps me and films the clinic as well. Linda and I have become a total team. Team Dancing Morgans as a matter-of-fact. Linda has become invaluable. She is always ready with the camera and shoots away.

When she is not helping me out, Linda is watching all the competitions. She manages to get lots of filming done. How she does it, I don't know. We check in with each other via cell phones just to make sure that all is ok in our Equestrian Games world.

I try to catch a nap in the folding chair in front of my stalls. I think

I sleep a little, maybe twenty minutes. Then I get up and brush and saddle the mares for our 2:30 performance.

My friend John Lyons rides after I do. I ask him, "John, I danced with your son several years ago in Spokane. How about you coming in and dancing with me on horseback after I finish my performance?"

John is game for the dance. "I'll be there!" he says. When I finish my presentation, I ask the gate stewart to open the gate and in comes the great John Lyons.

I ask Wayne to play a nice, slow song for our dance and explain that we are about to do a musical ride for the first time, and demonstrate how quickly the horses will get into the fun of something entirely new to them.

The music starts. The soft sweet sounds of "Shenandoah" waft thought the warm Kentucky afternoon. My mares respond perfectly to the melody. John and his gelding follow in-step, and soon the three horses are dancing to the music while John and I are cantering around the arena, easily holding hands. The crowds loves it. How could they not love the soft, beautiful and fun ride developing before their eyes? John relaxes and is having fun. So am I.

At the end of the music we ride over to the audience and they ask questions.

"Did you practice beforehand?" asks one woman.

"No," say John. "We just rode out and had fun."

"The key element is fun," says I. "John is an excellent rider, so we can just go along and ride to the music."

Someone hands John a portable mike. Bad idea. John clicks from fun-mode to his clinician-mode and begins his training pitch. It's a good pitch, but we are talking about being spontaneous here. I ride up and jokingly say, "John, give me the mike. We are here to explain that it is *just* fun, to ride to music, to share this dance with you, and to show the people gathered here something they haven't seen before."

John laughs and admits, "She's right."

"I'm a woman. Of course I am right," I quip back as the audience chuckles.

We both ride out and I ride over to do my meet-and-greet with the audience. I am asked to sign autographs. I sign away. It is very important to spend time with the people who come over and want to meet you. I came to be available. As much as they want to meet you, people need and want to share their dreams, their experiences, and their problems. I am here to listen. I answer no veterinarian questions. If Linda were standing here I would direct the questions to her, but she has magically disappeared. I eventually wind down with the dispersing crowd of people.

A storm rolls in. Thunder and lightning threaten the skies. I stay with the horses as long as possible, but we must leave. I am not very good at driving back in the dark. The rains come. The water is pouring down. We miss our turn. I cannot see the intersections.

Peering at her phone, Linda says, "the blue dot says we are not going the right way." Thank goodness for Linda, the smart woman and her smart phone. We make a u-turn into a factory lot.

Now looking up Linda says, "The gate is closing! The gate is closing!"

I gun the engine and slip through the gate just before it snaps shut. With Linda at her smart phone and me at the wheel, blindly driving, we slowly drive back to Pine Ridge. Out of the truck, we crash into bed. I sleep the sleep of the very weary.

Our eyes open to day three. The rain is now gently falling. Dark still cloaks the Kentucky mornings. Huge school buses pick up children standing waiting in the dark. School is often a 20-mile ride on these dark, fall mornings.

I am from out-of-town. The country roads in Kentucky are really just lanes barely wide enough for a small car. These roads are leftover, paved country roads. They were designed for horse and carriage. If you are a local person, you race down the narrow roads at breakneck speeds. Everyone speeds. Everyone drives fast. Not me. I drive a huge truck that takes both sides of the road and the middle too. When someone comes from the opposite direction, the offside of my tires scramble on the shoulder.

While the roadsides remain dry, there are no problems.

Last night, Mother Nature dumped water on the sides of the roads. Now we have mud. The routine does not change. One set of tires goes off the road when you meet cars head-on. Many places there is simply not enough room for two cars to pass. The traffic makes for an interesting journey on these dark morning drives into the Horse Park. The highway patrol has set up stations as you get closer to the park. Security is very heavy going into and out of the park. There are so many foreign dignitaries involved in the games. Sheiks from the far east. Local government officials. And very valuable equines. All must be protected. I just slow down when asked and rumble into the parking lot. Linda and I are greeted by the guys waving the lighted wands. They know us now and the morning chorus of "Good morning!" is welcome and sounds back-and-forth. Camaraderie is established.

We catch our first hitchhiked ride to Barn 1. I take the mares out, clean the stalls, fill the water, and away we go for our morning ride. The mares like to get out. They live differently at home. They move all the time in their big paddock and are turned out on nice meadows twice-a-day for a couple of hours. The mares don't complain. They are troopers. They are professionals and just make sure the show goes on. My first and only performance today is at 3 P.M.

I wander around in the misty morning with the mares. Attendance to the park in this weather is minimal. I am so glad that I am just performing today. We are asked to stay the entire 16 days of WEG. In the morning the invitation sounds wonderful. By noon, I know I cannot ask the mares to stay in their stall for 16 days. I want to leave this last show and perform the last dance with joy in my heart. I believe after 16 days of being at the Games, I would be really tired and so would the mares.

I say, "No, thank you," to the WEG organizers.

When the afternoon rolls around, the rain lingers. The rain is more like a steady mist. I am from Oregon so have come prepared for everything weather-wise. I ride in the rain, snow, and sun at home. Here is no different.

A couple of the Equine Village organizers come rushing up to me at 2 P.M.

Terry gushes, "Can you ride in a half an hour? All the other performers will not ride due to the rain."

I smile and say, "Sure. When do you want me?"

"Right now! The arena is empty. No one will ride."

I pull out the mares. I use the dressage saddle because my riding rain coat will cover that saddle. The sidesaddle would collect a puddle of water in the seat.

I trot them down to the Equine Village arena and proceed to perform every 30 minutes for three straight hours. The mares never miss a beat. We can ride all afternoon because these mares are used to working and are in shape. They like to perform, so doing performance after performance is easy for them.

At one point I want a little variety. I ask to borrow two belts. A couple of people hand me their belts and I fasten them around Bobby's neck.

I take off her bridle and ask an audience member to hold the bridle, with a strict warning, "Please do not leave with the bridle!"

The woman replies with a sincere smile, "I will not go anyplace."

The music begins one more time. I trot out with only the belt around Bobby's neck. Valentine floats in front of us, and we dance bridle-less. The audience is overwhelmed. Had I used a special rope or wire, then the bridle-less effect would not be as impressive. I simply use two borrowed belts. The audience became part of the performance. I return the belts, put Bobby's bridle back on her, and get ready for the next round of dances.

A gentleman with a thick accent speaks to me after the next couple of rounds.

"I am Swiss, and a German-FEI dressage judge. You, go out and trot a figure-eight."

What can I do? The Germans rule the dressage world, with the best trainers, riders, and show scores. This is not a request to be questioned. I go out and begin to trot a figure-eight with the two mares riding tandem. I make a perfect first part of the figure-eight. My brain panics. *I am riding in front of an FEI judge.* Valentine feels the panic and makes one footprint out of the second circle. Regaining my composure, I immediately relax and we go perfectly back on track.

I finish trotting the figure-eight with the tandem pair. I am laughing when I return to the judge.

Says I, "We did a *perfect* figure-eight." I use the high-pitch part of my voice to let him know that I know that Valentine put one foot out of the circle.

I then ask, "Do you want me to drop my bits?" I am using a Visalia western-style shank bit. In FEI dressage, the judge can ask to see the bits at the end of the ride to determine if they are legal and proper for the horse.

The judge replies, "I do NOT need to see the bits." He turns to the audience and says, "This woman has wonderful, light hands. She would have a gold medal if she where riding in dressage here. The horses are high level and her riding is high level. You are fortunate to watch her."

With those words he turns and walks away.

I sit on Bobby and look at Valentine, amazed. I weep tears of joy. My years of riding, *without* a western saddle horn, *with* a western curb instead of a dressage bit, with my cowgirl/draft-horse driving approach, has just been noted as gold-medal quality. My ability is validated.

I know that I love the performances and not the competition. In performance, you can make a mistake. You can take the bridle off and ride with just a couple of belts around the mare's neck. You can laugh at your mistakes. In competition, a winner or loser rides off the dressage field. I don't like to ever be a loser. I like performance and the standing ovations. His validation of my ability resonates in my soul.

I can ride.

We are invited to dinner at Bunny Thompson's lovely home. Bunny is Dustin Thompson's mom. They are the owners of the Pine Ridge Thoroughbred stables. Linda and I are really tired. The days are long, but to dinner we go. Gathered around the large table filled with wonderful, home-cooked, gourmet food, sit a vast arena of performers. Kristy Cook, from my hometown of Eagle Point, is there with her friends the Double Dans, trick riders and trainers from Australia. The Double Dans also have their two grooms from Australia with them. Turns out that they are all staying with John Fritch. John saves their day. John provides rooms for them. This troop of performers' original digs had been double-booked and they had to find a new place to stay. Once again, through the Eagle Point connection, we all wind-up sitting together at the same dinner table in Kentucky. All of us are exhausted. It is 10 P.M. All we want to do is go to our respective abodes and go to bed. I feel relieved to see that the young people, 40 years my juniors, are as tired as I am. I think I am tired just because I am 65-years old. We all feel exhausted because of the huge performance schedule.

Tomorrow is my last public performance.

CHAPTER 69
THE WEG EXPERIENCE

Linda and I hitch hike to Barn 1.

I know this is the last day of any more performances. I brush the mares for our morning ride. WEG films us and puts the video on-line. I talk about the last performance. I am ready to stop performing. I love the performance, but the time to stop has come. I am not the only star in this milky way of performers here at WEG, but I am certainly a very bright star here in Kentucky.

We meet-and-greet the public at the entrance gate. The mares know the routine. I enjoy our morning ride. I share my 11 A.M. lecture with trainer Lynn Palm. I have a wonderful time with Lynn. She is very technical, I am a very hands-on, show-the-audience and audience-participation person. We made a good team. I might as well just share the time left with everyone.

At 2 P.M. I dance my final dance with the mares. We hit every mark. I had asked Aaron Ralston if he would come and dance an exhibition dance with me. He shows up on his fine little stallion. Arron rides his stallion bareback and without a bridle.

We dance to "Happy Trails." We bring tears to the eyes of the spectators. Arron interviews me after the dance. We have a great time with the audience.

I ride out of the arena for the very last time to the music of "Happy Trails." I am finished dancing with the mares in public. I am really done. There is not a drop of regret in my blood. I quit at the very top of my game and my game is good. The game is over. Finished.

I ride back to Barn 1. Clean-up the mares. Hitch a ride back to the truck. I drive back to Paris, Kentucky. I hitch the trailer to the truck. I haul everything back to the Horse Park. Wind my way into the line-up of all the departing trucks and trailers. Tons of us are leaving. We have a four-day contract with WEG. Our contracts have ended and we are on the way out so the new performers can come in.

John Fritch, Dustin Thompson and Linda appear after I call them on the cell phone. The mares load-up. Everyone grabs stuff from the barn tackroom and tosses it into the mid-tackroom of the trailer. Linda jumps into the truck with me and we drive back to Pine Ridge. Our big event is finished.

I turn the mares out into the grass paddock. They are so glad to be out of the stalls. They trot around for several minutes and then put their heads down and begin to graze. The mares are done with all public performances. I think all of us, horses and I, feel relieved. The great pressure of driving cross-country to deliver the mares into the activities of the 2010 Alltech FEI World Equestrian Games lifts from my shoulders. I achieved my dream and beyond.

Linda flies home from Kentucky the next day. Dustin takes her on a flash tour of Lexington and Keeneland before he takes her to the airport. Dustin radiates as a tour guide. He is a wonderful host.

I just rest on the first day after leaving the event. The mares just graze. I plan to layover for two days before I drive back home. We all need to rest.

I feel strange to be alone for the first time in 20 days. Linda and I rode together, drove together, and shared much time, always together. I live alone on my ranch in Oregon. I can spend days at a time without seeing anyone. I make an adjustment whenever I travel with someone. Now I must make the adjustment to being along again. I miss the good company of my young veterinarian friend.

CHAPTER 70
TOURIST TIME

I need to have the oil in the truck changed. Dustin gives me directions to Paris and John recommends a place to have the oil changed. I, of course, get lost. I turn north instead of south and wind up in the small town of Carolina. I find a place to have the oil changed. The young mechanic used to be a student of John's when John taught Future Farmers of America at the local high school. I use the John Fritch connection again to assure I receive a really good oil change. The young man does an exemplary job. The big Chevy truck is ready now for the return trip.

I manage to find downtown Paris, Kentucky. This charming town is dotted with small antique stores. The stores display pictures of race horses and race horse memorabilia. I smile. In my part of the world, antique stores display western-ware, bits, and saddles. Horse people are possessed with the need to be surrounded by horses no matter what the event. I find myself in the heart of the race world, and the antique stores reflect the interest of the populace: racehorses.

I wander down the streets, moving from small store to store. I am not buying. I moved to a small house on my ranch. Luckily for me and my wallet, I have no room there for anything new. I now collect memories. In my long-running race, the memories are the most important to gather. As I wander down the sidewalk, I see the aluminum racing plates (horseshoes) embedded in the sidewalk, with the names of the race horses stamped in bronze next to the plates.

I stop and gaze up at the tallest three-story building in this town's world. I know that this building is the tallest building in the world because of a lovely sign proclaiming this tall fame.

I think about my small hometown of Eagle Point. We lost the charm that the town possessed. The old building-style was deemed unsafe and savagely replaced by square boxes of prefab sides and flat, uninteresting roofs. History in the west is brief and quickly replaced by the present. In the eastern part of the United States, history is valued.

When a country looses touch with its history, the country loses its soul. Perhaps the population of the west is filled with the restless genetics of the people who forged to the west as pioneers. The western population finds itself blocked by the Pacific Ocean and mills restlessly in California, Oregon and Washington states. I don't know the answer to the difference between the east and the west, but there is a memorable difference.

I manage to find my way back to Paris and to Pine Ridge Farm. Finding my way back to Pine Ridge Farms is a huge accomplishment for me. I finally figure out the lay of this small part of Kentucky.

On day two of my layover, Dustin takes me on the grand Lexington/Keeneland tour. Dustin opens every interesting door on this private tour. He holds a trainer's card, so he can go anyplace and behind all the closed curtains. I am going on the tour of a lifetime. Not only can he open closed doors, Dustin knows the industry. He treats me to a perfect "insider tour."

We begin by going to his friend's training stable. There are two brothers, young men in their thirties. Gus, and his brother, whose name I lose in the flood of new knowledge. Their father, the original Gus, was barn manager for 30 years at the world-renown Calumet breeding farm.

I am so thrilled to be in an actual training barn. I watch the breaking jockey ride the first filly. Everyone is very careful. They are playing with lives and too much money. The colt breaker gets up on the filly in the stall. Gus never lets go of her as he leads the 20-month old filly out of the stall, down the barn aisle, and into the beautiful indoor round pen. Once things seem to be going well, he unclips the lead shank and the colt breaker makes two walking sweeps around the round pen. He turns the filly once and then makes two more sweeps. Gus Jr. returns to the round pen and clips the lead shank back on the filly. This 15-minute procedure is repeated about four times with other colts. The colt breaker earns his money by the ride.

The breaker is quiet and knows his stuff. He rides a wildly-painted Harley motorcycle. Raw courage and finesse is written all over his face. I give him one of my cards. He looks at the pictures of the Dancing Morgans and he looks at me.

"You ride these horses?" he asks.

"Yup," I reply.

"I would like to see that," he smiles.

He climbs up on the Harley and roars off to his next job.

I see a set of nylon long lines hanging on the wall. I ask, "Do you guys start the babies in long lines?"

"Yes. Do you know how to long line?"

"I do," I reply. Then words tumble out of my mouth that I cannot believe I am saying.

"Do you want me to show you what I can do with the horses?"

"Yes," They both say.

"OK. Get me a well-broke horse and I will show you what I do.

They bring out a 3-year old Thoroughbred giant. "Moose" stands at least 18-hands tall. That's six-feet tall at his withers, with his elegant neck and head stretching up above that. I stand only 5'-4" tall. This horse's back towers at least a foot higher than my mares'. My heart skips a beat.

"OK. Let me show you what I do."

The first thing I always do is teach the horse to lead my way. Moose catches on immediately. The men just stare. By this time the farm's vet, Dave, comes in and stands watching this little old woman handle the horse. They all wear startled expressions on their faces.

I start tossing the lines all over the gelding. He just stands there. The horse knows from just a few moments of my leading him that I will not hurt him and that I am in charge.

I put the bridle on him. I put the surcingle (bellyband) on him and proceed to show them how I longline. The gelding is nicely-broke, but not very handy. Turning is hard for him with his huge body, but his willing mind gives me good turns.

I show the men how I hold my hands. How I use my hands, and how I give-and-take with my hands. Gus tries the new method. He sees how well the techniques work.

He asks, "So how do you start a young horse?"

Again, I cannot believe the words that come out of my mouth as I say, "Bring out one that you have worked with a little and I will show you what I do." I immediately think "SHUT-UP MERCER." But no, I open my mouth again.

They bring out a 20-month old filly. I begin my leading technique and the filly immediately figures out where I want her. My mind blanks, blanks but not blacks out. I can hardly believe what I am doing. I am standing in a huge racehorse training barn, with men who grew up training racehorses, and I am showing them how to long-line. The men get what I am teaching them. The filly just stands while I toss the lines all over her. They cannot believe that it does not take two men to hold her. I explain that with my technique, there usually is very little fighting. This technique makes things easy for the horse and the horse-person. Of course there is always danger while handling horses, but I have never had the strength of a man, so I use the finesse of lightness.

I soon have the filly long-lining well. She moves forward freely from my use and handling of the lunge whip. I let the whip trail behind me and flick it like the tail of a lead mare.

The two men give it a try. The method easily works for them too. My method works if you are willing to try it. These men are not stuck on their own system and are willing to try. A good deal for everyone concerned.

Dave the vet invites me into his lab. Dave is the local "maggot vet."

Dave prepares a blood agar petri dish for his maggots. He works in a spotless, sterile lab on the horse farm.

I ask him, "What do you use the maggots for?"

Dave replies, "I treat abscesses, mostly of the foot. I clean out the infected foot first, and then place the sterile maggots in to clean out any abscess I might have missed. In a bit I will check the progress. If the foot is healing well, I either wash out the foot or introduce more maggots. The maggot treatment works very well with foot abscesses."

I have read about this ancient treatment for humans, and now I see this procedure used for horses. I live in a very interesting and ever-changing world. Ancient medicine reworked and applied to the same problems of all living creatures. I always learn something.

The men ask if they can come to Pine Ridge to see me longline my horses. I say, "Sure. If you would like to bring anyone else, please come up around 4:30 today."

Dustin takes me next to the training track in Lexington. We arrive around 10:30 so there are no racehorses on the track. Racehorse training begins early in the mornings.

I am fascinated by the straw man's business at the track. This man buys clean straw bales. He sells the clean straw to the people at the track for the horses' stalls. When the dirty straw comes out of the stalls, the racetrack people pay him to pick up the straw that he first sold to them. He then re-bales the dirty straw and sells it to the mushroom farms. Here is a man who knows how to spin straw into gold!

From the training track, Dustin takes me to downtown Lexington. I have been nowhere except the Horse Park until now. I was so busy riding and lecturing at the Park, that I hardly saw anything beyond my small world there. I have done all the driving on this trip. Now, I sit in a snazzy little black sports car. Who knows what make the car is, I just know that it is a snazzy little sporty car driven by a delightful, young, knowledgeable man who is taking me on a horse person's dream tour. I bask in the rare experience.

Lexington, Kentucky comes in second or third on the Dustin Thompson tour route. Dustin finds a parking place and puts the parking sticker in his car window. We begin to walk around Lexington. On every street corner is a life-size horse statue. These statues resonate horse country as their brightly and uniquely painted coats differ greatly from equine-to-equine. One horse is painted like a sunset, then another one is painted like an Indian's tent. Every horse represents an artist and that artist's concept of a horse. I am in heaven. I stand and walk in a city where the heartbeat of the city is dedicated to horses. I believe that Lexington is unique in the world with this dedication to horses.

We make a quick, major, city-block tour.

Dustin and I eat lunch alfresco in the city center. In honor of the Alltech FEI WEG 2010, lunch vendors dish out local Kentucky food. I get to try Kentucky gumbo. The gumbo tastes pretty good.

We walk back to the car via a tent row of local artist wares. I buy nothing. I am here for the experience.

We jump in the car and Dustin says, "I am now going to take you to Keeneland."

"Sounds good to me!" says I.

I am starting to fade. At 2 P.M. and almost 20-days of travel, World Games, and a day of touring, I am fading. But I don't want to miss a single memory.

We drive through a huge gate-opening into a magnificent stone barn on the hill. Dustin brings me to Keeneland's original stone barn that is converted into a *library*.

I love libraries.

I enter the library. This library houses books and paintings dedicated to race horses. The shoes of famous race horses look out at use from their encased glass tables. I stand enchanted in this beautiful, quiet library. I ask the head librarian if I may film in the library. She says yes.

We strike up a soft conversation about libraries. I fall in love with Kentucky all over again.

Dustin and I walk to the car. I am bushed. I am really tired.

"Thank you so much for taking me to Keenland," I say. "I am really tired and ready to go back to the trailer and take a nap."

Dustin replies, "We're not done. I haven't taken you to Keeneland. I just took you to the library. I want you to see *Keeneland*."

I am startled and ask, "There is more to this tour?"

"Yes!" he says. "I am going to take you behind the scenes at the Keeneland race track."

I cannot miss one more incredible experience.

"Let's go."

I summon energy from the soles of my feet. I am not disappointed.

My eyes feel stunned when Dustin drives his smoothly-running Audi up to the back entrance of the Keeneland racetrack. My body is jolted by the rows of trees, the freshly mowed grass and the rows and rows and rows of racehorse stables. Visually, this back entrance to Keeneland feels like I have entered another world. In fact, I do enter another world. I enter the heart of the racehorse world at Keeneland, Kentucky.

Dustin, with his deep, smooth voice, gives me a personally-guided tour. His car hums past the empty racehorse stables. The stables smell empty, and are spotlessly clean.

Dustin murmurs, "You should see this place at 4 A.M. on a race morning."

I can *feel* the race morning. I can smell the warm heat of the horses as they come in from a morning run. I feel the smell of the sweat being rinsed from the hot horses' bodies. I can see the white sweat run down the legs of the horses as the water cascades off their bodies, down their legs, and down into the drains, and disappears.

I hear the men's voices, the horses snorting, and the sound of aluminum horseshoes striking the shedrow paths. Aluminum shoes ring softly, like tiny, silver coins dropping on cobblestones.

The stables are empty at this moment, but the gathering energy for the coming Keeneland race season hovers in the air. I feel like I am listening to the ever-present hopes and dreams of every racehorse owner, jockey, trainer and stable hand waiting to come onto the track with their dreams of winning this race.

I mentally ponder, "How is it that empty stables feel so alive?"

I know the answer. Dreams fill the air here at Keeneland.

Dustin speaks again. His voice turns into a soft southern drawl. "I'll take you to the Keeneland auction ring."

He parks the car and we enter the auction ring. This ring stands far removed from the old, dirty, decrepit Rouge Valley Sale Yard ring at my home in Oregon. No filthy old falling-apart seats here at Keeneland. No noisy cattle bawling. No overwhelming smells of animals' fear, dirt, and manure assails my nostrils in this sale yard.

Keeneland's sale ring looks like a theater stage. The auctioneer's bench stands, smoothly made of beautifully-crafted, golden-oak wood. The sale floor is covered in fresh and sweet smelling cedar shavings. The buyers' seats flow like rows of chairs in an expensive theater. This building houses one of the world's most expensive theaters. Horses parading across this stage sell for millions of dollars. The horse's sale price is based on bloodlines and expected potential to win races. Millions of dollars exchange hands on this stage. I can smell the money. I am out of my league here. The racehorse world. I know nothing of it or about it. I stand in awe on such a stage.

Dustin drawls in his soft, Kentucky voice, "Follow me."

I follow him.

We enter a courtyard filled with paths made of soft rubber tiles. Tall trees spaced in a pattern fill the courtyard.

Dustin explains. "At Keeneland, the jockeys mount up here in the courtyard. Each tree represents the horse's number on the track. This courtyard swells with people watching the jockeys as they mount up for their entrance onto the racetrack."

"This way," he drawls in his easy and alluring way.

At this point I would follow him anywhere in Keeneland. I feel like I am floating in a visual horse-heaven. Dustin leads me through a causeway under the grandstands at Keeneland. We walk through the muted light in the causeway and step out in the blinding sunlight on the entrance to Keeneland racetrack.

I look up at the vast, empty grandstand. I hear the far-off shouting and cheers of the racegoers. I hear the faraway thunder of the racehorse hooves, pounding the ground of the track. I feel the vibrations as the horses pound closer and closer to the finish line.

I ask Dustin, "May I step out onto the track?"

He says, "Of course."

I duck quickly under the low, white racing-fence. I stand with my feet and dreams firmly planted where other men and women's dreams will race by my footprints.

I turn to Dustin and smile.

"I am ready to run. I have had my dreams and they have come true here in Kentucky."

In my heart I know I am a winner. As I stand here on the Keeneland track, this race world jumps alive with the energy of the yet *un*won races, the *un*born winners and the *un*tried losers.

"Dustin, I am ready to go back to Pine Ridge and go home to Oregon. Seeing the racehorse industry with you as my guide shows me the essence of Kentucky. The essence is hope for future races and the glory of winning the current race. I would not have seen what you just showed me without your ability to bring me to this point in my life. Thank you for sharing your world with me."

I am more than ready to go back to Pine Ridge and rest. I must rest for the end of my journey.

Tomorrow I start my drive home to Oregon.

CHAPTER 71
COMING HOME

I sign-up "guys" for the trip home. John Fritch and his 14-year old son, Matt have never been west of Kansas City, Kansas. Matt has a week off from school, so we need to make the trip west in three days. Three days means we drive 14-hour days and make a thousand miles a day. My choice is to make a "guy" trip, sharing the driving with John, instead of making the trip home by myself. I can drive home alone, but I figure two drivers and a kid will be more fun. John possesses a commercial driver's license, and as a former Future Farmer of America (FFA) leader, has driven lots of school buses loaded with kids going to FFA meetings throughout the south. John is more than qualified to drive the truck and trailer filled with two Morgan mares.

Our first morning begins at the break of light. In October, light comes at 7:30 A.M. Matt calls the shotgun seat. Shotgun being the right front seat. That seat remains his for the next three days. Matt contorts his 5'9" body into sleeping positions, camera positions, and snacking positions. Matt is in charge of the "Jake brake" (the Jacob's compression brake on the Chevy Kodiak) for the next 3,000 miles. Matt and his dad work as a team.

I lead the mares out of the cool Kentucky morning into the trailer. They willingly step-up into their box stalls. The aluminum door breaks the morning quiet as I shut and fasten the handle. I look over the meadow where just moments ago, two black Morgan mares moved, silently nibbling the sweet bluegrass nourishment unique to Kentucky. I feel a tear slide down my cheek. I know that my experience here is truly over. A feeling of sorrow sweeps over me for the moment. My highest equine achievement now only stands as a memory. For me and my mares, the exquisite experience of performing at Alltech FEI WEG 2010 crosses the boundary from activity to memory. I will cherish this memory of Kentucky forever. I turn and crawl into the back seat of the huge Chevy Kodiak. I fasten my seat belt tightly. I have *never* ridden in the back seat of the truck. I usually command the driver's seat.

John starts the engine. He and Matt brim over with the excitement of the trip looming in front of us. We start our 3,000 mile drive. The westward route changes from my eastward trip. We take the more southern route towards Kansas City.

John ticks off the states as we rush through them. I teach the men the routine at the giant fuel stops along the way. John and I take turns pumping fuel. Matt races in to buy junk food. I quietly set out to change our fuel-food. Junk food does not make good traveling food. As with horses, food changes must be made slowly and carefully.

I drive as much as I can in daylight. My eyes will not work well enough at night to see where the road winds. Driving cross-country by myself, I can only drive in the daylight hours. John drives well at night. I take the day shift, he takes the night shift.

At one fueling point, a truck driver gives us a tip to shortcut from Kansas City to Grand Island, Nebraska. I finally give up the captain's chair in the gathering darkness. I am now the map reader. Matt does not know how to read a map yet. I can barely read the map in the dim overhead light of the back seat. We all feel nervous until, through the gloom of the dark and the flickering headlights of the automobiles on the road, we see our shortcut to Grand Island.

I know how to get to the Heartland Fairgrounds. I called ahead several hours ago to insure that the gate to the fairgrounds will be unlocked so we can slip in the 44-feet of traveling truck and trailer.

I used these fairgrounds on the way east. Now, after 1,000-miles of driving from Paris Kentucky to Grand Island, Nebraska, I stand on familiar footing, while the territory feels totally new to the Kentucky-bred father and son.

Matt jumps out of the truck in the darkness to walk the night fence-line of the outdoor arena. On his head he wears a magical light. Matt possesses a "miner's light." I stand transfixed. His headlight lets him move seamlessly around doing night-time chores. He closes all the open gates I could never have found in the dark. Then he helps me haul the water tubs and put out the night hay for the mares. The mares have been standing for the last 1,000 miles. They step out happily, roll, and trot around the arena and then put their heads down to drink and eat.

Once again I learn something, from someone so much younger than me. I *need* a headlight!

John and Matt begin to build their bed on the hay bales in the front stall of the horse trailer. I watch and finally say, "Have you guys ever camped before?"

"No," comes the soft, tired drawl from John.

They need "diesel" batteries to pump up the air mattress of their bed. Here, standing in the darkness at 11:30 and who-knows-what time zone, I am standing and these two southern, non-campers are murmuring about four *diesel* batteries to pump up a queen-sized air mattress. I know I am in over my head. All I can do is to go to my bed.

I feel every time they laugh or turn over on their bed. The gooseneck horse trailer rattles with their every movement. I have slept during emergency layovers with the horses in the trailer. You can feel their tails move. Matt and John's movements are felt too from my bunk in the front of the trailer. I drop into a very deep and tired sleep. The first 1,000 miles of the return trip home have fallen behind me in one, 14-hour day. There are only two more days and the mares and I will be home.

The next morning comes quickly. I pull myself out of bed. I feed the mares. They are always glad for their breakfast. They are such traveling troopers. The mares peacefully eat their hay. They know not that there is another 1,000 mile day in front of them.

I talk to John and Matt. Their hay bale bed slides apart during the night. The men remade the bed several times. Now rested, I can understand what they needed last night. The southern drawl translates to four "D-cell" batteries. So much for my comprehending the unfamiliar drawl of my two guys on this guy trip.

I start the drive this morning. John crawls into the back seat and rapidly falls asleep. Matt curls his lanky frame in the front seat and quickly goes to sleep too.

The mares load up, I start our drive. I drive and drive and drive. The inside of the truck remains silent as the two men sleep. When I stop for fuel they gradually come alive. We are close to Cabela's. This outdoor sports store stands in the middle of Nebraska's nowhere. I promise Matt that we will stop so he can wander around to his heart's content.

As we approach the middle of Nebraska's nowhere, I miss the turn to Cabela's. I am incredulous.

I drive five more miles before I can find an off ramp so I can turn around. Matt cannot believe that I missed the turn. He is visibly relieved to find that I really will turn around for him. I know this will not be a quick, half-hour stop. The men shop for at least a couple of hours in a hunting/camping/fishing version of male heaven. I know I am on a guy trip, and I am content to just sit and watch all the shoppers.

I strike-up a pleasant conversation with an older farmer and his wife. I ask him about the unusual, large hay stacks. The stacks look like they have been hand-stacked. He explains

"There is a huge machine that revolves on a very large disk. The hay turns on the disk and is piled up. It does look like an old, hand-stacked hay stack. The conical shape helps to shed the water and snow in the winter. The hay stack is protected by a fence. When the farmer is ready to feed that hay to the livestock, he simply removes the fence."

Once again I learn, another method for providing the winter feed.

I purchase two knit caps for the men to wear at night. In the four weeks since I started out from home, the night air has grown colder with each passing day. Matt presents me with my very own miner's light. I wear this light every morning, even now at home, and every night when we stop on this "guy road trip."

I had no idea how much help the miner's light on my head can be when I find myself in unknown places.

Sight-seeing and shopping done, I keep driving in the daylight. John and Matt sleep. We think we will drive until Salt Lake City and spend the night at Golden Spike Event Center. Darkness falls. John still sleeps. Matt sleeps too. As we draw closer to Wyoming, I know we cannot make three more hours to Salt Lake. Matt wakes up.

"Matt," I say, "let's take a vote. I know a place to stop in Rock Springs where I can keep the horses. I think we need to stop. What do you think?"

Matt votes "Yes."

Pulled from my memory of an east-west trip of years ago, I know that the KOA camp grounds in Rock Springs holds space for big trailers and has a couple of corrals.

I turn off on the exit that I barely remember. My eyes cannot see the dark road in front of me. John awakens.

Matt explains the situation. John agrees we should stop. I feel my way through the darkness, driving the truck, trailer and everyone's lives.

We pull into the packed campground. I ask John to plug us in. I will go into the office and make the arrangements. Turning us away once we are plugged into a camp spot will be difficult.

The lady office manager closes the till just as I walk in the door. I explain we are traveling with two horses and are desperate for a place to put the horses. I offer to pay cash without a receipt. Money talks and the woman is delightful.

She jumps in her golf cart. The water at the horse corrals is turned off for the winter. She helps me load the water tub and takes me and the tub to the one working water pump. She and I fill the tub and drive up to the corrals with the hay and the water tub. She grabs one side of the water tub and we expertly swing the water into the corral. I toss the hay into the corral. She drives me back to the trailer and I unload the mares. I wear my miner's light and quickly lead the mares to the corral. The woman's husband shows up in his golf cart. He bristles with disgust while she helps me. I thank her profusely and say nothing to the angry husband. I don't have to live with him. I gratefully hand this woman my card, money, and a piece of jewelry, and say, "Thank you. You gave us a much needed place to stay. Thank you for everything."

She smiles and says, "You are most welcome."

Her husband scowls and says nothing.

Matt and John use the D-cell batteries that I took from my battery-operated lantern. Their bed is pumped up, the hay bales placed so they will not come apart. They are ready for sleep.

I go to my bed and sleep comes slowly. I drove almost 1,000 miles today. We want to drive from Rock Springs, Wyoming, to Susanville, California. We have miles to go before we rest.

Morning comes. We plan on stopping at Little America in Wyoming. I need to get some good food into these men. Traveling on only junk food with a teenager who thinks he is a fussy eater is not good for anyone. The men are cheerful, but tired. I know an army marches on its stomach. I give my, "you are what you eat" speech.

The speech is simple. I start with this question while I look directly at Matt.

"Would you feed your FFA steer what you are eating on this trip?"

"Nooo," he drawls. I wonder if I will ever get used to the charming drawls, and believe that this drawl is truly how Matt talks. I am disarmed by the genuineness of his tone.

"Matt. What do you like to eat?" I ask. Matt forages on candy, potato chips and strange hot dogs from the truck stops. He also gulps some strange kinda soda and Gatorade. Too much sugar slides down his young throat.

Matt replies, "I like steak, potatoes, and that's about it."

"Ok. At Little America, you are going to eat dinner for breakfast and then no more junk food. We will load up with apples, milk, and some good snacks. Are you willing to try eating better for just one day?"

Matt is game. So is John. When we pull into Little America, Wyoming, we eat a Wyoming streak, eggs and potatoes breakfast.

We all feel better and more energized.

John will take the night-driving shift. I take the day shift. I know my way home and wake John and Matt as we cross the Continental Divide. John takes the wheel going down the eastern slope of the Rockies as we drop down into Salt Lake City, Utah. Both Matt and John find the raw beauty of the Rockies in fall incredible.

They cannot believe how big and flat the Salt Flats are. Both of them fall asleep as I take the wheel again to cross over the salt flats. John sleeps in fits and wakes up to see the same sight on either side of the truck as when he went to sleep.

I continue with the dayshift of driving.

We are going to stay with the Wolf clan in California. We have a little more than 1,000 miles to go today. Nevada stretches ever on and on. Again the men are surprised by the unending vastness of the West. I feel the pull of home with each mile that ticks off under the tires.

We drive endless miles through Nevada. The sky behind us hangs black with thunderstorms. I can feel the heaviness even though I am sitting in the truck, hurtling along at 80 m.p.h. heading west. I am as bad as an eager horse pointed home. My foot on the throttle grows heavy. The truck speeds up. Once I hit 85 miles per hour, I know I am driving too fast. Everything shakes in the truck and on the trailer. I ease up.

The men sleep. They wake up periodically and peer out the truck windows looking upon the vastness of the Nevada west.

John says, "I have seen more of nothing on this trip. This county is an expanse of nothingness."

My eyes feast on the rugged Nevada Mountains and desert. I feel I am coming home. The landscape feels familiar. I know this country. This country looks like parts of Oregon. I feel at home here.

Darkness falls early. We are four hours out from Susanville. I drive as far as I dare in the darkness. Finally, when we stop for fuel, John and I change seats. The rain finds us. Desert rain finds us. Thunder, lightning, and huge cloudbursts of rain plague us. The windshield wipers can hardly keep up with the buckets of water falling. We drive on and on in the drenching rain.

As we wind our way through the packed, dark freeways of Reno, Matt suddenly shouts,

"What is that stuff on the side of the road? It looks like snow!"

"Oh, my God! It's hail," someone shouts. I never figure out which one of us shouted. Truck, loaded with our lives, and trailer, loaded with horses, skids down the road on thousands of tiny ice marbles. Then it happens. In front of us appears four feet of water. The entire freeway overpass is flooded. Cars blast through the 60-foot long stretch of four foot deep water. John commands Matt to hit the Jake brake. Matt's quick reactions save the night. For a split second, the truck's diesel engine quits, then bursts back to life. We are alive. All of us. The humans and the equines are alive. The traffic keeps flowing. All of us are very quiet. I reach up and gently touch John on the shoulder and say, "Good job."

Matt says to me, "Make sure you have your seat belt on." I click it into position. We ride silently for about 45 minutes.

When we come to the agricultural inspection at the California border, the border agent says, "I bet you have been to the snaffle bit futurity in Reno."

I don't disagree with him.

"Yes, of course."

"Just drive on through. Hope you did well."

I reply, "Yes, we did well." I wanted to say, "Yes, we are alive."

He waves us through. John and I are emotionally exhausted by the narrow escape of a potentially fatal accident.

Then courage kicks in and we begin to make "gallows humor" remarks. I cannot remember exactly what we say, but our laughter sounds weak and shrill.

CHAPTER 72
KENTUCKY COWBOYS

I call Chet Wolf for directions to his ranch. The rain still falls. I can hardly see out the window. Of course we become lost and wind up on front of the state prison in Susanville.

Matt and I get out of the truck and guide John as he backs the huge rig up so we can turn around. We call Chet and Chet rushes over to lead us to his ranch.

As he is walking beside the trailer helping his dad back down the narrow road, Matt says, "I'm scared. The guard in the guard house is watching me. He has a big gun."

I am on the opposite side of the truck so I miss seeing the guard.

Chet pops out of the darkness in his little white station wagon. He breathlessly hisses, "Follow me right now. Hurry up!" Chet's voice is unusually urgent. Matt and I leap into the huge truck as John guns the engine and follows Chet's vanishing lights.

Once we pull into the Wolf ranch, park, and disembark, Chet explains his urgency.

"There is a serial killer locked up by the gate house. The killer is there for his own safety. The town of Susanville is up in arms about the killer. The prison has received death and bomb threats about the guy. You weren't in a very safe place."

Matt and I look at each other. We could *feel* the danger. John requests a shot of bourbon.

Matt wants to sleep in his new sleeping bag from Cabela's. He builds a secure, snug bed in the hay bales of the horse trailer. John sleeps in the guest room at Terry and Chet's house, and I crawl into my safe bed in the horse trailer living quarters. I fall asleep instantly. So close to home and so close to death makes for very deep sleep.

The next morning dawns full of energy. Eight people show up at the Wolf house for breakfast. John, Matt and I are three. Brian Wolf, his two boys ages 7 and 5, the hired man, plus a straggler who I never did figure out where he fit in. Terry makes waffles, Chet dishes up eggs, and I gather and wash dirty dishes. All of this breakfast activity happens before Terry Wolf hurries off to work. I stand in total awe of a working farm wife. The total maintenance and success of a farm and or ranch depends upon so many skills. The supreme skill of feeding the army of workers on a farm and ranch often falls on the slender yet sturdy shoulders of the farm wife.

Terry hurries off to her day job and we walk out to oversee the feedlot work of Brian. He chops the hay bales and feeds the chopped hay to young bulls and heifers in the feed lots. He also feeds a young group of six to eight bucking-bulls. The Wolfs support a rodeo bucking-bull breeding program. Matt stands transfixed by the bulls. These creatures are grey, with horns and an attitude that moves through the cold, fall air. The attitude simply translates as, "Don't mess with me." Matt doesn't mess with them. The heavy-duty pipe corrals will do nothing to stop one of the bulls from charging.

The pipe fencing *might* hold the bull, but who wants to take the chance?

Brian Wolf holds the job as the local vocational-agricultural instructor at the Susanville Junior College. Brian built the small agricultural and college rodeo program from nothing ten years ago into a viable working program today. Chet loads us into the white Ford pick-up. Matt and I crawl into the back seat, John and Chet take the front seats. Chet drives us to the college and Brian gives us the grand tour of the livestock and programs. The college tour is a total contrast to the Keeneland breeding farm and race track tour. This is a working college. Pens are handmade by students. The pipe corrals are forged by students learning to run a welder, posts are hand dug by students learning to wield a posthole digger. The horse stalls are built by students learning to build. Here stands a cohesive set of a working ranch building, pens, and efforts reflecting the future of California agriculture, truly built from the ground-up. The buildings reflect hopes and dreams of the future and of success that only begins with hard work.

Matt wants more than anything to ride a bull. Chet wisely takes us into the large hay barn and points to a hand-powered bucking-bull. No soft mats decorate the floor surrounding this mechanical bull. The bull has no head. The tail sports a handle that provides the human power of "push-and-pull" to make the vinyl-covered body buck. The human pushes the tail handle. The bull bucks. The human on the bull rides the up-and-down twirling movement of the hand-powered machine. Matt rides the bucking bull. John rides the bucking bull. No one gets bucked off. I even sit on the red, vinyl-covered hide. I don't get bucked off either as I only want very gentle bucks from my human tail-pusher.

From the college we head for the Susanville wild horse holding pens. John knows nothing of the wild horse situation in the west. He and Matt cannot believe the miles of pens containing at least 1,000 horses and burros rounded-up from the Nevada deserts and cruelly confined to "adoption" pens for the rest of their lives.

Without become political here, I can only see a reflection of the state prison, five miles away in Susanville. The prison seems to reflect sadness and hostility. The wild horse pens contain life sentences. I do not have a working solution for either the wild horses or the wild and sad men behind bars. I am uncomfortable in both places.

Our highlight of visiting the wild horses comes when Chet gets the truck stuck in the mud, but only for a moment. Chet, always the expert, manages to spin the tires just enough to grab the solid, wet earth and back down the slippery mud road to the parking lot of the BLM office. We passengers in the truck ride away wiser in the ways of the world.

Someplace in this journey we manage to find some lunch. We eat and then spend the afternoon looking at some cattle Brian and his wife, Michelle, want to purchase.

John finds himself at home here on the high deserts of the eastern slopes of Northern California. Cattlemen are cattlemen. They look for similar traits in the cows they purchase. Their animal problems are similar, but the geographical surroundings force different answers. The language of ranches and farmers remains fairly universal. "Make the crops and the livestock grow well. Keep everything healthy and try to wrest a profit from what Mother Earth provides."

Somehow we also become involved in pregnancy-checking cows for a neighboring ranch. Brian, with all of his education, is an expert at pregnancy checking cows. He knows by feel how far along in the pregnancy the cow is or if she is an "open" (not pregnant) cow. Brian is hired to pregnancy check approximately 100 cows this afternoon.

Brian needs to check 100 cows after working all day teaching college. The Wolf family continues to be an incredibly busy family. They work hard and play hard all the time.

John and Matt are not part of the working crew, but ever so gradually they step into the dance of working cattle. I always find watching men join a new team to be fascinating. The men all know the ritual. John stands back and watches the four men who are working the cattle in the chute. He watches until there is a moment where another man is needed and he steps forward and fills the space. Not only does John fill the needed space, John knows how to work the cattle. The other men see the smoothness and quietness of John's ability to work on the team and his cattle-handling skills. John is accepted on the crew.

Next comes Matt. Matt stands back waiting. His dad quietly instructs Matt to work by the chute, prodding the cattle down the line to the squeeze chute where the cow will be captured and palpated for her state of pregnancy by Brian. Everyone can see that this southern father and 14-year old son are a good, working team.

Strangely, this time I just stand back and film the crew working. I must be getting old. At one point in my life I would have stepped quietly into the cattle dance. I am for the first time in my life content to stand out of the fray and just to film and watch this dance. I have Brian's young son to keep me company. Brock can enter into the working fracas if he pleases or stay out of the way as his father or grandfather command. Brock and I often sit back and watch, or Brock runs around and plays the small games that seven-year old ranch children play when dangerous work is going on. He climbs the old wooden fences, kicks cow pies, or splashes in dirty mud puddles.

Suddenly a cow escapes the squeeze-chute. Six men try to push her back into the chute. The men are no match for the cow. The cow charges at Brock and I. He and I sprout wings and fly to the top of a fence out of reach of the angry, charging cow. I never take my eyes off Brock as he scrambles up the fence. We look at each other as the cow charges by. He is a young boy and I am an old woman.

I say to Brock, "Wow! You can run really, really fast!"

Brock says breathlessly, "I have been chased before. You can really run fast too."

I smile and reply, "I have been chased before."

Both Brock and I know to run fast and climb high fences and to GET OUT OF THE WAY!

The men all look our way whilst this chase is occurring. They see that the boy and the old lady are safe.

John only pauses to ask, "Did you get that on film?"

I look at him and reply, "Nope, Brock and I were too busy saving ourselves."

Everyone chuckles and goes back to work.

Small events makes up the nature of working cows. Accidents happen, but the work must go on. The escaped cow is captured by the horseback cowboys and the herd is pregnancy-checked.

The day is late. Darkness is falling. Matt, John, Chet and I load up into Chet's white Ford and head back to the Wolf ranch. Terry feeds another full crew of people. Tonight there are easily a dozen people sitting at the dining room table. Terry has worked all day at her day job and now feeds a huge crew for dinner. She never complains. Terry just steps up and does a job that must be done. I bus the dirty dishes and stay out of the cook's way. Terry and Chet are a team that feeds people often. Terry jokingly says, "Yup! We only had 40 people here for Thanksgiving last year!"

I believe her. I have no idea where everyone sat or stood, but I know that each person was welcome and well-fed.

Tomorrow we will leave this lively and vivacious ranch. Matt does not want to leave. After all that nothingness of the plains, he is falling in love with the west and the western lifestyle. Chet gives Matt a rope and teaches Matt and John how to swing a rope. They are both hooked on roping. I never see Matt without his rope in his hand for the rest of our trip.

Tomorrow we leave for home. I am just four hours away from the end and thus the beginning of my full-circle trip-of-a-lifetime.

Matt hates to leave the Wolf ranch. Who can blame him? He has ridden a mechanical bull, worked cows, and learned to toss a rope, all in one day at one place.

I load the mares one last time. They step up so nicely. They are such good mares. They don't know how close we are. They just load up as I ask them. I shut the door to the trailer. I am so glad to be going home.

Matt climbs into his front seat. John climbs into the back and I take the steering wheel.

There is much joking about finding my way home from the Wolf ranch. I listen smilingly. I am ready to go.

I drive all the way. The men watch the scenery change from high, open desert to the high pine desert around Alturas, California. We then drop down into the potato county of Klamath Falls, Oregon. John looks at the different machinery involved in potato harvesting. It's nice to travel with fellow farmers. We have similar interests and love farming.

I turn the truck onto Highway 140 from Klamath Falls. The aspen trees are just turning golden. The Rocky Mountains of Utah's fall foliage was two-weeks ahead of here when we passed through two days ago.

The truck winds its way up and over the 140 pass and we begin to drop down into the Rogue Valley of Oregon. I eagerly point out my farm from the road. I click the right hand blinker, turn onto Riley Road, travel the one mile, click the right blinker again, go 7/10 of a mile, and turn into my own driveway.

My little dog Suzie is waiting for me at the barn when I pull in. I hug her and kiss her head. I have not seen her for six weeks. I unload the mares. I put them into their stalls. They are so glad to be home. So am I.

The journey has come full-circle. I have just covered more than 7,000 miles with my Dancing Morgans. We have danced at the 2010 Alltech FEI World Equestrian Games. And now we are safely home. I hug my little Jack Russell one more time and walk down to my house.

I am done performing with the mares. I have been to that absolute top of the world in performances. I have had such an incredible time of my life in these past ten years with the Dancing Morgans. I can feel the time for change once again running through my veins and mind. I am not sure of this next creation of myself, but I know a new creation is coming. My life is not about finding myself, but creating myself.

If you are ever in the high mountains of Oregon and you meet an old cowgirl dancing down the trail with her two beautiful, black Morgan mares, you know that it is Carole Mercer and her Dancing Morgans. We are dancing to the soft, violin sounds of the wind in the pines. Our stage is the winding pathways of the mountains. Our joy is the beauty of the dance.

CHAPTER 73
FALL MORNINGS & CATTLE AFTERNOONS

Mornings are fall. Afternoons are summer. The men who have been leasing my fields all summer are moving their cattle to fall fields. There is a grand total of 58 head, counting mamas, babies, and a giant bull. The owners of the cattle are great, hard-working, honest men. They are just two men up against just two head under 60 head of cattle. The big stock trailer is backed up against the loading gate.

"In!" shout the men.

"Moo!" shout the cattle ("moo" means "go to hell" in cow talk).

"In! " shout the men.

"Moo" holler the cattle.

"May I help?" asks I of the Dancing Morgan fame. "My horses and I can push the cattle right into the trailer."

The men are skeptical, but in dangerous need of help. Here is an old cowgirl with a Dancing Morgan, offering to push very reluctant cattle into the trailer.

"OK," says the head man in desperation. "Go get a horse."

I trot off and saddle Bobby with my dressage saddle. Bobby and I are not only dancing partners, but we have worked lots of cattle together. Bobby and I move slowly into the milling herd and neatly separate out eight cows. We push them into the alleyway. The boss man gets in our way. I gently tell him he and I must work on the same side of the alley. He gets the message.

I ask my mare to "sic" a cow. Bobby reaches out and bites the cow on the rump. The cow springs forward, pushing the hesitant lead cow neatly into the trailer. The next cows jump into the trailer under the supervision of Bobby's snapping jaws. The boss man slams the trailer door shut.

He turns around and says, "Thanks. Will you help on the next eight loads?"

I can hardly stand myself. I love working cows with my Morgans. "Yup," I smile.

I trade off on my black mares. Bobby does the first load, Valentine pushes the second load. The mares and I load just two under 60 head of cattle in a total of nine loads. The head count of cows varies from load-to-load.

The men are very grateful.

People forget that I worked for the sale yard in Medford for 15 years. For 15 years I rode my Morgans up and down the alleyways, pushing cattle off the scales and into pen lots. I rode in the heat and dust of summer and though the ice and cold of winter. I rode every week of the year. I pushed a lot of cattle down the dark and twisting and dangerous alleyways of the Rogue Valley Auction Yard.

You can do the math. I worked one day a week for 52 weeks for 15 years. My mares and I have moved lots of cattle. Plus factor in 20 years of gathering cattle in the High Cascade Mountains as well.

I come well-prepared to push almost 60 head of cattle into a trailer. After all, I ride Morgans. I used to tease the cowboys that it took four of their Quarter horses to make one of my Morgans. I always brought one horse to work the sale yards or to gather in the Cascades. The cowboys always brought four horses per man.

I have Morgans. I only needed one horse, and that Morgan could outwork four quarter horses all day.

Pushing cattle today into the trailer was as much fun as going to WEG, just a different kind of fun.

The horses and I still have the ranch work ethic and the grace and style of ballerinas. My mares turned 17 this year and I am still 65 years old. Not a bad job for a bunch of ol' gals. I love the job and so do the horses.

The Dancing Morgans can and do still do it all. The Dancing Morgans are still the most versatile Morgan mares in the world. They have danced in front of the world at Alltech FEI WEG 2010 and have come home to do ranch work at their home at Rolling Wheel Ranch, Eagle Point, Oregon.

I am so fortunate to own Morgans. And I love the cow poop on the once-polished steel of the graceful dressage saddle stirrups.

CHAPTER 74
COMPLETE

I know that my daughter would have done wonderful things with her life. When Sarah's light was snuffed out, I had to pick up her torch and light the way. I could not be her, but every ride I made and every performance I did, I did so she would not be forgotten. I talked about how important the horses were to me and why I performed. Many people came up to share their stories and said I helped them. We all need help in some way or the other. Helping and listening gave me purpose to live again.

The long and short of my life is the moment I learned that I can create myself. My life is not about finding myself. My life is about creating myself. I am who I have created.

I like me again.

Cheers,
Carole L. Mercer
The Dancing Morgans
May 24, 2013

AUTHOR'S NOTE

Did this story strike a chord?

Please sing its praises to Amazon, and take a moment to rate it here:

http://www.amazon.com/The-Far-Side-My-Dreams/dp/1484867165/

As a private publisher, the best way to find interested readers is with your personal recommendation. IF you enjoyed this book please rate it on Amazon, and share my Amazon link on Facebook, Twitter, and with your real-life friends.

Great stories are meant to be enjoyed and shared. And true stories are meant to be learned from. Please pass it on and accept my, Bobby, and Valentine's most sincere, "THANKS!"

Carole L. Mercer

LEARN MORE!

Visit these links for more information about:

Carole L. Mercer: http://www.carts-carriages.com

America's Morgan Horse: www.morganhorse.com

The Kentucky Horse Park: kyhorsepark.com

Adopting Wild Mustangs: www.blm.gov/adoptahorse/

FEI World Equestrian Games: www.fei.org

6279533R00124

Made in the USA
San Bernardino, CA
04 December 2013